The editor would like to thank

Ruth Bayer for her beautiful photos and constant encouragement.
Caroline Wise for her invaluable proof reading and suggestions.
Martin Rose for his unwavering love and support.
Ian Foot for his memories and for continuing the legacy of Pagan Pathfinders.

All the wonderful Peepers who have contributed in some way to this book -
in thought, word, magic, song, dance, feasting and fellowship.

Most of all Jean, for all the wisdom she gave us so generously.

Ruth and Liz would also like to thank Stephen Thrower for his impeccable formatting,
and Katzi Kreitner for her beautiful cover design.

Tyto Alba

The Golden Bubble

by
Jean M. Williams

editor & contributor
Liz Wigglesworth

photographs
Ruth Bayer

CONTENTS

INTRODUCTION

Jean M. Williams started Pagan Pathfinders (or 'PP' as participants lovingly called it) in 1975, and held sessions in her Crouch End home every Monday night until 2012. I lived in the house for thirty years, and often attended sessions or bumped into members in the kitchen! The history of PP and how meaningful it was to so many people is thoroughly documented within this book, which Jean started work on many years before her passing in 2015.

Being Jean, she was highly organised and left a huge amount of detailed material behind. This was typical of her fastidiousness, a trait which enabled her to maintain a busy professional career as well as putting so much energy into PP, The Pagan Federation, and her other occult interests.

Liz was a member of PP for many years and was very close to Jean, who regarded her very highly - both personally and for her dedication to the group. Liz became a member of our extended family, and when it came to turning Jean's material into a finished book she grasped the challenge. This book is really Jean combined with Liz, who has done such a fantastic job of collating, editing, and occasionally adding material which may have been missing. Liz's years of experience within the group meant she had a complete understanding of its methods and working practices.

'The Golden Bubble' is a wonderful workbook and could not be a better introduction to anyone who is looking for inspiration within this field. I would like to thank Jean for everything she gave us, and her devotion to a group which continues to guide and encourage so many.

Jean would have been very proud of this book, and the hard work Liz has put into producing it.

Ruth Bayer
2021

Jean M. Williams, photograph by Ruth Bayer © 2021

PROLOGUE
IMAGINE A BUBBLE OF GOLDEN LIGHT

Make sure you're sitting comfortably with your back relatively straight. Close your eyes and let yourself relax. Put your awareness on your breathing, not trying to change it, but just observing it going in and out, in and out, in and out, letting yourself relax and observing any changes in your breathing; it may become slower and deeper .... (Pause).

Now put your awareness on your out-breath and imagine that your out-breath is carrying away any remaining tensions anywhere in your body. And it's carrying away the tensions not just through your nostrils, but through every pore of your body. Feel the tensions draining out of you ....

Let your out-breath carry away any tensions around your face and your lips .... and your eyes .... any tensions in your throat .... your shoulders .... any tensions in your solar plexus area .... your abdomen .... your pelvis. All the tensions are carried away on your out-breaths. See the tensions leaving you like dark smoke and sinking down into the earth ....

Now let your out-breath carry away any tensions in your mind, any thoughts of what has happened today, or might happen tomorrow .... any anxieties, or fears, or irritations, let them all go and sink into the earth, leaving your mind clear and still .... Feel that pleasurable state of deep relaxation of body and mind. Savour it. (Pause).

Now imagine that you are surrounded by a bubble of beautiful golden light that is shot through with effervescent sparkles of energy .... And now put your awareness on your in-breath and as you breathe in, let that golden sparkling energy flow into you, not just through your nostrils, but through every pore of your body. Feel it flowing into your bloodstream and fizzing along your nerve fibres, carrying away all discomfort, cleansing you, refreshing you, and energizing you .... Feel it going right down your arms to your fingertips and right down to your toes, all around your internal organs .... And now imagine it travelling up your spinal column into your brain and into your mind. Feel your mind becoming clear and bright, alert and focused, delightfully still and uncluttered ....

Now, if there is any part of you anywhere, body or mind, that has any pain or discomfort, breathe into that place and imagine that sparkling light concentrating there, carrying away the discomfort, bringing healing and boosting your own recuperative powers ....

Now imagine that golden sparkling light swirling through your aura and your aura expanding, the colours becoming clear and bright as that sparkling golden light cleanses and refreshes your emotional body ....

Now let the golden light sink down into the earth, leaving you feeling wonderfully relaxed, cleansed and refreshed and with a pleasurable sense of harmonious well-being. Let that feeling deepen. It is a precious treasure ....

Gateway to Inner Realms

The Golden Bubble meditation encapsulates the basics required by any spiritual or mental discipline: the ability to relax deeply and to focus the mind, to imagine something tangible to the senses, and to affect one's mental state. It is a gateway to the powers of one's own mind and to connectedness with others, to all living beings and the universe itself.

We start with awareness of our body and then focus on our breathing. Breathing is an automatic bodily process, but one that we can change and control at will, at least to some extent. It is also a connection to our environment and the life around us; as we breathe in, we take in air (which may be clean and fresh or polluted), we breathe out carbon dioxide which is taken in by plants and turned back into oxygen through photosynthesis. Watching our breathing without trying to change it is a good way to calm and focus the mind and to start the relaxation process. The focus is then narrowed down to the out-breath and the physical body, imagining each out-breath carrying away any physical tension. The suggestion that we imagine that our breath is carrying away the tensions not only through our nostrils but through the pores of the body, keeps the breathing rhythm relaxed and also preserves awareness of the body.

A classic way of promoting physical relaxation is to take the focus bit by bit from the feet up, starting with the toes, the feet, the calves, and so on, sometimes asking the individual to tense and then relax each part. A novice who is very tense and lacking in body awareness may find this a useful beginning, but it rapidly becomes tedious and counter-productive. I prefer to work from the head down, taking the attention in turn to each of the main areas of the body known to be tension-prone: the face, especially around the eyes, mouth and tongue, the throat and the shoulders, the solar plexus area, and the abdomen and pelvis. The focus is then taken to the busy conscious mind and all its preoccupations with recent experiences and future commitments.

As attention shifts to different parts of the body, the suggestion that they imagine the breath leaving through every pore of their body creates the sensation that it is going out through that part of the body, taking the tensions with it. When attention is turned to the mind and consciousness itself and participants are invited to let go of all their worries and concerns, at least for the time being, there is a feeling of peace and stillness that increases with each out-breath.

At this point, most participants feel pleasantly relaxed in body and mind, perhaps on the edge of sleep. In fact, this relaxation exercise can be effectively used at night to prepare for restful sleep. But our objective here is not sleep but further inner work. What is required at this point is a subtle change of tempo and pitch as participants are instructed to imagine that they are surrounded by a bubble of golden light shot through with effervescent sparkles of energy. Many will visualise the golden bubble, but for others it will be a sensation, an impression, or a feeling.

The golden sparkling light has cleansing, nourishing, healing and energising properties which are evoked as the exercise continues. It does not disturb the sense of deep relaxation and peace, but adds another dimension. Having established the image, participants are asked to transfer their awareness to the in-breath and, without changing it, allow the golden sparkling light to flow in, travelling to every part of their body. The in-breath will tend automatically to deepen as they do so and this in itself brings a sense of energy flowing in that dispels the tendency to sleepiness. The image of the golden light flowing up their spine into their brain and into their mind increases the sense of alert clarity and focus.

The relaxation part of the exercise may have made participants aware of pain or discomfort in some part of their body. An opportunity is now given to use the healing qualities of the golden light to bring relief by visualising it concentrating in the area of discomfort, carrying away the pain and boosting one's powers to heal oneself.

Finally, participants are invited to extend their sense of self beyond the physical body by imagining the golden sparkling light swirling through their aura, cleansing and expanding it. It is associated with their emotional nature, thus increasing their sense of calm and well-being. It also gives a sense of being more than their physical body.

The more frequently the Golden Bubble exercise is used, the more effective it becomes. The practitioner relaxes more quickly and more deeply; the sparkling golden light becomes more real; the sensations in the body of tensions draining away and the emotional feelings of calm, peace and well-being are pleasurable and healing. They encourage the secretion of endorphins, natural healing enzymes within the body.

This book is about inner exploration, personal growth, fulfilment and self-empowerment. It is about discovering one's potential, expanding horizons, exploring possibilities, developing the capacity to feel, to love, to express oneself, to trust the inner processes of the deep levels of the mind and thus to tap the wellsprings of creativity, joy and self-transcendence.

chapter one
PERSONAL MAGIC

The human brain is like Dr Who's space-time ship, the Tardis. Its outside dimensions are quite small, but within are vast unknown regions of inner space. I invite you to come with me on a journey into inner space and the realms of personal magic. Most of the techniques are simple and easily learned with a little practice. They don't require years of disciplined study yet can bring enormous rewards. They enable us to adventure safely into inner space and to bring back treasure, each adventure an enjoyable, enriching and uplifting experience that extends our boundaries. We can find our inner strength and courage, clarity of thought and deep wells of creativity.

The techniques can be readily adapted for personal use in dealing with life's problems and pursuing our goals, but I have found them most rewarding in a group context. There is something reassuring about the presence of others and the sharing of experience; it helps build an atmosphere that makes it easier to relax and to imagine. Many on-going groups have started out with just a few friends experimenting together, sharing their know-how. Some focus on just one thread such as the Tarot or the Zodiac, some on a particular Pagan Path; others may find a special book that inspires them. When I started Pagan Pathfinders in 1975, I relied for guidance on "Mind Games" by Masters and Houston (1972), adding elements from Pagan mythology to their mainly psychological approach. I had no particular training in running this sort of group, simply a background in psychology and a burning interest in the untapped potential of the human mind that led me into exploring Humanistic Psychology. When one of my friends suggested that I pull together my experiences and pass on what I had learned to others, I was shocked. "What, me? I've no experience in running a group!" But I made a start with a small number of interested friends and gradually built up my confidence. This was the shaky beginning of a group that flourished and ran for thirty-seven years. If I could do it, so can you!

Everyone that undertakes the adventure of running a group brings to it their own mix of interests and experience. My interest in the possibilities latent within the human mind led me first into eastern mysticism and Zen Buddhism and then, in the early 1960s, to Aldous Huxley's "The Doors of Perception" and some experiments with the consciousness expanding psychedelics, mescalin and LSD. I had met new friends who were Gardnerian Wiccans and was drawn into Paganism and magical disciplines. The psychedelics were taken infrequently and reverently in a carefully chosen setting designed to enhance the transcendental experience, with friends in support and time to absorb the experience afterwards. It certainly helped me begin the process of opening the doors of my mind.

In the early 1970s, the flower-power psychedelic movement started to grow up, partly due to the tightening up of drug laws, making mescaline and LSD illegal. Psychedelics sadly had become party drugs, sometimes with disastrous consequences. Psychologists such as Robert Masters and Jean Houston began to consider ways in which the same mind-altering transcendental effects might be achieved without drugs, through psychological and mystical techniques.

My experience of group work had been through attending every variety of Humanistic Psychology workshop then available. These ranged from simple encounter groups, learning to deal with negative emotions such as fear and anger creatively in interpersonal relationships, to unearthing the buried causes of these negative emotions and disempowering them through Gestalt therapy and Neo-Reichian body work, to transcending them and contacting the True Self with psychosynthesis and transpersonal work.

About this time in the early to mid-1970s, eastern mysticism became widely popular with the arrival of simple techniques for self-transcendence, firstly with the Maharishi Mahesh Yogi and then Bhagwan Shree Rajneesh. I noticed that many people who had been to a lot of Humanistic Psychology groups, and indeed many of those who had been facilitating groups, wanted to move on to the transcendental and were attracted to eastern mysticism, particularly to Rajneesh. I also noticed that many Pagan groups were very bad at handling negative emotions. There were too many fallings-out, often leading to an acrimonious breakdown of all communication. I thought that maybe Pagan Pathfinders could bridge this gap by providing a route into transcendental work within a Pagan context and also providing some techniques that would help people in their interpersonal relationships.

"The Science of Life and the Art of Living"

This phrase summarises the Pagan Pathfinders approach to personal magic. It is an adage of the Theosophical Society founded by Madam Blavatsky and arose from her studies of Hindu philosophy. It is also propounded by the Maharishi Mahesh Yogi who attributes its source to the Vedic scriptures, notably the Bhagavad-Gita. The Vedas are very ancient, their origins lost in the mists of time. In this context, the term "Science of Life" probably referred to what were then regarded as the natural laws that govern the universe, life and human society. In the context of the Pagan Pathfinders approach, it refers to psychological principles underpinned by modern scientific research. "The Art of Living" emerges as the imaginative application of tried and tested techniques and processes to one's daily life.

"Headology"

> "Granny Weatherwax had never heard of psychiatry and would have had no truck with it even if she had. There are some arts too black even for a witch. She practiced headology - practiced, in fact, until she was very good at it. And though there may be some superficial similarities

> between a psychiatrist and a headologist, there is a huge practical difference. A psychiatrist, dealing with a man who fears he is being followed by a huge and terrible monster, will endeavour to convince him that monsters don't exist. Granny Weatherwax would simply give him a chair to stand on and a very heavy stick."
>
> (Terry Pratchett, *Maskerade*, 1995)

Terry Pratchett's Discworld novels are about a flat world that is supported on the backs of four elephants that stand on the back of a giant turtle, travelling through space. It is a world run by magic rather than logic. Living on it are a number of witches, from young aspiring trainees, anxious to learn really powerful magic, to experienced, highly skilled older witches. Granny Weatherwax is regarded as the most skilled and powerful witch of all and is an expert in headology. The lesson that trainee witches have to learn is that magic is hard work and has often unforeseen consequences and costs. Why use magic when headology works just as well and is a lot less effort? Headology is a mixture of psychology, common sense and intuitive stage-management. It can be immensely effective.

Personal magic is very largely headology, but whereas headology is stage-managed by someone else, we can learn techniques to manage our own application of personal magic. The Pagan Pathfinders approach is a halfway house: the facilitator invites those present to examine an aspect of their life from a particular perspective and suggests a technique and scenario for exploring it and gaining insight. Participants can then continue to develop their skill in using these techniques on their own.

Magic and Science

> "Magic can be defined as the art of causing change in ways not yet fully explicable to science."

(Vivianne Crowley. "Wicca, the Old Religion in the New Millennium", 1996)

One of the most astonishing and exciting aspects of scientific advances is the way in which so many of them echo, but also demystify, the intuitive ideas and mystical or supernatural interpretations of what was regarded as magical from bygone ages up until the recent past. As Vivianne Crowley goes on to say, "In the future, much that is inexplicable today may be part of a psycho-technology which can be taught to us all." There is still a long way to go in understanding the way the mind-body works. One of the main discoveries so far is just how extremely complex it is. It is not like an engine that can be taken apart and understood, but is a dynamic, interactive, largely self-regulating entity, full of feedback loops working in nano-seconds, of which the conscious mind is one small but important part; and all this within the context of a living planet full of evolving, interactive life forms. Science can only nibble away bit by bit at this vast unknown mystery. Nonetheless, some exciting advances have been made.

Take the "Placebo" effect as an example

In a headology experiment worthy of Granny Weatherwax herself (but possibly more ethically ambiguous), a Texas surgeon and his team conducted research to evaluate two surgical procedures for osteoarthritis of the knee, debridement versus lavage (Mosely et.al. 2002). They recruited 180 people in need of treatment and divided them into three groups, one for each treatment and a third as a control group. The control group had the same anaesthetic and a mock operation involving small incisions. A video of an actual operation was played and the team enacted the passing of instruments, and splashing of water but there was no insertion of instruments or procedure. The evaluative measures were ratings of pain levels and self-reported mobility. The results showed no significant differences whatsoever between either of the procedures, or between the procedures and the control group, even over a two-year follow-up period. After two weeks, patients who got the sham surgery were doing better than the true surgery patients; most likely, Moseley said, because they had been spared the "trauma'' of surgery. He reported that after two years, the three groups had made similar gains in walking and stair climbing, and their pain had eased to comparable degrees. The conclusion was that neither surgical procedure had much success for many people with osteoarthritis of the knee and the money might be better spent on other treatment. But the findings were recognised as having considerable significance in evaluating the placebo effect, largely dismissed by medical researchers as unimportant and in some way "not real". Psychotherapists take a very different view and there is now considerable interest in analysing the components of the placebo effect in order to put together theoretical maps for developing an effective psychotherapeutic relationship. It has been suggested that a better name for it would be "contextual healing" and that:

> "There is more to medicine than diagnosing disease and administering proven effective treatments. This has long been recognized under the rubric of 'the art of medicine'."
>
> (Miller & Kaptchuk. 2008)

The use of the mind to heal both body and mind can, in a Pagan context, be seen as "The Art of Magic". Headology is the art of finding appropriate keys to this magic in the modern world, not only for healing body and mind but also for exploring our potential, finding our path through the maze of day-to-day living and discovering how richly creative and joyful we can be.

Pagan Pathfinders was not a therapy group. Its purpose was to encourage people to be self-reliant, to attain insight into their own minds but, above all, to discover their potential for enriching their lives, accessing their creativity and freeing them to participate more fully in the joyous adventure of living. It was also a place for forming deeper connections with others through group work and where we always remembered the importance of laughter.

Early enthusiastic participants began nagging me to write a book about the techniques I used as long ago as 1976. Although I made lots of notes and wrote up some imaginary journeys, I was too busy with my job and various other activities with which I was involved to actually start writing. It would have been a very superficial book. It is only after several years and feedback from many participants that I have developed a deeper understanding of what I was doing and why it worked.

Now that I am in the autumn of life, the time of harvest, I have the leisure to examine and analyse the rich treasure of the techniques that we explored, the exercises, pathworkings and rituals that we experienced together, and also to examine the contribution that recent research, especially from neuroscience, is making to the understanding of the workings of the mind. I am also aware that my work over the last 25 years with the Pagan Federation and my continued involvement over many years with Wicca have given me a far greater understanding as to why the Pagan viewpoint is so relevant to individual health and to the health of Planet Earth.

chapter two
BASIC TECHNIQUES OF PERSONAL MAGIC

The Golden Bubble meditation incorporates the three basic techniques of personal magic. These are:

- Deep relaxation
- Stilling the mind
- Active imagination

The first two are very similar to Mindfulness meditation, practised by Buddhists, Hindu yogis and other eastern mystics for over two thousand years and now an increasingly popular technique. Europeans started to get interested in the eastern techniques of meditation and its potential in the late Victorian era with the opening up of the Indian subcontinent and accounts of the strange magical society to be found in Tibet. Meditation techniques of a similar kind became part of training in many Western Mystery and Kabbalistic groups such as The Hermetic Order of the Golden Dawn and the Fraternity of the Inner Light, founded by Dion Fortune. But interest really blossomed in the 1960s and 1970s with the arrival in the West of teachers such as the Maharishi Mahesh Yogi with his Transcendental Meditation[1] and Bhagwan Shree Rajneesh's Dynamic Meditation. Buddhism also received a big surge of interest with the publication of many books on Zen Buddhism and the diaspora of Tibetan Buddhist priests after the Chinese invasion of Tibet, several of them senior Lamas. The Dalai Lama himself escaped to India in 1959 and has written several excellent books of Tibetan Buddhist wisdom.

In the late 1950s I was invited by a Buddhist friend to go with him to attend a Tibetan Buddhist ceremony at Friends House (a Quaker hall) on Euston Road in London. It was called the Ceremony of the Vajra Crown and was performed by a group of Tibetan monks, centred on the Karmapa, a very senior Lama. It involved a long period of chanting and the sounding of great chords played on 6-foot-long Tibetan horns. The Vajra Crown was then reverently taken out of its box and the Karmapa placed it on his head. He then entered into a meditative state merging his mind with that of the Bodhisattva of Compassion. After more chanting, those present were invited to approach the Karmapa to receive his blessing. There were at least 200 people there so this took some time. I noticed that most people approached with their head bowed as though he was too sacred to look at, but I was a psychologist and curious. I raised my head and looked into the face of the Karmapa. It seemed to shine like the sun and his eyes transmitted an almost overwhelming benevolent force. I was startled and momentarily transfixed, but I became aware of the pressure of people behind waiting their turn and bowed my head and moved on in a somewhat stunned state. This was my first direct experience of a dedicated human being transmitting what seemed to be a superhuman power. This was beyond mere charisma.

The Karmapa had been chosen as a young child and had spent many years in rigorous training. Mindfulness meditation is just a humble first step on that path and few of us have the dedication, or even the inclination, to forego an active life within our own society to that extent. Yet, as we shall see, Mindfulness meditation can make a valuable contribution to our well-being.

Mindfulness combines deep relaxation with emptying the mind of all the clutter of daily life by the simple technique of focussing on the breath as it enters and leaves the nostrils, noting any thoughts that intrude and gently letting them go. The effect is to bring a sense of deep inner peace that can be profoundly healing. Research has shown that just 10-20 minutes a day for as little as eight weeks can bring about measurable psychological and physiological benefits: a more relaxed and positive attitude, better sleep and increased activity in the left prefrontal cortex that deals with positive emotion, awareness and decision-making. MRI scans show that even after this short time the amygdala, the brain's fight or flight centre and region associated with fear and emotion, begins to shrink. Longer term, and combined with Cognitive Behaviour Therapy, it has been shown to help people with recurrent depression, addiction, anxiety states and other miserable conditions such as chronic pain and chronic fatigue syndrome. In 2005, the evidence was sufficient to lead the National Institute for Health and Clinical Excellence (NICE) to recommend Mindfulness-based cognitive therapy courses under the NHS, especially for depression which afflicts one in ten people. In the present day, Mindfulness has become increasingly popular and there are even mobile phone apps to facilitate it. Some companies offer Mindfulness training in the work place, showing a welcome trend towards accepting that productivity increases with a solid base of positive mental well-being.

In the Golden Bubble meditation, we amplify the essential first stage of deep physical relaxation by putting more emphasis on awareness of the body and letting go of its tensions, before moving on to focussing and emptying the mind. There has been a great deal of research on the psychophysiology of meditation (summarised in Tart, C.T. Ed, "Altered States of Consciousness", 1969). It started in the 1950s with the use of the electrical skin resistance meter (ESR), also called the "lie detector"[2]. The ESR involves placing electrodes on the hand to measure the skin's resistance to a small electrical current; the greater the resistance, the more relaxed is the person. Emotionally loaded thoughts cause the resistance to drop. Meditators consistently had readings that indicated deep levels of relaxation with occasional spikes as thoughts intruded. Versions of the ESR meter were produced that provided auditory feedback to the person using it: a note that was high to start with and became progressively deeper as the person relaxed. This feedback gave confirmation of increasing relaxation and helped to train the mind to recognise a state of deep physical relaxation.

In the 1960s and 1970s, research took a big step forward with the development of the electroencephalograph (EEG), a machine that measures the rhythms of electrical activity in the brain. Brainwaves are measured in two dimensions, frequency and amplitude.

Frequency: the number of cycles per second.

Amplitude: the size of the wave, indicating its strength compared to waves of other frequencies.

By correlating the amplitude of waves of different frequencies with specific mental activities or states, a very informative series of patterns emerged. The mental state mainly associated with high amplitude of the various frequencies is as follows, starting with the highest frequencies:

Beta (13-30 cycles per second). When brainwaves in this range are dominant, it indicates the normal thinking state: dealing with the outside world, active attention, problem solving. Recent advances in digital recording have revealed that even higher frequencies can occur in states of very deep concentration, usually around 40 cycles per second. These are sometimes called Gamma waves.

Alpha (8-12 cycles per second). Dominance in this range indicates a state of relaxed detached awareness, often with sensory imagery. It is described as the gateway to meditation and provides a bridge between the conscious and subconscious mind.

Theta (4-7 cycles per second). High amplitude in this range on its own indicates dream sleep.

Delta (0.5-4 cycles per second). High amplitude in this range on its own indicates dreamless sleep.

These are the mental states associated with each set of waves when they are clearly the most dominant, but the brain can produce patterns of brainwave frequencies with different amplitudes, like an organ playing many notes at once. A notable pioneering researcher in this field was Dr C. Maxwell Cade, a psychologist, physicist and long-term meditator. He had worked with Dr Ann Woolley-Hart at St Bartholomew's Hospital, London, on the use of biofeedback machines to explore the interaction between mind and body in such areas as reducing pain, controlling migraine attacks and teaching relaxation. He recognised the great potential of electroencephalographs and with the aid of Geoffrey Blundell, a gifted electronics engineer, he developed the Mind Mirror. The great strength of the Mind Mirror was that it measured and displayed the amplitude of the full range of brain waves, from 0.5 to 38 cycles per second, for both hemispheres of the brain at once.

Maxwell Cade was thus able to study the patterns of brainwave amplitudes produced by different activities and reported states of consciousness in a variety of subjects, from experienced long-term meditators to new trainees. He found that trainees could learn fairly quickly to become relaxed and to still the mind. In this state the Beta waves of normal alert consciousness were greatly reduced, while Alpha waves became the dominant amplitude. He described this state as the gateway to meditation and the bridge between conscious and subconscious levels of the mind. The first part of the Golden Bubble meditation is designed to induce this pleasurable state of relaxed, in-the-moment awareness.

As the meditative state deepened, Theta waves would start to manifest as well, leading to an experience of a blissful altered state of consciousness, the true meditative state. In this state, there is access to the creative inspiration of the unconscious mind, making available new insight, differences in perspective and access to the healing powers of the mind. The continuing strong Alpha waves provide the bridge to the conscious mind so that it is possible to remember the experience and make use of it. The second part of the Golden Bubble meditation is designed to lead people into this deeper level of consciousness where Alpha and Theta waves act together. Visual and other sensory imagery may become more vivid and there is a sense of merging with a greater whole.

In this state, Delta waves, normally associated with deep sleep, may also start to manifest in the Mind Mirror, while the subject remains awake. Maxwell Cade found this complex pattern developing in long-term meditators, able to reach the deepest levels. It seems that Delta waves give access to levels of the mind not available to our consciousness, but which play an important role in intuition, empathic attunement and possibly in psychic states.

Since the early days of psychology, it has been recognised that there are levels of the mind beyond our conscious thinking/experiencing mind through which we feel we live our lives. The subconscious mind is where our memories of what we have learnt and experienced are stored and is relatively easily accessed by the conscious mind. These memories include simple facts and happenings, emotional experiences, and also complex skills and patterns of experience that enable us to deal with demanding situations, crises and emergencies. The ability to keep calm and to focus the mind, engendered by Mindfulness, enhances the ability of the conscious mind to interact smoothly with the reservoir of useful data in the subconscious mind.

The third level of the mind is the unconscious. The Swiss psychiatrist and psychotherapist, Carl Gustav Jung (1875-1961), saw the unconscious as the realm of the Shadow, all those aspects of ourselves that we are ashamed of, frightened of, or embarrassed by, but also the source of creativity, intuitive leaps, poetry and spiritual insight. Dreams are an attempt by the unconscious to communicate with the conscious mind and Jung used the technique of Active Imagination to help interpret dreams and access the creative potential of the unconscious. Active Imagination involves being aware of mental images as they form, acknowledging them and recording them, but doing little to influence them. It can be seen as a way of visualising unconscious issues or wisdom and learning from it. As Maxwell Cade found, a deep meditative state enhances the ability to establish communication between the conscious and unconscious levels of the mind. Active Imagination is a very powerful tool in this context and was a central technique in almost every aspect of Pagan Pathfinders.

It is simplistic to think of the three levels of the mind as being discrete areas with boundaries. They are simply a convenient way of classifying different parts of a continuum. There is constant interplay between the conscious mind and the upper levels of the subconscious as we recall memories and experiences needed to carry on our daily lives. Some are deeper or happened longer ago and are more difficult to access. Some are too emotionally painful and sink down to the unconscious level.

Alpha waves usually vanish when the eyes are opened; Beta waves re-establish themselves as the dominant frequency, ready to cope with the everyday world. Maxwell Cade found that a few particularly gifted healers and meditators were able to maintain dominant Alpha waves with their eyes open and also a certain amount of manifestation of all the other types of wave, including Beta. He called this state the "Awakened Mind".

One of his colleagues, Anna Wise, continued his research in America. She writes:

> "In 1981, I returned to the United States, where I originally came from, with Max's blessings and a Mind Mirror, to develop my own work with the Awakened Mind. I began expanding the research into areas other than spirituality and healing. I measured artists, composers, dancers, inventors, mathematicians, and scientists. I measured CEOs in the boardroom and presidents of corporations. I found that the brain wave patterns of high performance, of creativity, the bursts of peak experience, were the same patterns that the yogis and swamis lived in. I measured the 'ah-ha' or the 'eureka' experience and found that the brain waves flared into an awakened mind at the exact moment of insight."
>
> (Anna Wise, 2002)

The Golden Bubble meditation is designed to provide a gateway into the realm of the unconscious and the Awakened Mind where the insight of the "Ah-ha" experience is obtained. It starts with the technique of deep physical relaxation and then focuses on stilling the mind to allow the Alpha rhythms to become established. It then adds the technique of Active Imagination with the introduction of the image of the Golden Bubble. It is important to stress that participants let the image arise and let the golden light flow in on each in-breath so that Delta waves can start to manifest. Many people will have a vivid mental image of being surrounded by sparkling golden light; others may only intermittently glimpse it, or they may have no visual imagery but simply imagine the sensation of the sparkling light on their skin and within their body. What is important is not the quality of the imagery, but the state of mind that is achieved.

The final stages of the Golden Bubble meditation reach for the transcendent. First, awareness is turned onto the quality of consciousness itself, evoking a sense of relaxed and focused clarity of mind that allows the Beta waves of thought to emerge without disturbing the Alpha/Theta state. Secondly, we move outside our physical body to the concept of our aura, imagining the golden light swirling around our body, cleansing, balancing and invigorating our emotional nature.

The Golden Bubble meditation is immensely restful, healing and restorative, and it is important that an opportunity is given to hold and enjoy the final state achieved. As participants gain experience and skill, they become able to return to the final state at will during the session, even if there has been talk and interactive activities. Every Pagan Pathfinders session begins with the Golden Bubble meditation. However, in Pagan Pathfinders it is not an end in itself, it is a preparation for what is to follow in the rest of the session. Once the everyday thoughts have been stilled, the mind awakened, we practise gaining access to the hidden wisdom of the unconscious, using tools such as visualisation exercises (perhaps meeting a guide who can impart wisdom), intuitive learning, the use of symbols such as those found on Tarot cards, stories and myths from around the world and reaching out to our higher selves through evocations of Gods and Goddesses. With continued and regular practice, participants could access this part of their mind more and more easily, awakening inner wisdom, calming the mind and increasing emotional wellbeing.

Endnotes

1. Which received a great deal of publicity after being taken up by the Beatles.
2. It proved very unreliable for this purpose as it measures only emotional arousal, not its cause.

chapter three
WHAT'S IT ALL FOR?

The purpose of the basic techniques of personal magic and meditation is not to produce a particular brainwave pattern. That is simply a means to an end. What we are seeking is an inner environment in which we can grow into our full potential, a dynamic state of wholeness and inner peace and harmony through which we can lead our lives, find our true companions and our ever-expanding roles in our communities; a state of joyous creativity and zest for life. This in itself is healing. But we seek more: a sense of self-transcendence, of unity with something larger than ourselves – a universe of incredible complexity and beauty in which we seem to dissolve, becoming one with a universal benevolence, a process of creative ecstasy and bliss, the source of all, in comparison with which we are infinitesimally small but at the same time as large as the whole immensity.

We may call this God, Jehovah, the Great Mother, Isis, Cerridwen .... groping for a metaphor to fix what is essentially a precious experience of the moment. It is all too human to want to grasp that moment, formulate and package it for use on demand, or even to proclaim it to others and try to found a new religion. But its occurrence is a grace, achieved by letting go, not by grasping for it. Such experience is available to all who seek for it, but the content is unique and personal to each individual.

Psychology is a young science that emerged from philosophy in the late 19th Century to focus on the study of the mind. The pioneering psychologist and Harvard professor, William James (1842-1910), studied the experiences of people venerated as holy and inspired in many different religions. He concluded:

> "When we survey the whole field of religion, we find a great variety of thoughts that have prevailed there; but the feelings on the one hand and the conduct on the other are almost always the same, for Stoic, Christian and Buddhist saints are practically indistinguishable in their lives. The theories which religion generates, being thus variable, are secondary; and if you wish to grasp her essence, you must look to the feelings and the conduct as being the more constant elements."
>
> (William James, "The Varieties of Religious Experience", 1902)

He characterises these feelings as "overcoming melancholy," as imparting "a zest, or a meaning, or an enchantment and glory to the common objects of life." (op.cit.)

The psychologist, Abraham Maslow (1908-1970), called these transcendental states "peak experiences" and placed them in the top level of a hierarchy of human needs that underlie human motivations (often referred to as the "Maslow Pyramid"). He called the top level of the pyramid "self-actualisation"[1] and described it as including, "creativity, spontaneity, problem solving, morality, peak experiences", all qualities that the techniques used in Pagan Pathfinders were designed to make more accessible. He describes peak experiences as especially joyous and exciting moments in life, involving sudden feelings of intense happiness and well-being, wonder and awe, and possibly also involving an awareness of transcendental unity or knowledge of higher truth, as though perceiving the world from an altered, and often vastly profound and awe-inspiring perspective. They usually come on suddenly and are often inspired by deep meditation, intense feelings of love, exposure to great art or music, or the overwhelming beauty of nature. Not surprisingly, Maslow became intensely interested in the research being done into psychedelics and the Human Potential Movement; he was co-founder of the Journal of Humanistic Psychology in 1961 and published his own ideas in "Religions, Values and Peak Experiences" in 1964. He is regarded as one of the fathers of the Human Potential Movement.

Many of the techniques used in Pagan Pathfinders are adapted from Humanistic Psychology which developed from the Human Potential Movement of the 1960s and 1970s. Humanistic psychology is largely about finding out how to realise one's potential by, in the first place, uncovering and exploring the factors in one's life that are unfulfilling and disempowering. These may be circumstances or the effects of past experiences. When I started going to humanistic psychology groups, I did not regard myself as a patient in need of therapy, but as an explorer wanting to explore my own nature and to add something more fulfilling to my life. After four years of experience of different types of group and learning about a lot of different techniques, both mental and physical, I wanted to take that next step of adding the enriching transpersonal element and knitting this into my growing involvement in Paganism and Wicca. This was what I wanted to explore and share with others through Pagan Pathfinders.

Combining the techniques of humanistic psychology with the focused awareness and meditation techniques of the mystical traditions, a powerful set of tools develops to encourage this letting go, to allow the experience of self-transcendence to creep up on us and surprise us with expanded horizons, new realisations, changes of perspective and valuation, and a wonderful sense of freedom.

Carl Jung, who developed the technique of Active Imagination, was fascinated by the universality of religion in all human societies. He carried out an extensive study of religious forms, myths and legends and was struck by the similarity of themes in different religions. Many of them were related to the elemental forces of nature: the ocean, storms and thunder, fire, rain and wind, earthquakes, sacred mountains, rivers, springs, trees. Others were related to human life and qualities: availability of food, pestilence, birth and death, love, war, beauty, wisdom; and to the great imponderables: creation, life after death, good and evil, tempters and tricksters, evaluation and judgement. Jung called these formulations the "Collective Unconscious" and saw myths as shared cultural dreams that give society an identity and cohesion, a focus for its spiritual life. The themes and personifications within the collective unconscious he called "archetypes", defined as "intelligent energies", patterns of universal forces that are seen within the individual, in society as a whole, and even in what we perceive as our world and our universe. They are cosmic forces that work within us, through us, and around us.[2]

> "All the most powerful ideas in history go back to archetypes. This is particularly true of religious ideas, but the central concepts of science, philosophy and ethics are no exception to this rule. In their present form they are variants of archetypal ideas created by consciously applying and adapting these ideas to reality. For it is the function of consciousness, not only to recognize and assimilate the external world through the gateway of the senses, but to translate into visible reality the world within us."
>
> (C.G. Jung, 1931)

Jung felt that modern life had become much too focused on the use of reason and intellect:

> "The more the critical reason dominates, the more impoverished life becomes; but the more of the unconscious, the more of myth we are capable of making conscious, the more of life we integrate. Overvalued reason has this in common with political absolutism: under its dominion the individual is pauperised."
>
> (C.G. Jung, 1961)

We made extensive use of archetypal images in Pagan Pathfinders, at every level, through the use of Active Imagination[3]. The first level was as an aid to creating an effect, such as the image of the Golden Bubble. This stage also included such imaginings as drawing up energy from within the earth, or down from the sun and moon, nourishing ourselves, or perhaps imagining oneself floating in the sea under a full moon, feeling oneself gradually dissolving and letting go. At a more complex level we mined the powerful archetypal images and mythic stories of gods and goddesses from many ages and places (myths from Pagan Europe, Ancient Egypt, Hinduism) designed to facilitate the dialogue between the conscious and unconscious. We explored the energies within the Tarot card images and representations of signs of the Zodiac. Everything was grist to our mill if we could see it assisting the process of self-discovery and expanding our horizons, opening the gates of creativity and renewing our sense of wonder and potential.

Endnotes

1. The term "self-actualisation" was coined by Kurt Goldstein (1878-1965) who saw reaching for self-actualisation as the basic human drive to become one's potentialities – the driving force of individual and social progress. Goldstein was a German neurologist and psychiatrist whose innovative ideas influenced not only Maslow, but many of the leading thinkers in humanistic psychology and humanistic therapies.
2. I have explored the use of mythological archetypal images to empower ourselves more fully in "The Gods Within" (Williams, J.M. & Cox, Z., 2008), a series of essays and evocations based on gods and goddesses of antiquity.
3. See also the talk on auto-suggestion in Part 2 of this book.

chapter four
THE PAGAN CONTEXT

I was brought up as a Church of England Christian. My father was a village parson who died when I was only four years old. Thanks to a remarkable organisation called "The Clergy Orphan Society", I and my older brother and sister received a reasonably good education at minor Church of England public boarding schools with prayers and hymns in our own chapel twice a day. I unquestioningly accepted the claims of Christianity to be the revealed true religion[1]. Questioning such basic truths was not encouraged at school or at home. However, my university experience as a psychology undergraduate changed my outlook dramatically. It started in October 1946, when most of the intake were recently demobbed ex-service men and women with considerably more life experience than my own. Before the end of my first year at college, while pondering all the different views and attitudes that I was coming across, the thought occurred to me, "Perhaps it's not true!", and a great weight of guilt and inner conflict fell from my shoulders.

After some years of freedom from any involvement with religion, I became interested in Buddhist philosophy and Eastern ideas on personal development through yoga and meditation. Then came Aldous Huxley's "The Doors of Perception" (1954) and its companion essay, "Heaven and Hell", describing his experiences with mescaline. It gave me a yearning for the sense of expanded horizons, personal growth and self-transcendence that he described, and coincided with my first contact with Wicca. I found the Pagan viewpoint instantly appealing. As I learnt more about the various European Pagan paths and also Hindu and Ancient Egyptian mythology, I realised what a rich source of archetypal material they provided and how full of wisdom they were. They expressed not only the formative influences within one's life, but the ways humans relate to each other as social groups and how they relate to the natural world.

All the Pagan paths are essentially nature based. They focus on the sense of connectedness to the natural world, the rhythms of the seasons, of sun, moon and stars, birth, growth, death and renewal; the way balance is maintained; on how fragile is the individual life, yet how tough, inventive and adaptable is life, a great flowing river; how much we owe to our pioneering ancestors, going back through all the stages of humanity and beyond, even as far as the single cell organisms setting out on this great life adventure. Pagans are also aware that life as we know it has evolved within the context of this planet, influenced by and also influencing the way in which the planet changes. Our planet is restless, changing its polarity, its climate, its oceans and landmasses. Living organisms have changed the composition of the atmosphere and the waters and winds, and been changed in turn by them in a wonderful interactive dance. Planet Earth is also in a context, a dance with the sun and the moon, both of which have phases and cycles that interact with and influence the planet itself and the life that has developed on it. At this point, the human imagination tends to become overloaded with the wonder and majesty of it all as it glimpses the scope of the universal cosmic dance. The sense of exaltation, of being in the presence of and part of something sacred, may give rise to images of gods and goddesses, such as Nuit, the Egyptian Goddess whose body is the starry night sky, Goddess of Infinite Possibility. Others may express their feelings in dance or song, in shared ritual, or in poetic imagery and language:

> "And before my face, beloved of gods and men, thine inmost Divine Self shall be enfolded in the rapture of the Infinite."
>
> (From the much loved Wiccan "Charge of the Goddess" by Doreen Valiente)

This is how the Pagan viewpoint was presented in the Pagan Pathfinders leaflet:

> "Paganism is an attitude of mind, a way of being that is in tune with the natural forces of the universe. Those on a Pagan spiritual path aim to heighten their awareness of their oneness with the Earth, the cycle of the seasons and the greater wheels of Sun, Moon and Stars, of Life and Death. The search is also within, to discover and manifest the powers latent within the human mind. We all have within us resources of energy, creativity and joyousness that remain largely unrealised. Pagan Pathfinders aim to explore and develop the Pagan way of being by tapping these inner resources so that we may participate more fully in the ecstasy of the Cosmic Dance."

The intuitive feeling of connectedness to all life is not confined to Pagans, but is shared with many others, especially those in the ecology movement and New Agers responding to their psychedelic experiences. In the late 1960s and 1970s, this intuitive feeling received wonderful scientific confirmation from the lateral-thinking scientist, James Lovelock, when he put forward his Gaia hypothesis. The very name, Gaia, the Greek Goddess of the Earth,[2] perfectly captured the concept.

The Gaia hypothesis emerged from Lovelock's work for NASA to try to determine whether Mars could support any life of the sort found on Earth. Using spectroscopy to analyse the composition of the atmosphere of Mars, Lovelock concluded that it could not. So how had life arisen on Earth in all its amazing diversity? Lovelock defines Gaia as:

> "... a complex entity involving the Earth's biosphere, atmosphere, oceans, and soil; the totality constituting a feedback or cybernetic system which seeks an optimal

> physical and chemical environment for life on this planet.... the entire range of living matter on Earth, from whales to viruses, and from oaks to algae, could be regarded as constituting a single living entity, capable of manipulating the Earth's atmosphere to suit its overall needs and endowed with faculties and powers far beyond those of its constituent parts."
>
> (James Lovelock, "Gaia: A New Look at Life on Earth", 1979)

Lovelock is a highly respected, world-renowned scientist with many patents for inventions and awards for his diverse contributions. Born in 1919, he is now over a hundred years old. He recounts how his hypothesis was received with interest and respect by physicists and climatologists, but with angry rejection by biologists as counter to the Darwinian theory of evolution. Over the decades since he first put forward his Gaia hypothesis, a great deal of evidence to support it has been collected and it has now been upgraded from a "hypothesis" to a "theory". Professor William Hamilton, a leading evolutionary biologist, was originally sceptical, but in 1999 described it as a "Copernican" insight, as shattering to current thinking as Copernicus's theory that the Earth and other planets went around the sun; what was now needed was a Newton to describe how it worked.

To many Pagans, unravelling the science of the totality of Planet Earth as a living, self-regulating entity increases their sense of awe and wonder, but also adds a deep sense of humility, even shame. How could we have ever thought the Earth was there for our benefit to use as we liked? Like children in a sweet shop, we have greedily plundered the Earth's resources, used our technology to modify plants and animals, destroyed habitats, cut down vast tracts of rainforest, part of the very mechanism that helps to regulate our atmosphere, and we have proliferated to the point where our own survival is endangered, especially when our own activities contribute to the melting of the ice caps so that the rise in sea level reduces the amount of inhabitable land.

At one point, Lovelock was in a state of despair, believing that humanity had already gone too far and Earth would inevitably become uninhabitable to humans and many other species, but more recent information about the rate of change in temperature and other measures have led him to modify this prediction; we still have a chance to redeem the situation and a responsibility to try:

> "We are the intelligent elite among animal life on Earth and whatever our mistakes, [Earth] needs us. This may seem an odd statement after all that I have said about the way 20th century humans became almost a planetary disease organism. But it has taken [Earth] 2.5 billion years to evolve an animal that can think and communicate its thoughts. If we become extinct she has little chance of evolving another."

But he also says:

> "... if we fail to take care of the Earth, it surely will take care of itself by making us no longer welcome."
>
> ("The Vanishing Face of Gaia: A Final Warning", 2006)

In a 2012 BBC Radio programme in the series "The Life Scientific", presented by Jim Al-Khalili, Lovelock commented that if human activity causes catastrophic global warming and humanity becomes virtually extinct, Gaia will eventually restore balance, but Earth cycles can take millions of years whereas human cycles are numbered in thousands.

Ever the dispassionate scientist, Lovelock summed up his position in his opening remarks to a 1999 conference at Oxford University:

> "Gaia is a theory of science and is therefore always provisional and evolving. It is never dogmatic or certain

> and could even be wrong. Provisional it may be but, being of the palpable Earth, it is something tangible to love and fear and think we understand. We can put our trust, even faith, in Gaia, and this is different from the cold certainty of purposeless atheism or an unwavering belief in God's purpose ... I have put before you the proposition that Gaia, in addition to being a theory in science, offers a worldview for agnostics. This would require an interactive trust in Gaia, not blind faith. A trust that accepts that, like us, Gaia has a finite life span and is provisional."

Darwinian evolution also is a theory of science and therefore "provisional and evolving". As genetic research progresses, it is becoming apparent that the processes of DNA are a lot more complex than were at first envisaged. While acknowledging that Darwinian "survival of the fittest" is a major factor driving evolution, it is now thought not to be the only factor. Two other processes so far identified seem to play a part: epigenetic switching and gene transfer.

Epigenetic switching is a process whereby environmental effects can switch genes on or off and bring about heritable changes to the genome. Identical twins start their development with identical sets of genes but recent studies have found that their genomes can start to diverge in small ways quite early. A striking example comes from a major study at King's College, London, where a pair of twins had developed what seemed to be quite different personalities: one was happy and confident, the other suffered from bouts of depression. Their genes had diverged significantly due to different life experiences.

Gene transfer is a process by which genes can transfer from the cell of one entity to another. This can happen between unicellular and multicellular entities and between species. The process is complex and still the subject of much exploratory investigation. Medical research has already made some progress in removing faulty genes that cause inherited illnesses, such as

Huntington's chorea, but few illnesses are caused by only one identifiable gene. Such research offers hope of freedom from some crippling ailments, but more worrying is the growing enthusiasm for genetically modified crops. The major ecological charities are concerned that gene transfer may result in unexpected catastrophic environmental effects by the inadvertent transfer of modified genes to the local plant life. Gene transfer is also considered to be a major cause of the development of antibiotic resistant bacteria.

In general Pagans strive to be aware of their environment, to cherish it and to understand our impact on it, whether good or bad. Often Pagans are at the forefront of ecological campaigns, trying to prevent what they view as unsound practices. We constantly ask ourselves: how can we take command of our own environmental input and how can we help others to do so?

The Pagan context for Pagan Pathfinders seems to have expanded to include the science of life itself and the belief systems it has engendered. We must beware of belief systems; they often comprise nuggets of information sown into the collective mind by the media and often lag far behind the cutting edge of ongoing research. The true scientist never forgets that the body of scientific knowledge is based on an evolving set of theories, constantly being expanded and refined, and occasionally superseded, replaced, or engulfed within another overarching theory. The Pagan viewpoint tends to be holistic, knitting together the micro- and macro-cosmic, the inner and outer world; through imagination and imagery, poetic language, music, dance, and joyous exuberance. What I call the "Pagan viewpoint" is not confined to Pagans. Every year a close friend gives me the latest "Trees for Life" calendar. Each month is illustrated with a beautiful photograph of woodland or an unusual tree and usually has a quotation from some wise and passionate lover of trees. In August 2013, I came across this:

> "On a fair morning the mountain invited you to get down and roll in the new grass and flowers ... Every living thing sang, chirped and burgeoned. Massive pines and firs, storm-tossed these many months, soaked up the sun in towering

> dignity. Tassel-eared squirrels, poker-faced but exuding emotion with voice and tail, told you insistently what you already knew full well; that never had there been so rare a day, or so rich a solitude to spend it in."
>
> (Aldo Leopold)

My heart trembled and my eyes prickled with tears at the sheer wonder and magic that he evoked. He did not merely describe a scene, but infused it with the joy and euphoria of his own emotional reaction to it. I had never heard of Aldo Leopold but Google soon showed me what I had missed: another great man with his origins in the nineteenth century, but active well into the twentieth, he is well-known in America as the founder of the Wilderness Movement and a prolific writer on the glory of the changing seasons in the wild places. Jung, too, featured in the 2013 calendar, in a more sober vein, as befits an eminent old man reminiscing about his early life:

> "Trees in particular were mysterious and seemed to me direct embodiments of the incomprehensible meaning of life. For that reason the woods were the place I felt closest to the deepest meaning and to its awe-inspiring workings."
>
> (C.G. Jung, "Memories, Dreams, Reflections")

William James describes these moments as "melting moods", which can be transforming:

> "Especially if we weep! For it is then as if our tears broke through an inveterate inner dam ... leaving us now washed and soft of heart and open to every nobler leading."
>
> (William James, "The Varieties of Religious Experience" 1902)

When I was a little girl in the Cotswolds, we used to get wonderful sunsets and night skies full of stars. I would look at them and feel this prickling of the eyes and the heart full to bursting with joy and wonder. The adults would also admire the sunset or night sky, but with a cool aesthetic appraisal that lacked any intensity of emotion, so I learnt that the adult way was to suppress that reaction of the heart and appraise what I saw more objectively. Later in life, I got a camera and tried to capture anything especially beautiful as a picture to show my friends. It was still to a large extent a way of keeping the "melting mood" at bay. It took psychedelic experiences and a close friendship, openness and contact with the natural world and its rhythms that came through my involvement with the Craft and Paganism, to allow me to regain my child-heart and that sense of living in a magical world zinging with life and potential. The techniques of Pagan Pathfinders are designed to evoke these experiences through active imagination, beautiful language, music, dance and ritual. But humankind's roots are "out there", in nature. Nothing imagined quite matches the direct experience of leaning against a tree and feeling the surging life within it, or touching a rock with an awareness of its weight and the slow rhythms of its formation and destruction, or visiting a place that was sacred to our ancient ancestors who had their own wisdom and understanding of life. To root our indoor exercises in real experience, we made use of my garden when the weather permitted and had annual trips to ancient sacred sites, the sea, or the countryside, for more direct experience and to make these places more vivid in our imaginary journeys.

A Pagan would have no hesitation in describing these experiences of heightened and joyous awareness as "magical", and might find themselves in the unlikely company of the eminent scientist and arch-atheist, Richard Dawkins. He identifies three types of magic: supernatural magic, stage magic and poetic magic[3]. In his view, stage magic is fine as it is known to be enjoyably clever trickery. Supernatural magic is acceptable and even enjoyable as long as it stays in the realms of fairy stories and fiction, but when it is found in the belief systems of adults, it is not acceptable as it precludes any possibility of it ever being explained, "Because anything 'supernatural' must by definition be beyond the reach of a natural explanation." Dawkins' definition of poetic magic is where he makes common ground with Pagans:

> "We are moved to tears by a piece of music and describe the performance as 'magical'. We gaze up at the stars on a dark night with no moon and no city lights and, breathless with joy, we say the sight is 'pure magic'.... In this sense, 'magical' simply means deeply moving, exhilarating: something that gives us goose bumps, something that makes us feel more fully alive. What I hope to show you in this book is that reality – the facts of the real world as understood through the methods of science – is magical in this third sense, the poetic sense, the good to be alive sense." (Dawkins, op. cit.)

I think many Pagans would be in considerable agreement with Dawkins. The differences are largely ones of attitude and stance. In the first place, Pagans actively seek these deeply moving experiences as part of Pagan practice: in their seasonal celebrations, in their lunar rituals, in their daily salutation to their favourite tree or to the brave blade of grass growing between the concrete paving stones, in their awareness of the life all around them, visible and invisible, of which they are a part. Secondly, such feelings are in a sense an act of worship: the experience is both a blessing and a healing, "an occasion for reverence"[4] that is a balm to the inner being. Such experience is a source of comfort in times of stress and pain. Pagans are aware that Nature is not always benign and that life and death, change and decay, storm, flood, earthquake and tsunami are all part of the same process. To feel a part of an on-going process makes one's own pain less personal and one's empathic understanding deeper. The sense of connectedness is like a lodestone that directs our moral compass in making the difficult decisions that we all face from time to time.

Pagans would tend to disagree with Dawkins on what he calls "supernatural magic". In the main, Pagans do not pray to the divine to perform miracles, but attempt to mobilise the archetypal energies of Nature in its widest sense to bring about change. The forces may be poetically clad in the form of gods and goddesses, or elemental powers, or sun or moon, in order to define the type of energy to be directed. Our understanding of what is "natural" and what the human mind is capable of is constantly changing and expanding under the impact of scientific research in cell biology, neuroscience and psychology. Therefore, I return to Vivianne Crowley's useful definition of magic:

> "Magic can be defined as the art of causing change in ways not yet fully explicable to science." (Crowley, op. cit.)

Paganism and Science

The Pagan attitude differs from the strictly scientific one by what I call "giving the benefit of the doubt": unless a process is proven to be effective beyond reasonable doubt, the scientific view tends to regard it as not useful; the Pagan may well think there is enough of a hint of proof of a truth, perhaps tying in with old lore and intuition, to be worth treating as if it were true, pending future research developments. What follows are examples of areas where science begins to explain what many have intuitively felt in themselves, maybe through meditation, or use of other mind-expanding techniques.

The Moon

In all ages and cultures, the moon has been regarded as being mysterious and magical, and the full moon as especially powerful. Its effects on the tides and marine life have long been recognised. More recent research with sensitive modern instruments has found that the effects are detectable in quite small bodies of water and affect the life forms that live in them. Life originated in water and our bodies are largely water; it is thus not particularly surprising to find that the phases of the moon affect humans. Researchers at Basel University, Switzerland, undertook a study of sleep patterns with 33 volunteers spending two nights each in strictly controlled conditions in darkened rooms. The decision to look at sleep patterns in relation to the moon's phases was an afterthought, not the original purpose of the research. They found that at the full moon the volunteers took longer to fall asleep, spent less time in deep sleep, generally slept for less time and reported poorer sleep. There was also a dip in melatonin production, a hormone related to our body clocks. The study was small, but suggests that as well as our body clocks having a response to the time of day, they may also have a response to the phases of the moon.

Endorphins

Editor's note: Jean was fascinated with the study of endorphins and in Pagan Pathfinders she ran a series of sessions dedicated to understanding and working with them. She had unfortunately not finished this section of the book, but it feels wrong to leave out altogether a subject she felt so passionate about. What follows are transcripts of her talks on endorphins, which were given over several sessions and were the result of extensive research. She also wrote a series of pathworkings (guided meditations) to help us understand and work with endorphins and these can be found in Part 2 of this book.

"Introduction to Endorphins" - Talk by Jean Williams (2010)

Endorphins have been discovered mainly in the last 35 years or so. The initial research was in the 1970s and William Bloom wrote his book, 'The Endorphin Effect', in 2001, so he has been doing this work solidly for the last nine years, probably longer.

The research started off looking at drug use and drug addiction and looking for ways in which they could find alternatives to morphine and opium, which wouldn't be addictive, by examining first of all what went on in the cell. By this time they had the techniques and the equipment to look at this cellular level and analyse this microchemistry, biochemistry, and they found that there were indeed sorts of receptors in the cell which allowed the opium/ morphine active ingredients to get into the cell and latch onto it and then affect it, so the question then arose: if there are receptors already in the human cell, was this because the human body was capable of producing something similar which would work in the same way? And lo and behold they did find that this was so.

A lot of the initial research was in the States, but it was a couple of researchers at Aberdeen University who identified the constituents of endorphin initially. They called it enkephalins, presumably because they thought it was generated by the brain, but the American researchers who took that up came up with the term endorphins, endogenous morphines, which was the term that stuck with it. So far they have identified about 20 types of endorphins and they are all to do with good feelings, making you feel good, making you feel happy and things of that sort, and variations according to where in the body they are.

They are part of a family of biochemicals known as neuropeptides and these include all the other indicators of emotion, so adrenalin which gives you feelings of fight or flight and things like that, but endorphins are the ones to do with making you feel good, which is very useful. But all of these neuropeptides carry information around the body and they too are part of an even bigger group of biochemical agents called amino acids, of which DNA is one. They are all to do with the information system within the body. One of the things that they came to a conclusion on was that you think of the body as a mechanical type of device, but basically it is an enormously complex information system. Everything is influencing everything else and the influences go in every possible way, and they found that endorphins could be produced in particular parts of the body. So if you have a pain in a particular part you can do mental exercises to reduce the pain in that part of the body, but they can also be produced in the mind. They can be produced anywhere in the body and they can work together, and you can build up what he calls a cascade of endorphins in the body which he says in the really higher states leads you into the 'bliss fields', as he calls them, and that is what he is trying to teach: techniques for people to access a state of wellbeing, a state of being happy and contented, or any aspect of good feelings, and to be able to increase these within the body so that instead of just dealing with one particular aspect of your body, that you can get this feeling of it spreading throughout the body.

So what he says is that the result of all of this is a real understanding that the nervous system, the immune system, the endocrine system, are all part of this information system throughout the body. They all interact with each other and can all influence it, so that if something happens to you from outside, it affects your mood and the production of things, but then you can fight back by changing your mood, by using some of his techniques to keep the good feeling going and that sort of thing. I haven't got to the bit in the book yet about people who have really bad things happen to them in their life and how it strengthens you to cope with that sort of thing, but I will get there. This is one of those courses when the person telling you about it is only one chapter ahead of you.

So there is continuous communication going on throughout the system. It is a busy information system. He says that people say, 'Oh, surely how you are feeling is just biochemistry', but it is not just biochemistry. It is biochemistry for looking at the biochemistry of the body, but it is emotion if you are looking at the feelings of the body and consciousness of what you are actually feeling and the biochemistry influences your mood. Your mood, what is happening to you, what you do with your mind, what you imagine, what you remember, influences the biochemistry. It is going backwards and forwards all the time and the idea is to gradually gain some kind of mastery of it.

The other thing is that all cellular creatures have these endorphins, from the smallest blob to the most complex structures, so you may like to think of those little one cell animals being happy little blobs. He relates this to the old spiritual practices. What he is saying is that it is actually quite simple to get to a state of happiness and expanded awareness, without going through years and years of mental discipline and meditating for hours. At one stage of his life he was a meditation junkie, spending five or more hours a day meditating because it was so lovely. The fact that it is in every sort of cellular creature he relates to the connection of all life, to what has been called 'chi' in China and 'prana' in India and things like that, the sort of life force. He relates this to what he calls the 'bliss field', this sort of connectedness to everything and the sense that you are not only connected to everything, but part of everything, so you can expand your awareness and feel this sense of being part of this huge thing, so that you almost are the huge thing, the huge cosmos, the planet and so on.

There is nothing to say that you can't have different sorts of neuropeptides all happening at once. You probably need them, you probably need adrenalin, but you can also have endorphins making you feel good ... Also things like anger, which are usually regarded as unpleasant feelings and to most people are, you can also sometimes find an exhilaration in being angry, 'I'm not going to put up with this anymore', you are going to fight back and deal with whatever it is.

Editor's note: After this introduction, the group then utilised William Bloom's technique of calling to mind "mental strawberries". We had to think of a list of things which trigger happy memories or feelings for us. As Bloom states:

> "The strawberry represents the positive trigger, memory, sight, smell, taste, event or encounter which can focus your attention away from hellish circumstances and connect you with a different, more benevolent reality. Even in the worst situation, a strawberry can trigger endorphins and enable you to connect with the benevolence of life."
>
> (William Bloom, "The Endorphin Effect" 2001)

So a strawberry might be the feeling of warmth and joy you experience when greeting an old friend, the sight of a beautiful flower, the taste of honey, or the sound of a particular piece of music. If you compose a mental list of these strawberries, in theory you can call them to mind to trigger endorphins and hold onto that pleasurable, happy feeling. Here we see techniques for personal development and science aligning.

"Endorphins Part 2" – Talk by Jean Williams (2010)

William Bloom says – I certainly find it is true of myself – that we all too easily see something pleasant, or we have a pleasant feeling, or something that gives us a smile and feel a lift of the heart and then we move on quickly. We are busy, busy, busy all the time. We don't stop and enjoy it. His theory is that by that we are cutting ourselves off from our own natural healing powers and that if something attracts you, like if you see a beautiful flower, or a lovely cat, or a person that you really love that you are greeting, put your awareness on that moment, put your awareness on feeling a moment of joy and pleasure, because that is a very healing thing. It encourages the endorphins and, if you pause, it lets the endorphins gather momentum, as it were, go to a deeper level within you and spread, because he says that endorphins are produced all over the body in very specific areas, so if you see something, maybe something very beautiful with your eyes, the endorphins will be produced in the vision section of the brain at the back of the head, but if you then pause and appreciate it, it then spreads to other parts of your mind and even down into the body because you feel it in your solar plexus and your heart. You let go. A little bit of relaxation spreads all the way down. The pleasurable feeling spreads all the way down.

He says that by rushing around and always thinking about what we are doing next, and worrying about things, and trying to meet all the demands on us and so on, we are actually cutting ourselves off from a natural healing process and building up trouble for ourselves in the future. So he is saying that this is an important part of it: being aware and pausing, so that that awareness can really be appreciated and so on. It doesn't have to be for long, but it does make a difference and if you are in a stressful situation then produce one of your mental strawberries. Think of a picture. He recommends that in your work situation, or places where you do a lot of work at home, put things that are strawberry triggers, as it were, like a picture of something you really love, or a flower, or a stone, or a shell, or if there is something that for you reminds you of a happy time, or gives you pleasure just to look at it, then you can just pause for a moment and look at that and let yourself relax a bit, let yourself heal a bit, which seems to me to make sense.

He says that the sort of pleasure that you get from seeing something beautiful, or something valuable to you, something precious, something you love, actually releases the tensions in the face, round the eyes, round the mouth, tensions in the solar plexus, round the heart and that sort of thing, so that through this we can actually mobilise our endorphins and increase our sense of wellbeing. So it is pausing and being aware, letting the awareness develop and the pleasure develop and treasure those moments, treasure the triggers, whether it is a person, a flower, an idea, a memory, or whatever.

He stresses also that bodily awareness is important. I think I described it last week as there is always a sensation, a bodily feeling of tension, or relaxation, or tightness, or pain, or discomfort of some sort and that is another aspect of the emotion you are feeling, so that if you are angry you have your shoulders hunched, if you are afraid you have your solar plexus and stomach all tensed up. So he stresses the importance of being aware of what you are feeling in your body and relaxing it.

So the more that you can let the pleasurable feelings develop and the more the endorphin effect spreads through all of the body, the more benefit you get from it, the more pleasure you have in your life, the happier you are, which we all like to be.

Another thing that he says is that if there is something wrong, if you are hurt in an accident and you break a limb, or you have a cut, or you have toothache, or whatever, or you have emotional pain from having a row with someone, or someone is injured that you love and you are anxious about them, or someone even dies, whatever it is, that you should treat your body and the hurt with tenderness. I think very often if we are in pain, or something goes wrong with our body, we tend to feel that it has let us down. We are almost cross with it. I was very cross with my heart for developing problems, you know, how can it do that? I have always treated it well and taken exercise and things like that. It took a long time before I said no, really my poor little heart has been beating all these years, year after year, day after day, of course it has got a bit worn out. You have to learn to treasure it and love it and he says you have to cradle it, cradle the bit of you that is hurting, either mentally or physically, and similarly if you are in emotional pain, be kind to yourself about it and treat yourself gently, treat your body with affection, respectful affection for your own body. He talks about you as being the mind, but being dependent on the function of this incredible mammal which is highly strung, but very efficient and we should look after it and treasure it and cradle it and generally nurture and nourish it.

"Endorphins Part 3: The Curled Deer" – Talk by Jean Williams (2010)

I want to talk about something William Bloom calls the 'curled deer' and it is about nurturing yourself and really good rest and sleep. One of the things he stresses is being kind to yourself and looking after your animal part, your animal aspect, your body, by loving it and I realised that to some extent I have been rather bad at that. I get cross with my body if it lets me down, I get cross with my heart for daring to have a faulty heart valve. I tend to think I shouldn't have these flaws, I shouldn't have these things, it is something I have done wrong, which is very puritanical and goes back to something wrong with the British culture. What he says is that you should really appreciate the way that your body keeps going and nurture it and love it and heal it by sending it loving and nourishing, caring thoughts.

This takes it a little bit further with this curled deer because he says imagine that you have a little deer in your abdomen, a little baby deer, and it is curled up with its nose on its tail, deeply asleep and safe, and that if you visualise this and imagine it, or imagine yourself being that little deer, whatever comes easiest to you - it is important to have flexibility and find out how it works for you - that you can really feel yourself relaxed and nurtured and safe and that you sleep really well, so he is saying that when you are going to bed at night, or just taking a nap -- he is very much in favour of the short nap when you are feeling a bit tired after lunch, for instance. He says in his workshops he always has a ten-minute break after lunch where everybody visualises being a curled deer fast asleep, and some people really fall quite deeply asleep in that time and it is very restoring, so this is one of his basic developments of the process.

After you have visualised your strawberries and dwelt on them and enhanced the idea, thought about it and increased your awareness of it, do that first and then visualise this curled deer, yourself as a curled deer, or a curled deer within your body, and let yourself really relax and feel that safety and that love and that nurturing of yourself.

On top of that he then builds what he calls this micro-cosmic orbit exercise. What he is saying is that when you get to this deep state of relaxation that comes from really feeling good within yourself, then you are like a magnet drawing in energy from the cosmos around you. He says that the way you can harness this energy is to start by getting your own micro-cosmic orbit going, which is sort of like a breathing exercise, where you envisage the in-breath is drawing energy up your backbone, over the top of your head, and on your out-breath it goes out down your front and then it just circles around you like that. Then you can take that further and link it into the macro-cosmic orbit of the earth and the sun and the wider cosmos.

I have left out one little bit. One thing you should do to complete the circuit of linking up the spine and coming down the front is to put the tip of your tongue on the roof of your mouth, sort of halfway back on the hard palate, and then you just sort of breathe, drawing that air up the back and down the front. Then you just visualise that this is connecting gradually to drawing in the bigger energies around you from the earth and the sun and the cosmos. It is so that it makes the connection. This comes from Chinese medicine. It makes the connection between the two parts of the body. The great masters of Chinese medicine say it is also quite a cooling way of breathing. I have come across that in yoga classes.

At any rate, what I thought we would do is we would try going through the exercise as he sets it out and then I will add a little bit of connection to Pagan gods at the end, just to add our own particular stamp on it.[5]

Editor's note: We then explored the endorphin effect through a series of pathworkings (guided meditations) which are included in The Pagan Pathfinders Workbook, Part 2 of this book.

Conclusion – The Pagan Context

I am more interested in religious experience than in belief systems. The English language has many words to describe religious experience: "mystical", "numinous", "spiritual", "sense of mystery". None of these words necessarily imply a belief system. Whereas a believer might clothe their religious experience in images of their faith, there is no specific dogma that binds all Pagans together. An eclectic Pagan might deliberately focus on their concept of the Goddess of the Moon, the Lord of the Greenwood, an Elemental, or an animal-headed God of Ancient Egypt, realising that religious imagery arises from within the human mind as metaphors and representations of their hopes and fears, aspirations and ideals; of the archetypal forces that they sense within themselves, within society and within the forces of nature.

A particularly intense peak experience is often described as "religious". The characteristics seem to be that it persists for more than a brief "eureka!" moment; it includes a sense of being in a wonderful timeless moment, of being part of, connected to, or in touch with some energy/power/presence much greater than oneself. There may be a sense of momentarily grasping great cosmic truths, an awareness of being within a wonderful unfathomable mystery, an on-going process in which everything is connected and unfolding in a wonderful harmony that transcends the mundane, limited human viewpoint.

Pagans are sometimes referred to contemptuously as "tree huggers". If you have never leaned against a tree, put your hands and forehead on the bark, relaxed, and given the experience your full attention, you don't know what you have missed.

Endnotes

1. Compared with some current Christian sects, the literalness of the bible did not feature strongly. The six days of creation were interpreted as metaphors for epochs; Darwinian evolution was a perfectly acceptable explanation of the wonderful way in which God worked.
2. Suggested to Lovelock by his friend, William Golding. The association with Pagans, Greens and New Agers sadly did not enhance Lovelock's reputation among scientists.
3. Richard Dawkins, "The Magic of Reality", 2012.
4. An apposite phrase used by Mike Stygal, former Pagan Federation president.
5. See 'The Curled Deer Pathworking' in Part 2 of this book.

chapter five
PAGAN PATHFINDERS MEETINGS

Editor's Note: This and the following chapters were not completed by Jean before she passed away, so have been contributed to or written by the editor, at all times with care and consideration, keeping in mind the original intent of the book which was to help and encourage others to run their own group.

****

I organised Pagan Pathfinders to suit my own inclinations for how I liked to interact with people within the Pagan and humanistic community. Others may choose quite different arrangements and be just as effective, or indeed more so. However, it may be helpful to describe my approach and the reasons that lay behind it.

The General Organisation and Social Context

Pagan Pathfinders was a weekly group, held in my house on Monday evenings. The year was broken into three sessions, similar to school terms: Autumn, Winter/Spring, and Summer, each lasting ten to twelve weeks. Applicants were asked to commit themselves to regular attendance for at least one session in order to have continuity, build up familiarity with the techniques and type of content, and to get to know other people in the group. My preference is for a group of people that I get to know and who get to know each other, rather than dealing with groups of strangers. In such a way trust is built up, enabling deeper experiences in the group. Nothing was more pleasing than finding that people who met at Pagan Pathfinders were arranging to meet together elsewhere as friends and perhaps pursue Pagan interests together. I myself made many long-term friends through Pagan Pathfinders.

A meeting lasted about two and a half hours: half an hour for people to assemble and meet together beforehand over a cup of tea, an hour-and-a-half of work, and half an hour afterwards for more tea and a bit to eat, grounding oneself back into the real world – a vital step before making the journey home. As Aldous Huxley says, the reason why we cannot stay in a state of exaltation is that we cannot function effectively or safely in it. I kept to a fairly strict timetable, aware that some people had quite long journeys home afterwards. The working hour-and-a-half started on time, whether people had arrived or not. I have a built-in time sense, it seems, and rarely over-ran by more than 15 minutes. Other group members who prepared exercises for the group occasionally over-ran by more.

I made no charge for Pagan Pathfinders. I had room at home for a group of up to about 15 people. I had an adequate salary and minimal expenses (mainly candles) and I rarely had to buy any biscuits, even for personal consumption, as those attending kept me fully supplied. People also brought grapes, crisps, chocolate, sushi, guacamole and all sorts of delicacies, as the concept of grounding became an excuse for a small feast and general social.

We met first in a room with a big table on which the tea and food could be served. When the group was well attended, this was a very convivial time with people squashed up together chatting away. It is important to encourage newcomers to interact with other group members. It can be quite intimidating to join a group of people who all seem to know each other and who are talking away on subjects of common interest. Someone feeling socially awkward and unwelcomed is likely to find it impossible to relax and participate in what follows.

Applicants were always asked to write a letter or email about themselves and their Pagan interests and often I met them or we spoke on the phone; in this way I made sure I had some information about them that I could use when introducing them, that would encourage other members to talk to them. If someone was obviously not managing to join the talk, I would spend some time talking to them myself and then collar one of the group members with a common interest and organise a conversation between them. It is also important of course to consider security if hosting in your own home, so a good idea to scope the person out first.

Applicants were not required to have any previous experience in group work, but an interest in Paganism and personal development was implicit. As it said in the publicity leaflet: "All those prepared to adventure into inner space, whether new to Paganism or experienced, can benefit. An interest in personal growth and transcendental experience is assumed."

The Meeting Room

The room where we worked was prepared in advance by the removal of several items of furniture to provide as much clear space as possible. Cushions were dotted around and candles lined up on the mantelpiece and bookcases, and also placed at the four corners to mark the Elemental Quarters: North, East, South and West. Of course you are free to use whatever colours you feel best, but we placed a green candle in the North representing earth, yellow or white in the East for air, red in the South for fire and blue in the West for water.

Over the years, a treasure trove of accessories was acquired, constructed or donated by group members: altar cloths, elemental symbols, chalices, wands, candle holders, percussion instruments, incense, even robes and head-dresses. While all these contributed to the atmosphere and sense of occasion, none was strictly necessary. For Pagan Pathfinders as I conceive it, the necessities are subdued lighting (preferably candlelight), space to move about and to sit, the where-with-all to play music, plain paper, pens for writing with, and crayons, pens or chalks for drawing. In addition, some exercises require special items (e.g. Tarot cards) and most seasonal celebrations and other informal rituals included some form of cakes and wine.

Aspects of a Meeting

The object of Pagan Pathfinders was to combine the ancient methods of spiritual development with the modern techniques of inner exploration used in Humanistic Psychology, within a broad and eclectic Pagan framework.

The emphasis in Pagan Pathfinders was doing and experiencing rather than discussing or lecturing. Each meeting was designed to be an interesting, enjoyable and enriching experience, as well as to further the development of disciplines, skills and understandings that would be of value to participants in their daily lives. Methods of exploration are drawn from a wide range of religious disciplines, both Western and Eastern, and also from Humanistic Psychology and the Personal Growth Movement. Similarly, god-forms and archetypal images are employed from diverse Pagan pantheons, astrology, the Tarot and other sources. Pagan Pathfinders meetings are thus suitable for people who want to learn some of the basic skills common to most Pagan schools, without committing themselves to any one path. The path of attendees varied greatly, from New Age seeker, to eclectic Pagan, to ecologist, to Wiccan, to Druid, to Heathen and to Hedgewitch.

Techniques used in Pagan Pathfinders meetings included: deep relaxation, auto-suggestion, heightened awareness, active imagination, trance work, energy raising, empowerment of the true will and healing. Participants were free to share ideas and techniques and often worked together in pairs or as a group. Examples of all of these practices are set out in Part 2 of this book.

It was key that the meeting began with grounding and centring. Combined with the different atmosphere of the meeting room which was already created with dim lighting, candles, incense and such like, taking a moment to pause, clear our minds of everyday thoughts and worries, trying to dwell in the now, grounding ourselves in that room, at that time, was very important. This would usually be done by the group beginning standing and stretching or wiggling about, shaking out tensions, perhaps doing some simple yoga stretches, or just standing tall and rooted. We might then do some breathing exercises, tuning into our breath, paying attention to it going in and out, thus focusing the mind and helping to clear room in the mind for whatever work we were to do. Partner work (see below) such as massage or polarity healing is also a good grounding exercise, as is chanting together as a group. The aim is to loosen up physically and mentally, with regular practice conditioning ourselves into knowing that now is the time for deeper work and for concentration. This would be followed by the Golden Bubble meditation and then whatever deeper work was planned for that evening.

Example of a meeting programme

If not celebrating a seasonal festival such as Beltane or Yule, a typical evening's programme would involve the following:

1. Arrival and chat over tea and snacks.
2. Clear the space for the meeting.
3. Light candles and/or incense.
4. Session facilitator announces the beginning of the meeting.
5. Grounding. Begin seated with relaxed breathing followed by a seated meditation (see Part 2), or alternatively;
6. Begin standing. Ask participants to stretch, breathe deeply, shake out tensions and negative emotions. Do a moving meditation (see Part 2).
7. Option for partner work (see below).
8. Golden Bubble meditation (see Prologue).
9. Pathworking and/or ritual (see Part 2).
10. Option to discuss pathworking together; what participants saw, felt or learned.
11. Close the meeting by standing together in a circle, holding hands, feeling the energy flowing from hand to hand, around the group, from one person to the other, feeling the connection, fellowship and trust. Revel in that feeling for a while.
12. Finish by all saying something akin to "Merry meet, merry part and merry meet again!"
13. Dispel the working atmosphere and ground everyone with food and tea and chats, sharing the experiences.

Notes:

1. Usually the group leader will lead the meditations by reading them aloud, or from memory, unless someone else is conducting the session. It is important to think of the voice as a wonderful tool, capable of transporting people out of the everyday world and into the inner realms of their mind. Read slowly and allow pauses for people to absorb what has been said and time for their mind to go on a journey.

2. If there has been a ritual for a seasonal celebration, or in honour of a particular deity or element, this will usually end with food being passed around the circle (such as a bowl of small cakes or biscuits) and a chalice of wine, each person taking a sip and maybe offering a toast.

At the end of each session the participants will hopefully feel a sense of having gained some wisdom and guidance, a sense of resolution, a blessing or gift, or a better understanding of their own purpose and true will and how to achieve what it is they need.

Pathworkings

As mentioned previously, pathworkings were integral to Pagan Pathfinders and one was done at almost every session. A pathworking is a guided meditation, whereby the participants enter a relaxed and transcendental state and go on a mental journey, guided by a speaker (usually the leader), during which they may meet archetypes representing key psychological themes such as higher wisdom, confidence, expansion, true will, or self-acceptance, or they may meet the higher aspects of themselves, as well as deity archetypes and guides. Each time a story unfolded, such as a journey to a moonlit sea cave where you would encounter a guide, perhaps a wise crone who may share lessons with you. Through regular practice participants should find themselves able to enter this trance state and bring back valuable lessons from their subconscious mind. It was always prefaced with the Golden Bubble meditation and at the start of every pathworking we slowed our thoughts and breathing, entering a trance-like state. Often the start of the pathworking involved going down some stairs, or through a door, a symbolic representation of leaving behind the everyday and stepping into a deeper realm of consciousness. The pathworkings were where Jean utilised Pagan imagery and archetypes to explore psychological themes, such as those mentioned above, and psychological techniques to achieve higher states of consciousness, gaining deep wisdom and exploring our own inner potential. She used imagery from Celtic mythology, as well as Egyptian and Eastern mystery traditions. These metaphors and symbols helped us to tune into our own potential and knowledge, however hidden we may have thought it was.

Pathworkings were designed to access inner wisdom from the subconscious mind, to seek guidance (either generally or perhaps asking a specific question), to interact with deity and energy archetypes and to aid relaxation and a sense of connection to the universe all around us. Jean used her background in psychology to pinpoint five psychological themes people could work through, using pathworking as a tool:

- Lost, neglected, or repressed aspects of yourself.
- One's higher wisdom.
- Confidence, expansion, stature, the gods and goddesses as higher versions of self.
- Direction and decisions.
- Self-acceptance, appreciation, value, strengths/weaknesses.

Editor's note: Jean wrote further about pathworkings:

For these longer exercises, many people prefer to lie on the floor so that they can achieve a more comfortable state of total relaxation without aching backs or painful ankles distracting them. Some people, however, have difficulty staying awake under these circumstances and need to sit up!

It is recommended that the 'trip' or guided fantasy (pathworking) should be the last item of the session so that the previous things are a preparation for it. Participants are thus already relaxed and centred, their brains functioning in the imaging rather than the intellectualising mode. Nonetheless, some further relaxation and preparation for the trip is also advisable in order to awaken all the imaging faculties – hearing, touch, smell, muscle sense, as well as sight.

We usually use an induction based on that given in the book 'Mind Games'[1]: the finding of a door at the back of a cupboard, the discovery of a stone staircase going down, or the finding of a boat on an underground river, for example. However, halfway down the stairs we introduce a landing on which is a door set in a stone arch. This door leads to one's own secret magical temple. The temple is furnished with a waist high altar on which is a candle. The altar is flanked by two pillars, one black and one white. There is also a wooden chest in which to keep one's magical weapons:

> A wand for the element of fire, wrapped in scarlet silk.
> A sword or dagger for the element of air, wrapped in yellow silk.
> A cup or chalice for the element of water, wrapped in blue silk.
> A pentacle for the element of earth, wrapped in green silk.

Each participant also has within the chest a talisman which is put on before embarking on the trip. The design of the talisman is whatever seems appropriate to the individual and it serves as a source of power and protection. I am often asked whether working with powerful archetypal images in this way is dangerous as many books utter dire warnings about it. In my experience, it is extremely rare for participants in these trips to encounter any difficulties or problems that threaten to seriously disturb or overwhelm them. Therefore, the more common problem is that people over-protect themselves from anything that might be mildly disturbing. A number of simple precautions are taken of which the use of the imaginary talisman is one. It can be of considerable help in giving people the confidence, the courage and the power to confront unpleasant aspects of themselves as disturbing and alarming archetypal images. Some of the trips are quite challenging – the object is personal growth and there is no change without a certain amount of pain, but the pain is far outweighed by the sense of enhanced freedom and energy that growth brings.

Some people who have not used their imaginations in this way before may find the very process itself disturbing; they feel themselves being swamped by images and feel that they are losing their grip on their usual way of being in control of their world. These people need reassurance that they can control their own state through the use of their talisman and also through simple grounding and breathing exercises. If they feel overwhelmed or frightened, they should take deep breaths and feel the floor, put their attention on their bodies and their physical sensations. But they are also encouraged to trust their own higher self to guard them, so that they can feel free to let go and explore these new inner realms that are so exciting and rewarding. They are told that there is within them a self-protecting mechanism that will prevent them from going too far and trying to deal with more than they are able to absorb in one session.

Another protective device is the magic circle. When the secret temple has been entered in the mind, the candle lit and the talisman put on, the participants can be asked to draw in their mind's eye a circle of blue fire right around the temple and themselves; this creates a safe place in which they can leave their everyday self while the deeper levels of themselves go exploring.

On returning to their temple from the trip, the participants can be instructed to seal each chakra of the body with a symbol of their choosing (such as a pentagram, a yin-yang symbol, etc) and then to draw a double helix of golden light around themselves, from their toes to the top of their head. This is to ensure that the opening up process that goes on in the trip does not leave them in an overly vulnerable state afterwards.

Finally, the participants are brought back to everyday reality and the here and now by counting slowly from twenty to one and by instructing them to take several deep breaths to bring themselves back into their bodies, to feel the floor, and then to open their eyes. Tea and biscuits are then served as the final grounding procedure. Care should be taken to see that everyone is properly back and in touch with other people and that they eat and drink something. It can be very dangerous if someone leaves in a bit of a daze to drive themselves home.

Occasionally people will go very deeply into a trance state, or fall very deeply asleep, and be very reluctant to return to the outer world. Their hands and feet should be held and they should be told again that it is time to return to everyday reality; another count down from twenty to one should be carried out and every five numbers they should be told to take a deep breath in and out and to feel your hands in theirs; they should be told firmly that when you reach 'one', they will open their eyes, feeling relaxed, refreshed and alert. They should then walk about a bit, if necessary being drawn to their feet and propelled up and down, taken out into the fresh air for a few minutes and then given something to eat and drink. This usually only happens to people who are very tired and/or tense and an alternative method of treatment is simply to let them sleep on and awake naturally. On no account should they be allowed to go home alone until fully awake and interacting with other people.

In Part 2 there are many examples of pathworkings which could be used in a Pagan Pathfinders type meeting. Many followed the format above, but as participants become more experienced, it is not always necessary to 'visit' the temple first in order to enter the inner realms. In the transcripts please note that the dots ("....") signify a comfortable pause, to allow the participants to absorb what is being said, or to allow them to experience things on a mental journey.

Before every pathworking the session leader should ensure the group is relaxed and centred, focused and with their minds ready to go on a journey. You can do this with the exercises at the beginning of Part 2 and also the Golden Bubble meditation.

Special Place

Foundations are important in all mind expansion work. It is important when doing guided meditations to have a special place in your mind, a sanctuary that is yours and yours alone. Only you know the sign or words needed to enter it and when you visit it in your mind, know that you are safe and protected. It is a mental trigger that inner work is about to begin. The magical temple is an example of such a place. Pathworkings often start with each person visualising their special place. It might be underneath a particular tree, a woodland cottage, a quiet room, a garden, a temple, or a sea cave, anything that feels right for the individual person. A pathworking to help find your sacred place is in Part 2, 'Spring'.

Partner Work

A key element to Pagan Pathfinders was group experience and partner work. This might take the form of:

- Sitting together and trying to tune into each other's energies, feeling with the mind for any tensions, psychically trying to heal the partner and sending positive energy to them.
- Trying to sense each other's aura, trying to feel/see the colour and shape of it (see 'Colour Healing Pathworking' in Part 2 of this book).
- Practising "aura brushing", whereby one person sits and one stands, sensing the seated person's aura and literally brushing around it with their hands, brushing away negative energy.
- Taking it in turns to give a shoulder massage.
- Polarity healing, which is a bit like reiki, transmitting healing energy through the hands to your partner.

You first rub your hands together very fast, then hold them apart and feel the energy flowing between them, trying to feel it as a ball of healing golden energy, tingling and sparkling, then without actually touching, transferring that energy to the other person.

- Trying to sense each other's past lives and also work on divination, such as drawing Tarot cards for each other and trying to interpret them.

All of these things build trust and develop the group's psychic skills. A session often began with partner work. We would also often discuss our experiences during pathworkings with partners after the meditation. Discussing it embedded the journey in the memory and helped us to interpret hidden meanings or messages.

Music

Pagan Pathfinders sessions often involved the use of music. Sometimes the session would begin with a moving meditation, for example we would all curl into a ball and picture ourselves as a seed, then as suitable music played we would gradually uncurl and grow and stretch up to the sky, up to the sunlight, expanding our bodies and consciousness together, drawing in vital earth energy, energising ourselves. Examples of such meditations are in Part 2.

It is important to have a stock of music for such purposes which can be prepared beforehand. Use whatever works for the group. An example is "A Night on the Bare Mountain" by Mussorgsky, used in the infamous goblin movement meditation (see Part 2), or "Danse Macabre" by Saint-Saëns. "Tubular Bells" was another favourite and pieces from "The Planets Suite" by Holst worked well. There is a wealth of meditation music available on the internet. Music can be a very useful tool to aid relaxation and transport the mind into a different level of consciousness, away from the mundane worries and tensions of the everyday. Through dance and movement meditations we can loosen the body, dispel tensions and break down inhibitions, leaving us ready for deeper work to follow in the session.

Creative Writing and Drawing

One of the key aims of Pagan Pathfinders was to realise our own potential and work with it. People were challenged to try new things, learn new skills and unlock their own inner wisdom. Creativity and spontaneity were encouraged. There was often space in the meetings for some creative writing, for example attendees were asked to compose poems or invocations relating to the seasons, or for particular gods and goddesses. If people preferred to draw, crayons were also provided so people could draw an image that had come to them during a pathworking or ritual, whether it be a random image, or a deity or symbol. People were also encouraged to write their own parts in rituals, as well as invocations or statements of gratitude.

Blind Walk

An annual tradition which took place every summer in Jean's garden was the 'Blind Walk', fondly remembered by many. Each person took a partner and one of the pair closed or covered their eyes. They were then led around by the other seeing person, through the beautiful, slightly wild garden, their hand directed towards things which might have a particular feel. Sometimes this would be a beautifully soft rose petal, sometimes the rough paving slab, sometimes soft grass brushing the back of your hand, sometimes a dip in the bird bath, sometimes plunged into the earth. We would be instructed to listen, smell, taste (if appropriate) and touch, to wonder at how we have evolved to receive such beauty, to have such an aesthetic experience. We wondered at the burgeoning life all around us and tried to sense nature and the planet as aware, sentient, alive and conscious. Jean encouraged us to tune into the Earth Mother, the planetary soul, to see ourselves as connected to it and as constantly reaching forward to a better state of spiritual evolution and connectedness with all things. We were also asked to remember the mess we make, heedless of the treasures of evolution, the carelessness with which we treat our Mother Earth. The idea was to sense without seeing, to open ourselves to other ways of perceiving the world, as well as enjoying the mischief and fun. It brought the group together in laughter and strengthened the bond of trust between us.

Drawing up Energy

Many of the pathworkings focus on drawing up energy from elemental sources, such as the earth, the moon, the sea. This is a fundamental technique used in Pagan meditation or workings and is common in Wiccan magical work, for example. As you will see from the examples in Part 2, the idea is to close your eyes and sense the natural energy fields all around you, to see them growing in strength and size in your mind's eye, vibrating, pulsing, expanding, and to absorb them into you, energising and healing yourself, drawing them into your core being, and then perhaps to send them out to others, or to nature itself, in healing work. Imagining one is a tree, sending roots down into the earth and drawing up green earth energy is a good way to start. You could spend 5 or 10 minutes doing this before any pathworking or ritual commences.

The Golden Bubble itself is another example of drawing in positive energy, cleansing and energising your body and mind. A moon pathworking may involve drawing down silvery energy from the moon. In most Pagan ideologies, the moon symbolises women's mysteries, love, emotion, healing, intuition, divination and a calm sense of peace. Thus by visualising energy flowing from the moon to you, you draw those qualities into yourself. You could do the same with the sun, drawing in energies of joy, creativity, health, success, growth, determination and strength. You can work with elemental forces in this way using your own ideas of what they correspond to (for example in some systems the moon is a male force), but there are also many 'tables of correspondences' readily available online and in books.

The Elements as Metaphors

Editor's note: A common theme at Pagan Pathfinders was to work with the qualities of the four elements. They can be seen as metaphors for inner work, each representing different aspects of ourselves. As Jean explained:

As someone with one foot in the realm of psychology and science and the other in the realm of magic and mysticism, I am fascinated by the parallels that emerge between these worlds. Psychology recognises that there are four main mental functions:

- Cognitive: the thinking, intellectual, problem-solving function (Air).
- Emotional: feelings of love, hate, anger, happiness, etc. (Water).
- Motivational: purpose, goal setting, intention, willpower (Fire).
- Sensation: the mind interprets and evaluates the physical sensations (Earth).

These four functions correspond to the four elements of air, water, fire and earth, that featured for centuries in theories of illness and medicine before modern technology brought about a revolution in medical practices. But the four elements still feature in the realm of magic and mysticism and provide a useful structure for inner exploration and for tapping powerful archetypal sources of empowerment.

The first three functions also correspond to the three Primordial Virtues that are the aspiration of followers of the Western Mystery traditions: Wisdom, Love and Power (or Will). They manifest in the sphere of Malkuth on the Kabbalistic Tree of Life, ie the sphere of everyday life.

Each of the four functions and the four elements rarely work alone; there is a constant interplay between them. Recent research using new technology, such as Magnetic Resonance Imaging, has revealed more of the amazing complexity of the human brain. Old ideas about how mental functions mapped onto the brain have had to be jettisoned as the capacity for different parts of the brain to communicate, support and supplement each other gradually becomes apparent. Decision-taking used to be considered a purely logical process, but it has been found that emotions play a big part: the person who, through brain injury, has lost the ability to connect with the emotional function is completely unable to make decisions. On the other hand, the person who has the emotional function, but has lost the connection to the cognitive function, may well become an addictive gambler, seeking always to re-experience the thrill of a win.[2]

Most people are stronger in some mental functions than others. The pattern of strengths and weaknesses is a vital part of our individuality, but we can also learn to understand our inner patterns by using the metaphor of the elements. Using active imagination, we can explore the archetypal energies within the elements and how they interact with each other. We can come to understand why we procrastinate, why certain events or people undermine our self-confidence, how we handle being angry or react to those who are angry with us, what combination of functions make us feel happy, creative, excited, etc. This insight into our own natures enables us to bring the elemental forces into more harmonious balance within ourselves through active imagination and archetypal images.

In practice, if you were working with the archetypal energy of earth, you might do any of the following in a meeting:

- Earth-related movement meditations: for example, a simple tree meditation. Find a place to stand and become a tree, feel your roots going into the ground and your branches reaching up to the sky. Stretch your arms up as though they were branches swaying in the light breeze. What kind of tree are you? Feel the nourishment coming up through the roots, the earth energies and the wind as it blows through your branches and leaves. See the clouds passing over you release their rain and gently wash you and cleanse away any negativity as you feel the warm shower of rain moistening your leaves and branches and the earth around you, nourishing and renewing you. Now the day is coming to a close and the animals around you go to sleep. As you watch over them, you see the stars like diamonds in the sky and the moon, its pale luminescent light envelops you whilst all around you is still .... until gradually a new dawn appears on the horizon and the sky is filled with sunlight and the birds sing. Experience the feeling of the sun on your leaves, warm and energising, life-giving and healing. And absorb the sunlight into every part of your being, radiating sunlight out to your extremities mixing with the earth energy .... Leaving the tree now you thank the tree for allowing you to share in its energy .... and return to the room.

- Tap into the qualities traditionally associated with earth – groundedness, our roots, stability, deep wisdom (inner and of our ancestors), fertility and growth, unconditional love, abundance, thanksgiving and harvest; do we experience them in our lives, could we improve these aspects of ourselves, what can we learn from them, how are they manifest in us? You might choose to do this session around harvest time and conduct a Lammas ritual.
- You might do a Blind Walk or a summer trip to a sacred site to connect to the earth.
- You might do a pathworking to meet an Earth Goddess, an archetype of earthly qualities, and seek her wisdom (for example Gaia, Cybele, Danu or Demeter) or perform a ritual dedicated to her.

Working through all the elements in this way will help to bring these elemental qualities that we all possess into balance within ourselves.

Gods and Goddesses as Archetypal Images

Whether you view the gods and goddesses as actual physical beings we can worship and connect with, or as archetypal forces, they can be worked with in pathworkings and ritual. Much as you can work with the elements as metaphors, you can connect to a particular deity when working on a particular element of yourself or the wider world.

> "Within this context [Pagan Pathfinders], the god-forms are regarded as representations of archetypal forces, not as 'spirits of place' or discrete entities ... In Pagan Pathfinders ... we seek to contact these archetypal forces in order to access our sources of inner wisdom and to enhance particular inner qualities."
>
> "The Pagan goddesses and gods are not images of idealised perfection. They are fundamental forces within Nature and within the human psyche."
>
> (Jean M. Williams & Zachary Cox, "The Gods Within", 2008)

Some examples of deities and their associations are:

Arianrhod – priestess of the moon, shapeshifter, goddess of change, beauty, death and renewal.
Artemis – wild and free goddess of the new moon, representing strength, feminine power, and personal integrity.
Demeter – representing fertility, abundance, harvest and gratitude.
Pan – representing wildness, a connection to the earth, joy, the primal life force and sensuality.

The Morrigan – representing strength against adversity or unfairness, courage, justice and wisdom.

Many more can be found in the above cited book.

Tarot & Astrology

Often in Pagan Pathfinders we would use Tarot and astrology as tools to learn things about ourselves, or as a basis for inner meditation work. These were sometimes run by others in the group with a particular interest in the subject. Included in Part 2 is a Tarot session by a long-term "Peeper", Lisa Stockley, who also wrote the Virgo/Libra session in the Autumn section of Part 2.

Ritual

As part of the process of increasing our awareness of the unity of all life, with each other and with the natural world, it was inevitable that early on in Pagan Pathfinders we would start to weave into our work awareness of the changing seasons by including the eight festivals commonly celebrated by Pagans.[3] These are as follows:

- Imbolc – 1 February
- Spring Equinox
- Beltane – 30 April/1 May
- Summer Solstice
- Lammas – 1 August
- Autumn Equinox
- Samhain – 31 October
- Winter Solstice

A stated aim of Pagan Pathfinders was to teach basic ritual practice and to enable participants to experience group celebration. A wonderful feeling of fellowship can come from this. Our approach was largely rooted in the traditions and seasonal characteristics of Britain.[4] The rituals were simple and often included improvisation, periods of meditation, music and dancing. The emphasis was on the meaning of the seasonal change, the inspiration and inner nourishment to be drawn from it and the inner change to be targeted. As Pagan Pathfinders grew and flourished, the preparation of seasonal rituals was often undertaken by members of the group so that over the years a body of ideas and approaches developed. The ones presented in Part 2 are an amalgamation of ideas and experiments, by no means all my own, that highlight our practice over the years.

Pagan Pathfinders was not a stable esoteric group, people came and went. For this reason, the emphasis of the seasonal rituals was on inner work and personal significance and insight. However, often the group had enough ongoing members and people with experience of group ritual to develop a strong sense of cohesion and the atmosphere at the end of a ritual was often exhilarating and empowering.

The allocation of roles in a ritual was constrained by the numbers attending. If the group was small, roles would be doubled up. In general, the allocation was a mixture of volunteering and cajoling.

If most of the group members were relatively inexperienced, they would be provided with a script but told that they could improvise if moved to do so. Experienced members might be given free rein. Occasionally, all those present would be given a meditational period in which to compose an invocation, even if only a few words. The quality of invocations prepared was often astonishing and moving and examples are included in this book.

Jean on Meditation

Since I started down the Pagan path, books and teachers stressed the importance of inner work. As my orientation was at first towards practice based on magic, I worked on creative visualisation, both as part of a voyage of self-discovery (imaging stuff from the subconscious and transpersonal areas of the mind) and also as a training in focusing the intent for the practice of creating sacred space and the formulation of spells. The first instruction of a book or teaching devoted to this kind of work is more often than not, 'Sit down, make yourself comfortable, and close your eyes.'

When we close our eyes, we 'go into ourselves'. For some people, this means running a movie of images generated by our imagination, supported by a bank of visual memories that provide the details and colours – like the holodeck of Star Trek's 'Enterprise', employing virtual reality and holographic projection to place the user anywhere they feel like going. The practice of visualisation in a relaxed state resembles dreaming, but with more control over the subject matter; it can be used to plant a preconceived intent into the mind at a more subtle level of consciousness, or to open up the conscious mind to messages or images from the unconscious or transpersonal sides of ourselves.

In recent years my own journey of self-discovery has led me to India, a place where many different religions and practices can be observed and experienced in a form that has changed little for thousands of years. My experiences have led me to read material about Eastern spiritual practice; in a sense, a logical progression, since much of the 'energy work' that modern Wiccan practice advocates to its students is based on the Tantric notion of the 'esoteric body' and its chakras. A fair amount of Eastern meditational practices do involve visualisation; but what a seeker will soon discover is that many crucial practices in Yogic, Zen and Tibetan discipline are intended to be experienced with the eyes open.

The reason for this, I believe, relates to the concept of duality. Duality is not the juxtaposition of opposites like yin and yang, light and dark, masculine and feminine, that together make up a whole; duality is the notion that a sentient being has a discrete existence from the world or universe that it believes that it inhabits. But shamen, yogis, Sufis, Tibetan Buddhists or Bonpos and other mystical core traditions within most world religions tend toward non-dualism: we are all one. We are stardust: as

Crowley says in the 'Gnostic Mass', 'There is no part of us that is not of the Gods.' A shaman in trance is able to communicate with plants and animals, not only because everything is alive, but also because there is no division between the shaman and the other beings, being all part of the same luminous 'ground' of higher existence. What this can mean in practice is that the consciousness shifts from the notion of 'observer' and 'observed' to a state in which we 'forget' that we are 'present' at the scene, lose our grasp on 'self' and undergo a transient merging with what we are looking at. Those who have read Wordsworth, Blake, Keats and other visionary poets will recognise that certain poems are inspired and composed within the afterglow of such realisations.

This experience is often enjoyed in an accidental, involuntary way; sometimes by being in a beautiful place and just getting lost in the scenery, sometimes through absorption in a work of art (painting, poetry, drama, music), often through the acts of creating or performing the art, sometimes through ritual, sometimes during sex, if we are genuinely focused on our lover. In Tantra, it is taught that the eyes should be kept open during sex: the ecstasy isn't about your own fantasy gratification, but about the transcendental union with another – the eyes keep you 'present' and in contact with your love(r).

So, Sogyal Rinpoche maintains in 'The Tibetan Book of Living and Dying' (1992), should it be with meditation. The eyes should be open because the non-dualistic realisation is the most revolutionary, liberating state of awareness: you are the same as what you observe – and what you observe is luminous, energetic and divine. However, I must now admit that this kind of practice – a conscious decision 'To see a world in a grain of sand, and a heaven in a wild flower' [5] – is not at all easy, especially from scratch. Luckily for some of us, we have encountered that one-ness accidentally and spontaneously, without knowing what it meant. Having once been there, the knowledge of it can be used to purposely return to the same space in a meditation. However, the challenge begins when we find that place (having relaxed and let go of all the rubbishy mental chatter): how long can we focus and stay there before the mundane part of us begins to grasp onto desires, paranoias and niggling little insecurities? It must be a serious discipline to achieve. I wouldn't claim to have accomplished it.

But using the 'eyes open' approach may offer other bonuses for some of us: for those who find visualisation very difficult, and for those who get too physically relaxed when they close their eyes and tend to fall asleep. Closing the eyes may even encourage dualistic thinking: 'The world is ugly, stressful and distracting, and to fly away from all that I need to just close my eyes and turn within.' Fine, but that postpones the acceptance of an essential truth: that the world is you and that by accessing your true 'mind' you can see the divine right before your very eyes.

Tips for Meditation

Andrew Harvey writes in 'The Direct Path' (2000):

> "The best way to treat the thoughts and emotions that arise in meditation is with spacious compassion. Your thoughts and emotions are after all your family, the family of your mind. A great Tibetan practitioner, Dudjom Rinpoche, used to say, 'Be like an old man, watching children play.' So, during your session, practise letting whatever thoughts and emotions come up rise and settle like waves in the sea. Whatever you find yourself thinking, however weird, 'irrelevant', trivial, or even 'scandalous' – do not identify with your thought but 'watch' it rise and settle, without any constraint. Don't grasp at it, or avoid it, or flinch from it, or feed and indulge it; don't cling to it, or attempt to trace its origin or understand its 'truth'. Don't follow a 'train of thought'. Thuksey Rinpoche used to say when he taught meditation: 'Be like the sea gazing at its own waves, or the sky gazing at the clouds passing through it.'"

And from 'The Tibetan Book of Living and Dying' by Sogyal Rinpoche, (1992):

> "What should we 'do' with the mind in meditation? Nothing at all. Just leave it, simply, as it is. One master described it as 'suspended in space, nowhere' .... I often compare the mind in meditation to a jar of muddy water. The longer we leave the water without agitating or stirring it, the more the particles of dirt will sink to the bottom, letting the natural clarity of the water shine through. The very nature of the mind is such that if you only leave it in its unaltered and natural state, it will find its true nature, which is bliss and clarity. So take care not to impose anything on the mind, or to tax it. When you meditate, there should be no attempt to control and no attempt to be peaceful. Don't be overly solemn or feel you are taking part in some special ritual; let go even of the idea that you are meditating. Think of yourself as the Sky, holding the whole Universe."

Endnotes

1. 'Mind Games: The Guide to Inner Space', Robert Masters and Jean Houston, 1972.
2. For a fascinating read about recent research on decision making, see Jonah Lehrer, "The Decisive Moment: How the Brain Makes up its Mind", 2009.
3. The dates can vary.
4. As Jean came from a Wiccan background, many of our rituals were drawn from Wiccan practice. However, we were influenced by many different spiritual traditions, even celebrating Diwali, the Hindu festival of lights.
5. 'Auguries of Innocence', William Blake.

chapter six
WHERE TO GO FROM HERE

Practical Notes on Starting a Group

Jean's great wish was that others would be inspired by Pagan Pathfinders and would go on to start their own groups. Pagan Pathfinders in fact still continues today, run by a long-time attendee of Jean's group. Other groups have formed across the country, influenced by it. I like to see it as a web, with the original PP and Jean at the centre, and spiderweb-like strands stretching off to other groups, all inter-connected.

There are several things to consider before starting such a group:

1. Decide on the purpose of the group. Will it be purely mind expansion work, based on meditation and pathworking? Will it perform rituals and celebrate the seasons? Will it follow a particular Pagan path? Is the goal group cohesion and group work, or individual inner work, or both? Will it focus on working through particular things, such as the elements as metaphors, or the moon cycles, for example? Will it concentrate on exploring aspects of the divine feminine, such as many women's groups do?
2. How many people will be in the group?
3. Where will the meeting be held? If it is to be in your house, are you comfortable with strangers in your house? Take

precautions and always meet people before they join. If you need to rent a room, will there be a charge and how will this be paid for?

4. Think about the timing of the meeting. Jean mentioned she stuck to the timing very firmly because she was aware people had a long way to travel to get home and the meetings were on a Monday night.
5. How will you advertise the meeting? Jean was a very active member of the Pagan Federation (PF) and would put adverts in the London Pagan Federation newsletter as well as the 'What's On' section in their magazine, Pagan Dawn. You could find out if there is a PF newsletter near you by contacting the local representative (see their website for details). You could advertise in places like Health Food shops where you frequently see adverts for meditation classes. Word of mouth, Facebook and MeetUp are also options, but it depends how open you want the invitation to be.
6. How will you check people out? They could be asked to write an introduction letter or email, or you could arrange to meet people or talk over the phone.
7. Will you run the group yourself or have a dedicated helper? Will you ask attendees to occasionally take turns running sessions?
8. Will you be strict with regular attendance? This does build a more stable group, but it is probable that people will drift in and out at times.
9. Will you charge for the sessions? In my view any charge should be limited and aimed at covering practical and time-based expenses, rather than enriching the group leader.

Flowing Onwards and Outwards

As mentioned above, some attendees of Pagan Pathfinders were inspired to set up their own groups, as it is hoped this book will inspire readers to do. Below are some comments from two of them.

Yvonne's story

> When the time came to leave London, I said to Jean, 'I shall really miss this group'. She said, 'Why don't you run a group?' I asked, 'Will you support me?' She replied, 'Of course.' That's all I got. I said to a friend that I'd got nothing from Jean in the sense of notes or suggestions of what to do. She replied 'No, you won't', so I realised I was on my own.
>
> I had begun making some notes on the group during the last year that I was there. I also did some reading. In my new town I looked for people to start a group with. I advertised at local moots and in a Pagan magazine. I decided to start a group as soon as I had three people. At first I made copious notes, searched for suitable music and researched for ideas online. I took into account the season of the year, the moon phase and the astrology.
>
> I had formerly run antenatal classes for the NCT, so I was used to inviting strangers to my house, asking them to take their shoes off, sit on cushions, doing some relaxation and gentle movement with visualisation. I also had a strong interest in Tarot and had begun work on a deck derived from the Greenwood, so I incorporated ideas from that and worked on visualisations for the cards linked to seasons.
>
> I saw entering the work of the evening as going through a series of doorways. First they rang my bell and entered my house. So I prepared my house. Before people came I burned

sage and carried it round the whole ground floor. Then I burned incense and carried that around each corner of each room on the ground floor.

My house was a similar age and layout to Jean's Edwardian North London home and so the room I used for the group was very similar with glass doors to the garden. If we needed an altar, I set that up. I used candle light only, so as they entered and took off shoes they entered a candle lit prepared space. We sat around a dining table with candles and I offered tea and invited them to bring snacks. Sitting chatting around the table was a chance to move into a different psychological space. I had soft music playing and also used an oil burner to lend atmosphere and lead the emotions. Then we moved into the group room. I invited someone to light the quarter candles and others as necessary.

Following Jean's format, I led them to stand, stretch and move to music that was chosen to reflect the theme for that evening, then to sit down and I led a relaxation. Each move was deepening the psychological place we were in. It joined us together as we focused. Coming out of the relaxation I spoke and introduced the evening's work. I tried to always tell them what to expect as I believed that would generate trust that would build up over the weeks to help them to relax more. Then we followed with the work I had prepared. After the work we did a closing and then we put out the candles and returned to the dining room for refreshments and talk.

For the sabbats, my husband (who was not part of this group but was very supportive) lit a fire in the garden, so that at an appropriate time I could open the glass doors and lead them into the garden. We often had dried herbs to throw on the fire.

The most I had in the group was six plus me, and it continued for five years, although we did not meet every week, and not all came every time.
I think leading the group made me do a lot of research and work for myself. I learned about oils and incense. I guess I followed my own interests and what worked in the group. At the start I took notes and did a lot of preparation. By the end I sometimes only decided what to do about an hour before they arrived. As I got more experienced I gained confidence. Looking back now, I think about what it was for. It was definitely for me, as I worked and transformed a lot. Then it was for the people who came; although only one stayed in touch, the others let me know through feedback that they gained a lot. Thirdly, I think it was for something else. Something that we might call Otherworld or the collective unconscious. There all we do leaves a trace, for others to find and use.

Ian's story

It wasn't really on my mind to start a PP, but Jean wanted it to carry on after she retired and the strength of Jean's will should not be under-estimated. She could persuade people to do things in a very gentle, quiet way, but in a way that you couldn't turn her down. I think I was worried I wouldn't be capable of stepping into her footsteps. However, three of us, Hannah, Peter and me, started to run a PP group. It was tricky at first to get publicised and to find people. We put flyers in bookshops, for example Atlantis and Treadwells (in London).
We started holding the group at Atlantis Bookshop. It was a tiny, basement room and we had to charge people to cover

the cost of the room hire. Jean never charged anyone and after a while I thought it would be better to carry on and do it in my house as I wasn't comfortable with charging. Also hiring a room means you are dependent on a good turnout.

I had some of my own ideas for the sessions, but Jean also sent me a lot of her pathworkings, meditations and rituals, so I had a foundation of those to go on, but I didn't want to do it quite as a carbon copy. I wanted to use some of my own ideas, but also wanted to keep it recognisably PP, running it in a similar way, starting off with some exercises or guided meditations and quite often doing a little ritual. Sometimes I used my own, sometimes Jean's. Of course we kept the Golden Bubble – not all the time, but it is nice to bring it out and do that. It is the signature PP meditation.

I think the main challenge has been that Jean did a PP every Monday and always had ideas. She would repeat things and did have a stock of things to use, but she always had an idea for the evening and I find that quite challenging. Our PP only meets once a month and there are two of us running it, but it is still a challenge to come up with good ideas. I meet up with my co-organiser on an evening before the session to come up with ideas. Sometimes it almost writes itself, it is very quick; other times it takes hours. Maybe a lesson there is to keep it very simple, like Jean.

My best advice for someone starting a group like PP would be to try to bring in mirth and reverence. Have some fun and do something more serious with it. People want to enjoy themselves, but also feel that they are developing, learning and getting something out of it.

We have had some memorable sessions in our new Pagan Pathfinders group. A while ago we were doing some sessions exploring the Goddess Bride in her different aspects: one as

Goddess of poetry, so we did an evening on poetry; one as Goddess of healing, so we did an evening on healing; and the last one was exploring her as Goddess of blacksmithing and smithcraft, so we actually did some metal casting with white metal by melting it in my fireplace and casting little metal pieces. We got a lot of people for those. We always advertise what we are doing first, mainly on Facebook, so people tend to pick things to go to.

I have been asked what I get out of running the group. I feel it was a real transition stage at the start because I had always come along and taken part and been sitting at Jean's feet, so it was quite a transition to be actually leading it. At the time I was living for a while down near Avebury and I went to visit West Kennet Long Barrow. It was a nice summer afternoon, but there were no tourists about. I went inside on my own and felt like it was a transition almost from pupil to teacher. I had a strong sense of that feeling while I was in there. It really was a transformational experience, realising I had to change, I had to step into a different role to the one I had previously had.

I find it is very enjoyable to carry the group on. It is also a good way to remember Jean and carry on with her meditations and pathworkings, which we all love. It is a way of carrying on her legacy. I still learn from it and it helps develop me personally as I am constantly having to think of ideas and plan evenings. It challenges me.

To someone thinking of starting a group I would say keep it simple at first and if you want to make it more elaborate, or come up with more interesting ideas later on, do, but to start with base it on the materials Jean provided and her ideas. You don't need a lot of people to start off either, you can have just a few people and do meditations and simple rituals. But also have fun and make friends! You can make it a regular part of your social life as well. It is a good place to meet like-minded people. I have lots of good memories of PPs past and things we have done together."

Now What?

Part 2 of this book is a Pagan Pathfinders Workbook. It follows the Wheel of the Year, which roughly equates to the Pagan Pathfinders' terms. Each term was somewhat planned in advance and sessions were themed to fit with the time of year. For example, in winter, the time of hibernation, more work was done on deep hidden wisdom; while at the equinoxes work was done on bringing balance into our lives. Part 2 contains many examples of meditations to start the session (seated and standing), pathworkings and rituals. There is an example ritual for every festival, but do create your own as the leader, or together as a group. The more personal it feels, the more powerful it will be.

I'm sure Jean would say "Good luck! Go forth and multiply!" And a final reminder, I found a large note scribbled in Jean's notebook, right at the beginning of Pagan Pathfinders in the 1970s, which reads:

"REMEMBER THE IMPORTANCE OF BEING SILLY"

Paganism is an attitude of mind, a way of being that is in tune with the natural forces of the universe. Those on a Pagan spiritual path aim to heighten their awareness of their oneness with the Earth, the cycle of the seasons and the greater wheels of the Sun, Moon and Stars, of Life and Death. The search is also within, to discover and manifest the powers latent within the human mind. We all have within us resources of energy, creativity and joyousness that remain largely unrealised.

Pagan Pathfinders aim to explore and develop the Pagan way of being by tapping these inner resources so that we may participate more fully in the ecstasy of the Cosmic Dance.

Pagan Pathfinders was founded by Jean Williams in 1975. The object was to combine the ancient methods of spiritual development with the modern techniques of inner exploration used in Humanistic Psychology, within a broad eclectic Pagan framework. All those prepared to adventure into inner space, whether new to Paganism or experienced, can benefit. An interest in personal growth and transcendental experience is assumed.

MEETINGS

Pagan Pathfinders meet weekly on Monday evenings, 8.00 - 10.00pm, at a private house in North London (nearest tube, Highgate; nearby buses to Finsbury Park).

Sessions start in October, January and April; they run for 10-12 weeks. Newcomers are normally admitted only at the beginning of a session and should be prepared to commit themselves to regular weekly attendance for that session.

The group is small (12-15 people), friendly and informal. Comfortable clothes are worn. There is no charge, but members usually bring biscuits, fruit or other snack to share.

AIMS AND TECHNIQUES

Pagan Pathfinders place the emphasis on doing and experiencing rather than discussing or lecturing. Each meeting is designed to be an interesting, enjoyable and enriching experience as well as to further the development of disciplines, skills and understanding of value in all walks of life.

The methods of exploration are drawn from a wide range of religious disciplines, both Western and Eastern and also from Humanistic Psychology and the Personal Growth Movement. Similarly, god-forms and archetypal images are employed from diverse Pagan pantheons, astrology, the Tarot and other sources. Pagan Pathfinders meetings are thus suitable for people who want to learn some of the basic skills common to most Pagan/occult and meditation schools, without committing themselves to any one path.

Some of the main techniques are:

Deep Relaxation

A prerequisite for all meditational and magical work is the ability to relax deeply, physically and mentally. In this state brain rhythms change; we have access to the unconscious mind and can tap mental powers that we in the West are only just beginning to realise are available.

Auto-Suggestion

In a meditational state, alpha waves become predominant in the brain; it is then possible to use auto-suggestion to heal ourselves and to change habits and attitudes that restrict us. We can also use it to help us identify and achieve our goals.

Heightened Awareness

Turning out to the world with increased sensitivity and receptivity is as important as turning inwards. We therefore give attention to tuning in to our bodies, increasing our awareness of our relationship to the Earth and to each other. We discover that we can achieve states of greatly enhanced perception with all our senses without the use of drugs.

Active Imagination

The development of the skill of vivid imagery is fundamental to all magical disciplines. It is also a powerful tool for growth and self-transcendence since it enables one to get in touch with the great creative forces of the unconscious. Through pathworkings (guided journeys), we meet the Gods and Goddesses of mythology, explore the Elemental Kingdoms and find guidance from the images of the Tarot. These enable us to contact our own inner wisdom, explore our inner conflicts, define our goals and discover our True Will.

Energy Raising and Empowerment of the True Will

A number of physical and mental techniques are explored to release our latent energy flows in a balanced and harmonious manner so that we are at peace with ourselves and in tune with our True Will.

Psi

Deep relaxation and alpha brain rhythms are thought to be the basis of extra-sensory abilities. We work to develop our powers of intuition and clairvoyance and practise dowsing skills.

Healing

Healing is an inner process that takes place within the individual. Many of the techniques described above can be used to facilitate this process, helping to boost one's own recuperative powers. Relaxation, active imagination and the psi faculty are combined with simple physical massage or polarity healing to bring a sense of calm and well-being.

Seasonal Celebrations

The wheel of the year and the changing seasons are celebrated with informal rituals which focus on their inner significance for the individual and the ways in which each participant can use the seasonal energies for their own empowerment.

Sharing Ideas and Techniques

Pagan Pathfinders is not a one-woman show! Participants with some experience of our objectives contribute pathworkings and exercises or introduce us to their own area of expertise. All participate in the informal rituals.

To attend, apply by post to:

Pagan Pathfinders

enclosing a stamped
self-addressed envelope
or phone Jean Williams on

PART 2

THE PAGAN PATHFINDERS WORKBOOK

INTRODUCTION

"Let beams of golden light stream out from the hall to make contact with Pagans all over the world, feeling that warmth of belonging to a wonderful community, that community that is rooted in the myths and traditions of the Pagan past, but reaching forward into the future to create something new and wonderful."
(Jean Williams addressing a Pagan Federation Conference)

This section of the book is designed to be a workbook, a roadmap for someone starting their own group. It is divided into terms based on the seasons, much as Pagan Pathfinders was. In each section there are exercises, meditations and rituals chosen to complement the themes of that season – for example in springtime one might focus on aspects of personal growth, while winter is more about stillness and contemplation, and summer inspires celebration and gratitude. It is not designed to be strictly followed word by word or page by page, but more to serve as inspiration from which to form your own way of doing things, whatever works best for you and the group.

A typical meeting programme was outlined in Chapter 6. It would always begin with some stretching and settling in, becoming aware of our bodies and our breath, and relaxing. This is important in order to take the participants' minds out of the mundane everyday, to focus them on the here and now, and to enable them consequently to attain deeper states of meditation. Jean used certain exercises to facilitate this and to prepare the group for inner work. Some examples of these are set out after this introduction. After these tuning in exercises, the Golden Bubble meditation always preceded pathworking or ritual (see Prologue). Some ideas of exercises for the start of the session are:

- Stretching: curling up and down, circling arms and shoulders, touching toes, etc.
- Grounding: walking, rocking and swaying to music, dancing to music, movement meditations (see following examples).
- Shaking out tension in our limbs, wiggling around (often with humour).
- Breathing: tuning in to basic breathing and deeper yoga breaths.
- Sitting meditations (see following examples, such as the seed meditation).
- Partner work such as massage (see Chapter 6).
- Finally relaxing and energising with the Golden Bubble meditation.

Then followed the pathworking, ritual, or other planned activity.

As described in Chapter 6, an important part of Pagan Pathfinders was celebrating what Pagans call the Wheel of the Year, the cycle of the seasons, with group ritual. This gave a tremendous feeling of fellowship, as well as giving participants a chance to learn basic ritual and to gain valuable insights. In this part of the book are examples of rituals used in Pagan Pathfinders. They do not adhere to one particular Pagan tradition but are drawn from many. This was a valuable way to learn about different paths and different god and goddess archetypes. Rituals may of course be conducted according to your own tradition and way of doing things. It is not the intention of this book to offer an in-depth 'how to' ritual guide for complete beginners, although basic terms are explained. There are many other books and resources available for that.

In Pagan Pathfinders the constants were candles in each quarter representing North, East, South and West, as well as elemental symbols: a pentacle for earth, a feather for air, a wand for fire and a cup of water. We always began by holding hands in a circle and being quiet and still for a moment, feeling the energy of the group flowing around the circle and taking our minds away from the everyday, into the ritual setting. We would cast a circle[1] and call the elemental powers to be present. Then the ritual would begin. Often a deity would be invoked or evoked and some beautiful examples of things to say can be found in 'The Gods Within' by Jean M Williams and Zachary Cox (2008), as well as in this section of the book. A member of the group might personify that deity and carry out a certain role, for example blessing the participants, or offering wisdom and insight. The ritual would end with cakes and wine being passed around, before bidding farewell to the elements and closing the circle.

An example of a typical meeting programme is set out in Chapter 6, as well as further explanations around pathworkings and rituals.

Following this introduction are some preliminary exercises, after which you will find the beginning of the Pagan Pathfinders Workbook with sections for spring, summer, autumn and winter. The term begins in the new year, with an Imbolc celebration. Imbolc celebrates the first breath of spring, the expectation of new growth, a time of new beginnings, planting the seeds of projects for the year ahead. Brigid/Bride is a Goddess who is honoured at Imbolc, Goddess of inspiration, poetry and healing. You may place Brigid's crosses on the altar, snowdrops and white candles. Celebrate the wonder of the turning year and the burgeoning life within the earth.

---

[1] There are many books and internet resources available describing ways of performing these preliminary ritual acts. At Pagan Pathfinders different people took on the roles each time, so it was rarely the same.

GROUNDING AND CENTERING

Spoken by the Guide:

Stand with your feet (preferably with no shoes) about shoulder-width apart and close your eyes. Take three really deep breaths, letting yourself relax ....

Put your attention on your physical sensations, just being aware of them without trying to change anything. Notice what you can feel, what you can hear, what you can smell .... Notice your breathing .... Notice the temperature of the room on your skin .... Feel the ground beneath your feet .... Be aware of the pull of gravity and how your muscles interact to hold you upright. Make sure your knees are not locked back, but are very slightly flexed.

And now imagine that there is a piece of elastic from the crown of your head to the ceiling and, as you relax, you are drawn up taller, your neck and backbone elongating. And let your shoulders drop back and down. Let your breathing become slow and deep .... Put your attention on your breathing as it comes in and out of your nostrils and let your mind become still .... And discover that, although you are standing up, you can become very relaxed and centered within yourself, and that this relaxation allows you to expand...

SEED MOVING MEDITATION

This is an example of an expanding and contracting moving meditation.

Spoken by the Guide:

Curl up in a little ball on the floor, as tightly as you can and imagine that you are a tiny seed lying under the soil, and the earth is dark and cold and winter is on the land. You are sleeping, dormant, dried up and shriveled ....

Now gradually the season changes, the sun becomes stronger and penetrates down into the earth, warming it, and the gentle spring rain falls, and you begin to expand. As the music plays, physically begin to unfurl as you go through the process of growth. Imagine yourself first putting out a tiny root that reaches down into the soil, minute root hairs seeking nourishment. And then you put up a tiny shoot, wiggling its way among the grains of soil until you reach the air and light. As you grow and put out leaves, begin to come to your feet; let your leaves grow strong and shapely and your flower buds form and swell and unfurl until you are fully grown into blossoming beauty, turning to face the sun and letting your perfume flow delicately on the gentle breeze. *[Play music]* So now, as the music starts, let the seed that is you begin to grow ....

[When the music ends] Notice what sort of a flower you are, the colour and shape of the blooms. What the leaves are like. The height of the plant. The smell of its perfume. And be aware that this is your own inner beauty that you have allowed to flower and give its gift of delight to the world. So now, still feeling that the flowering plant is there within you, open your eyes and walk about, allowing yourself to be wholly beautiful ....

And now once more stand still and close your eyes. Summer is passing and the seed capsules of your plant are beginning to swell. The flowers wither and shed their petals and the seeds ripen. And when they are ready, the pod bursts and they are scattered on the soil. The wind blows and covers them with a fine layer of soil and leaves. And remember that always, as you let your inner beauty emerge, it sows the seeds for further flowering. Let those seeds sink into the dark fertile soil of your inner nature so that they will grow and flower in their season .... And then take three deep breaths and open your eyes.

CLOUD MEDITATION

This could be used as an alternative to the Golden Bubble meditation.

Spoken by the Guide:

Relax and let your breathing become slow and deep .... And, as you relax, let your head grow up towards the ceiling. And your neck become longer .... And put your attention on your breathing as it comes in and out of your nostrils, in and out, in and out ....

Imagine that you are sitting on a little cloud floating in a perfect blue sky, feeling very relaxed and at peace. Feel the gentle breeze on your face, blowing away all tension as you breathe slowly and deeply. And you feel very calm and serene as you float on your little cloud in the sky ....

And now in the distance you see what appears to be a fall of golden light. And your little cloud floats closer and closer to it. And now it takes you right into the light-fall and you feel this golden sparkling light pouring all over you, tingling like effervescence on your skin .... And it swirls all over and around you, exhilarating and refreshing you .... And as you breathe deeply, absorb the golden light into your body, not just through your lungs but through every pore of your skin .... And you feel it swirling around, permeating your whole body and mind, filling it with a sense of well-being and vitality, lifting your spirits and making you feel light and full of effervescent joy.

And now your little cloud floats on, out of the light fall. And begins to float gently towards the earth. Floating down very gently, it sinks down into the ground .... And you take three deep breaths, and become aware that you are back in the everyday world, but still feeling relaxed and light and full of effervescent energy.

PLANT IN THE WATER MOVING MEDITATION

Spoken by the Guide:

Stand with your eyes closed. Imagine a beach at low tide. There are rocks covered with seaweed and little pools and ribbed sand, decorated here and there with small pink and white shells. The seaweed has become dry and lifeless and dull looking from its exposure to wind and sun .... You are one of these seaweed plants, fastened to a rock, lying there on the sand ....

And now the tide turns, responding to the forces of gravity and the moon's influence. And wave by wave it advances slowly, until it just touches you and recedes again, touches you a little more, and recedes again. The next wave immerses you for a brief moment and recedes again. And the next wave immerses you for longer, until gradually you become totally immersed in the water ....

As the music plays *[play music]*, imagine yourself as this seaweed plant, becoming alive and beautiful, all the cells of your fibres becoming full of water, your tendrils becoming supple, translucent, glowing with subtle colours of green and yellow and red. And as the water ebbs and flows around and through you, you are swayed hither and thither. Let yourself move with the music, remembering that your roots are firmly fastened to the rock, but your tendrils flow and writhe and intertwine with the movement of the water, gathering nourishment from the sea, becoming totally relaxed and loose as you give yourself to the watery element ....

[When the music ends] And as the image of the sea ebbs away, become aware once more of your human body, but now feeling relaxed, cleansed and refreshed .... And take three deep breaths and open your eyes.

TREE MOVING MEDITATION

Spoken by the Guide:

Stand up with your eyes closed. And now imagine that you are a tree. Your feet are becoming great roots reaching down deep into the earth, your legs and body are the trunk of this tree and your head and arms are the branches .... Feel your roots penetrating deep into the earth, drawing up moisture and nourishment and providing a firm foundation .... And feel your branches spreading up to the sky and the sun shining on your foliage. The wind rustles your leaves and with the sun's light you draw nourishment from the air. A shower of rain washes your leaves and soaks down into the earth releasing more nourishment for your roots ....

Notice what sort of tree you are, what your leaves are like, how tall you are, whether you are bearing flowers or fruit. Notice what condition this tree that is you is in. How well rooted are you? Have you grown in a well-balanced shape? Is the wood of your trunk sound? How healthy are your leaves? Are there any dead or dying branches or any patches that have become over infested with insects, or impaired in health in any way, or not grown to its full potential?

As the music plays *[play music]* imagine all the elements working together to nourish and increase the well-being of this tree that is you .... Feel the rain washing your leaves and soaking down into the earth releasing nourishment; the earth feeding the roots and supporting the whole tree; the sun providing warmth and light and combining with the air to nourish the leaves. Let your branches sway to the wind and reach up to the sun and your leaves rustle as all the elements combine to bring you to a state of glowing health ....

[When the music ends] Notice how you feel as the tree and notice how the condition of the tree has changed .... Let that tree become part of your innermost being .... And take three deep breaths and open your eyes.

STONE MEDITATION

The session leader places a stone in the centre of the room and guides the participants to sit in a circle around it. Also in the centre of the room is a small bowl filled with water and a cloth for drying.

Spoken by the Guide:

Sit in a relaxed state and focus on the stone in the centre of the circle. Breathe deeply and rhythmically until calm and centred .... Meditate upon this stone, until the stone breathes with you. The stone may change colour or shape, just watch and accept this. Identify with the stone ....

Return to yourself .... Pass the stone around, with each person taking a turn to pause and visualise pouring into it any physical pain or tension you have in your body. Focus on transferring that into the stone. Then take the stone and wash it in the bowl of water, washing away that physical pain or tension, cleansing you as you leave it behind. Dry the stone and pass it to the next person ....

Pause to allow all to do this.

The second time around, pass the stone around with each person pausing to visualise any emotional pain or tension, worry or anxiety, sadness or anger. Focus on transferring that into the stone. Then take the stone and wash it in the bowl of water, washing away any negative emotion, cleansing your inner being and emotional self. Dry the stone and pass it to the next person ....

Pause to allow all to do this.

The third time around, pass the stone around the circle with each person pausing to visualise positive emotions – pleasure, desire, love, joy, security, bliss, companionship – and as you hold the stone, pour these emotions into it. Instead of washing the stone, pass it to the next person to pour positive energy into it ....

Pause to allow all to do this.

When it has gone around the whole circle, place the stone in the centre and meditate on it. Become the stone again and experience it as you have helped it to become, purged of pain and distress and charged with pleasure, happiness and love .... The stone is infused with the essence of each person; become one with everyone else here. Link hands and feel the energy of the circle of people, linked in fellowship, trust and love ....

BETWEEN EARTH AND THE HEAVENS (DRAWING IN ENERGY)

Spoken by the Guide:

Mankind is between Earth and Heaven. Our feet are on this Earth, representing our connection with matter, our present home, but our heads reach up to Heaven, representing the home of the spirit that is on another plane. Constantly there is a tension, a stirring between the two planes. So now be aware of your feet on the ground. Feel the ground beneath you and the pull of gravity .... And be aware of your head reaching upwards .... Contact the power within the Earth, the power of life, the power of fruitfulness, the power of gravitational forces .... And with your arms and hands, draw up that power from the Earth. Feel the green energy flowing up your arms, into your whole body, energising you and healing you ....

And now contact the power of the spiritual place, represented by the Heaven above. And draw down that power with your arms and hands .... Now feel it mingling with the Earth power within you ....

As the music plays *[play music]* continue this as a dance, drawing up the Earth power and drawing down the Sky power so that the two flow and mingle within you, joining forces to give you power and strength and wholeness of being ....

[When the music ends] Be aware that you have roots in both the world of matter and the world of spirit and that your inner sustenance depends on keeping in contact with both planes and letting each enhance and complement the other .... Then take three deep breaths and open your eyes.

MARS DANCE – A MOVING MEDITATION

Spoken by the Guide:

Stand with your legs about shoulder-width apart and your feet firmly planted on the ground and breathe deeply, right to the very base of your abdomen .... Imagine yourself surrounded by scarlet light, rich and vibrant. And as you breathe, imagine that you are drawing that scarlet light into yourself. Feel yourself filling with vibrant energy .... Let it build up and as you continue to breathe, let the energy build up within you even more so that you feel that you are glowing, becoming incandescent with it, brighter and brighter as the vibrant scarlet energy builds up .... Then when the music starts let that energy out! Let it out in a joyous dance of power and self-assertiveness, let it flow out from your hands and through your eyes. Feel that you are master of the universe! So let that scarlet energy build up within you, fueling your power centres, and when the music starts, let your dance be a statement of your courage and your will and your power ....

Play energetic music for a few minutes while the group dance.

Now as the music ends, hold an expanded, assertive stance with your arms raised .... And then let the surplus energy drain down into the earth, but feel how it leaves you empowered, with the fires of your will fueled for the future.

GOBLIN AND COURTIER MOVING MEDITATION

This infamous and fondly remembered exercise encapsulates Jean's view that a sense of humour is crucial in any group working, and the key to effective spiritual practice is a healthy mix of mirth and reverence.[2] *The exercise requires two different types of music, one fast and full of mischief, such as 'Night on a Bare Mountain' by Berlioz, or 'Dances Macabre' by Camille-Saëns, and the other slow and elegant such as Gluck's 'Dance of the Blessed Spirits', or a Mozart Gavotte, or 'Tubular Bells'. Two excerpts of each are required, each lasting two to three minutes.*

Spoken by the Guide:

We all have within us an imp or goblin that loves to play practical jokes, to cock a snook at serious people, to pinch and poke and frighten people. Let that goblin out! When the music starts, let that goblin emerge. Open your eyes and do a really nasty goblin dance. Be a spiky, mischievous, malicious creature, leaping and prancing, pulling faces, sticking out your tongue .... Be as nasty a goblin as you possibly can!

Play goblin music for 2-3 minutes.

Change music suddenly ....

"Now become a courtly, elegant person, dancing gracefully and courteously .... Let emerge your most charming, beautiful and gentle self ....

Play courtly music for 2-3 minutes.

Change back to goblin music ....

---

[2] Doreen Valiente, 'The Charge of the Goddess', see Bibliography.

Let the goblin out again! ....

Play goblin music for 2-3 minutes.

Change back to courtly music ....

.... And again let the courtly, elegant you emerge and dance gracefully ....

Play courtly music for 2-3 minutes.

When the final piece of music ends ....

Realise that both these extremes exist within you and that each needs to be expressed from time to time. It can become easy to move from one to the other and neither need dominate. Each contributes to the rich texture of your personality.

TUNING IN TO A PLANT MEDITATION

The session leader instructs the participants to take a plant growing in a pot[3] *and place it before them, then go through a preliminary relaxing and restoring exercise (eg the Golden Bubble meditation, or Cloud Meditation), finishing with a few moments of quiet, staying very relaxed.*

Spoken by the Guide:

Let your mind remain clear and empty, noticing only your slow deep breathing .... Now open your eyes and observe the plant – but observe it uncritically and non-conceptually. Don't think about it, but just let the image of the plant arrive, letting yourself be very deeply relaxed and letting your breathing be slow and deep. You are just completely in the here and now, observing the plant ....

And now let your eyes close and relax even more deeply .... And visualise the plant and discover how vividly you can see it in your mind's eye; see its colour and shape, and as much detail as you can. Notice any aspects of it that are vague, where you can't see the detail ....

Now open your eyes again, still staying very relaxed, and look again at the plant, just letting the image arrive. You may notice details that you failed to notice before, brought to your attention by your attempt to visualize the plant. Continue to observe the plant for a while ....

Again let your eyelids close, and relax even more deeply. Take five deep breaths, discovering as you let out each breath that you can sink to an even deeper level of relaxation .... And let your intuitive and empathic faculties become very alert and sensitive. Tune in to that plant .... Slowly open your

[3] Or place one plant in the centre of the circle if there are not enough plants available.

eyes again, observing the plant and also tuning in to its inner nature so that you can sense the inner life of the plant. Sense its roots, its stem, its leaves, its flowers (if it has any) .... Through your psychic and empathic faculties, let your human consciousness act as an amplifier for the plant consciousness. Discover what it is like to be that plant. Imagine that you are that plant, merge with it and feel being that plant from the inside. Discover its state of health, its needs and how it feels about humans, about you in particular ....

[After a few minutes] Now let your eyes close and withdraw your consciousness from the plant, being aware of your separate identity .... You may find that you seem to have gained something from your contact with the plant, perhaps drawn some healing energy or calming influence. If so, send feelings of gratitude to the plant, send loving attention and awareness of the plant's needs, and perhaps a promise to give it water or fresh soil afterwards....

Now let the image of the plant fade and your mind become empty for a few moments .... And take three deep breaths and return to the here and now.

CHAKRA OPENING EXERCISE

This beautiful exercise was written by Kay Bridger, a long-term attendee of Pagan Pathfinders. Jean often led the group in a chakra opening meditation before doing a deeper pathworking or ritual.

Spoken by the Guide:

Close your eyes and settle your weight .... Take a deeper breath and as you release it, feel your body becoming heavy and still .... And another ....

In your mind's eye, see a golden bubble forming around you, shot through with effervescent sparkles. As you breathe in, this golden energy travels into your lungs, into your blood and permeates your body, bringing ease and relief to any sore or tired parts ....

The light of the golden bubble begins to clear and you see that you have travelled. Before you is a peaceful place in nature, and you find a comfortable place to sit for a while ....

Feeling your connection where your body meets the earth, visualise your sitting bones sending down roots, breaking through the soil, travelling down, down through tree roots, rock, groundwater, seeking the energy centre of the earth beneath. When you find it, that warmth, that tingle of earth power is drawn up your roots. With each breath you draw it higher. It is good strong red energy and as it reaches your sitting bones, it warms and energises your base chakra. See or feel it collecting there, expanding your root chakra to a warm glow.

You say to yourself: I am safe and secure ....

Reach down your roots again, this time for orange earth energy. It rises up easily, up your roots, up your legs, through your root chakra, and into your sacral chakra, warming the place just below your belly button. See or feel it collecting and expanding there.

You say to yourself: I am confident in my sexuality ....

Reach down your roots again. Each time the energy comes up more easily. Feel a little frisson of joy as warm yellow light rises up your roots, your legs, through your red root chakra, your orange sacral chakra, and up into your solar plexus, just below your ribs. Breathe into it, let it expand like the sun on a hot day.

You say to yourself: I stand in my power ....

Down your roots you go again, slipping easily through to find pulsing green earth energy, green and serene. Let it travel up again, through your three lower chakras, noticing how vivid and strong they seem .... The green energy pools and gathers at your heart chakra. Take time to breathe in and nurture this heart of yours. Let it replenish itself with green light.

You say to yourself: I am loved, and I am loving and compassionate ....

Reach down your roots again. Joining the underground streams, your roots find cool blue energy, the blue of summer skies, and this energy is lighter and travels faster. Up, up it comes, through roots, legs, root chakra, sacrum, solar plexus, through the heart centre, and up into your throat. Hear the breath in your throat as you open to the blue light. Let it expand here. Now notice a second stream of energy coming from above. The blue of the heavens is available to you too. Let it find a thread down to the top of your head to flow down into your throat chakra.

You say to yourself: I easily speak my truth ....

This time let your energy rise up the column of your spine, up towards the heavens, seeking above you, beyond the atmosphere, out into the stars, and the deep indigo blue of the night sky. Breathe this in to you, and let it flow down, down, through the air, joining your body at the top of your head and energising the space between your eyebrows, your third eye chakra. Let there be an expanse of tranquillity there.

You say to yourself: I trust my intuition ....

Once more, follow the thread upwards, beyond the blue until you find a beautiful violet light. Breathe this light gently in until it flows easily down into your crown chakra, right at the top of your head. Feel it a little like static just above your scalp, a fast turning ball of violet light.

You say to yourself: I am guided by Spirit, by the Divine, and my own Higher Self ....

As you sit, savouring the peace and balance in your body, the golden light of your bubble returns and forms around you, sealing all the rejuvenated energy in. But if there is any that is more than your needs right now, simply allow it to flow down your body, passing each chakra in turn, and down your roots, into the earth beneath you. Let it be your gift to the earth, released with gratitude ....

Now, before you allow the golden bubble to return you, take a moment to check back with each chakra. Notice how strong each one is, notice if any one is more or less vibrant, and remember this information. Bring it back with you.

Take a couple of deep breaths as you start to recall your roots to your body. Pull them up out of the bedrock, out through the groundwater, the soil, and back up into your body.

Notice the golden bubble, ready to bring you safely back to conscious awareness. Take a big soft breath and let it go, maybe as a sigh.

Feel for your fingers, your toes. Let your eyes blink a little. Get ready to move. Welcome back to your beautiful body. Let it move a little, or a lot.

Below is an example of how to begin a ritual, cast a circle, invoke the Elements and close the ritual. As mentioned before, at Pagan Pathfinders there were people from many different traditions and so the words spoken would differ every time. Part of the magic of this was that the words spoken came from the heart, rather than being learned from a book and merely recited, so this example (taken from a Midsummer Ritual) is just to provide some foundation stones..

BEFORE THE RITUAL

Cleansing

Begin with the group standing in a circle.[4]

Now all close your eyes and become centred. Find inner stillness and silence .... Breathe out all tensions, anxieties and preoccupations. Let them sink into the earth and be absorbed .... Now visualise sparkling golden light surrounding you .... breathe it in. It cleanses and refreshes you .... Let the golden light expand and fill the room, cleansing and purifying it.

Drawing the Circle

It is common practice for the circle caster to walk clockwise (deosil) around the outside of the circle of people to create the sacred space, saying something like:

I draw around us a circle of blue fire. Visualise it springing up from the ground, tiny flames at first, growing higher and higher, surrounding the group and then the whole room .... This space becomes a sacred space between the worlds, protected and set apart from the everyday. The circle is cast.

---

[4] In our case, due to the shape of Jean's living room, this was called the "PP sausage"

Invoking the Elements

After each invocation the whole group may say, "Hail and welcome!"

EAST/AIR: I call upon the Powers of the Element of Air to be present and to aid us. A soft breeze blows from the East into our sacred space, bringing the perfume of flowers and the song of birds. Breathe deeply. We feel ourselves becoming light and swift; our minds become clear and focused, our intellects sharp as a sword in the services of truth. Hail and welcome to the Powers of Air!

SOUTH/FIRE: I call upon the Powers of the Element of Fire to be present and to aid us. Fire blazes in the South; we see the flames and hear the crackle of burning. Its heat pours into our sacred space, bringing a feeling of energy and restlessness. As we breathe in the power of Fire, we feel impatient with restriction; we long to be active, to change things, to be changed. Deep within, the force of will awakens. Hail and welcome to the Powers of Fire!

WEST/WATER: I call upon the Powers of the Element of Water to be present and to aid us. Cool water flows from the West into our sacred space. We feel the gentle rain on our faces, moistening our lips and trickling into our mouths. As we drink in the power of Water, we feel the ebb and flow of the inner tides of our emotional nature; we reach out, yearning to love, to laugh, to pour ourselves into living life to the full. Hail and welcome to the Powers of Water!

NORTH/EARTH: I call upon the Powers of the Element of Earth to be present and to aid us. From the North, the smell of earth and of green things growing infuses our sacred space. Our roots go deep within the soil to draw up the Power of Earth. We feel strong; enduring; determined, obstinate. Physical wellbeing enriches us and we tap the resources for all we want to achieve. Hail and welcome to the Powers of Earth!

AFTER THE RITUAL

Thanking the Elemental Powers

We thank the Powers of [Air] for their presence here tonight and for their gifts. We bid you, Powers of [Air], Hail and Farewell!

Here the whole group may say, "Hail and Farewell!"

Repeat for each Element.

CLOSING THE SACRED SPACE

It is common practice for the circle caster to walk anticlockwise (widdershins) around the outside of the circle of people to close the sacred space while saying something like:

See now the circle of blue fire dying down, sinking down, back into the earth, as we let our sacred space dissolve and we return to the everyday world .... The rite is ended! Merry meet, merry part and merry meet again!

SPRING

Requirements

- On the altar place a candle, cakes and wine to share and a tealight for each person. Optional altar ideas include: a Goddess figure, flowers (snowdrops if possible), incense, elemental symbols.
- Cloak for Bride
- Quarter candles & means of lighting

Roles

- Narrator (may need a small candle)
- Circle Caster
- Elemental Officers
- Goddess Invoker
- Bride
- Officer of Lights
- Cakes & wine officers [1]

All enter the room and bow to the altar then sit down.

The Narrator leads a relaxation and cleansing meditation (see examples in this Workbook). Then asks all to stand for the circle casting and invoking of the Elemental Guardians, including lighting the Quarter candles.[2]

The Narrator asks all to sit.

---

[1] Responsible for passing round the cakes and wine to the group, or sometimes offering them to the person taking on the role of a deity to bless, before passing them round.

[2] As previously mentioned, there are many books and internet resources available, describing ways of performing these preliminary ritual acts.

Options: Chakra opening exercise, or simply instruct all to relax and centre again, being aware of the protective circle of blue fire[3] *and the Elemental Guardians.*

The Narrator continues with an introduction to the ritual, as follows or similar:

> Imbolc is one of the ancient Fire Festivals, sacred to the goddess, Bride or Brighid, the ancient Celtic Goddess of inspiration and creativity. She was a Triple Goddess - of enchantment, fertility and wisdom. The Great Mother gave birth to the Sun Child at the Winter Solstice. At Imbolc she brings him forth to her people, representing the first stirrings of Spring, the awakening after Winter. The nights are still long but we notice that daybreak is a little earlier day by day. It is a time for new beginnings.
>
> Tonight we will celebrate the Feast of Bride as the bringer forth of the inner Sun Child within each of us – the inner fire of creativity. At midwinter, we celebrated the boundless possibilities of the New Year, the new beginning, the new directions. Now we feel the fire of our will flowing into creative endeavour. As yet the fire is in the form of light rather than heat. We become aware of new ideas taking shape, of clarity as to what steps to take next; we prepare for action. Procrastination, doubt and sloth are set aside as a new lust for life arises within us.
>
> But to find the light, we must first enter the darkness. Let the Quarter lights be dowsed.

---

[3] This is an image often used when casting a protective circle.

Elemental officers put out the Quarter candles.

> In the dark let us prepare for the coming of Bride .... We share with the life within the earth the stirrings of new growth. We resonate with the seasonal change, the growing light, and feel the urge to expand, to embark on new ventures. We feel new ideas taking shape, new aspirations – our deepest creative potential beginning to grow within the dark.

Short period of meditation.

In the dark, Bride dons the cloak and stands. The Narrator says:

> Let us now invoke the Goddess Bride.

Spoken by the Narrator or another:

> Bride, Lady of Light, we invoke you.
> Bright Maiden, Goddess of growth,
> You stand upon the horizon of Spring,
> Eager to awaken the dormant Earth.
>
> Bride, Lady of Light, we invoke you.
> Bring us the Light of the returning Sun.
> Come forth, Lady of Fire, we yearn for you.
>
> We seek your blessing; we seek your gifts.
> We go deep into the darkness to seek for you.
> Here in the darkness we wait for you.

Short pause, then the Officer of Light lights the candle on the altar and hands it to Bride. The Officer kneels and says:

Bride is come! Bride is welcome!

All repeat three times.

Bride reads her Charge:

I am she of the golden hair
Queen of the white hills,
Rider of the white swan,
Mother of the King of Glory.

I bring to you three gifts of Fire:
The first is the flame of creative aspiration;
The frenzy of the poet and artist,
Aye, even the lover's passion
For union with the Beloved.

The second flame I bring
Is for purification and testing -
The Flame of Truth.
For with this flame,
All your dross and weakness
Are made clear and cleansed from you,
So you become as a true and tested sword.

The third flame I bring is the greatest of all,
For it is the Healing Flame,
Born out of the Love that gives all;
The maker of Peace and Harmony.

But I do not give these gifts one by one;
I give them as one,

In the form of the growing Sun,
My child, the Lord of Light!
Draw near, each one of you,
And receive the gift of Inner Light.

All rise and take a taper or tealight from the Officer of Light and light it at Bride's candle. Bride steps to the centre and all dance or sway in a circle of lights around her. All sing a popular chant, if known:

Lady, spin your circle bright,
Weave your web of dark and light.
Earth, Air, Fire and Water,
Bind us as one.

The Narrator says:

Let the Officer of Light relight the Quarter candles
that the Elemental Powers may be drawn into this
web of Light.

The Officer of Light relights the Quarter candles.

The Narrator continues:

Let us offer unto Bride cakes and wine, that she may
bless them to sustain and nourish body, mind and will.

The cakes and wine officers present them to Bride silently or with their own words. Bride blesses them silently or with her own words. The Officers then stand one on each side of her so that people can come to partake.

The Narrator says:

> Let each one of you in turn approach the Goddess and dedicate your inner fire to Bride by giving her your light to hold while you partake of cakes and wine.

Bride blesses each and returns the light.

The Narrator says:

> Let us stand before the Great Goddess and thank her for her gifts of fire and for nourishing us. Make your affirmation to her that you will use her gifts well.

All raise lights in homage to Bride who raises her candle high.

The Narrator concludes:

> Now we bid Bride farewell as her light fades [Bride extinguishes candle].
>
> Take her gift of fire into your inner being as you extinguish your physical light [extinguish lights].
>
> And now let us thank the Elemental Powers for their presence and close the Quarters and the circle.

Elemental Powers thanked, circle closed. This is now a time for the group to socialise and possibly feast together.

A SPECIAL PLACE AND FULL MOON PATHWORKING

Editor's Note: See Chapter 6 for an example meeting programme. Pathworkings should be done after the group has relaxed and tuned in. Regular practice of the Golden Bubble meditation beforehand, for example, trains the brain to know it is about to go on a journey and engage in inner work. Have pens and paper available in case people wish to record their experiences. Always ground people back in reality afterwards, perhaps with stretching, touching the ground, talking together and sharing some food.

Requirements

- Usual candles and optional incense
- Chalice of water on the altar

Option to cast a circle in a similar form to the closing described at the end of this Pathworking.

Spoken by the Guide:

It is very useful to have an imaginary place that you can take refuge in, a place that is very beautiful and peaceful and secure. If you haven't got such a place already, I hope that you will find it in this little journey.

Imagine that you are on a path going to your own private, secret place. You may find that you are going to a cave, or a building, or a place in your own house, or a magical house, or it might be just a place out of doors that is safe and secure and beautiful. But this place is magically guarded. Only you know the magic sign or the magic word that lets you enter it. So imagine now that you are coming towards your secret, special place. You are coming to that hidden entrance and you make the sign or utter the word that allows you to enter .... It reveals the magic doorway, the magic way in. Your special place is very attractive, comfortable. It is however you want it to be. You can make it just as you want it, with somewhere comfortable to sit, somewhere to look out to something beautiful, a beautiful item there that you can contemplate, whatever you want. Maybe your special place will develop as you become more familiar with it, so enter your special place and feel its calm and beauty surround you. No creature, being, or entity of any sort can come here unless you invite them in. Here you can be completely yourself, relaxed and happy, a place you can come to to restore your energies, your confidence, your well-being. A place of healing ....

Let yourselves relax even more deeply in your special place and imagine that you can see the full moon, either through a window, or a doorway, or if you are out of doors you can just see it in the sky; a beautiful, bright full moon. The moon, the light that illumines the darkness when the sun has sunk below the horizon. Moonlight reveals a rather different world, a different aspect of reality. There are no colours, but somehow the world becomes magical and mysterious in the moonlight, unfamiliar, yet fascinating. It enables us to see things in a different light from the everyday, a more magical way.

We can think of our lives as being a journey. It seems as we sit in our special place that that journey of our life is taking on a symbolic reality and there is a path before us that we are following. Sometimes it is difficult and sometimes it is easy, sometimes the way ahead is obscured by obstacles, or it is hidden in mist, or we come to bewildering divisions of the way and don't know which way to go. Sometimes the path we are on seems suddenly to crumble beneath our feet, or to disappear into a bog, or become too narrow for us to continue and perhaps we have to take a detour, or find another way, or simply push through, however uncomfortable it is.

So now see your path, your current life, by moonlight. See if you can identify what the difficulties are, the blockages, the problems. Is it too steep, or too crumbly, too muddy, too rocky, misty? What is it that makes your path ahead difficult? ....

Try to pinpoint it as some sort of an image rather than just as a concept .... Feel intensely your desire to find a way through, to continue your path, to find the way through the difficulties or around the difficulties. See them by the light of the moon in a different perspective. Perhaps they will suddenly look much simpler than they did by sunlight ....

Imagine the full moon overhead. Relax yet more deeply, but mentally focused on your path, on what you saw as the difficulties and problems you need to face on your path. Each one of us is in a sense alone on our path, in that we individually have to make our decisions and find our way, and yet in a sense there are always companions, people we can turn to, people who love us, people we love.

So imagine that you are on your path, walking along it by moonlight, seeing a different perspective, a lunar perspective, letting your lunar nature guide you, letting your intellectual solar nature go into the dark because the sun is the other side of the earth at the moment. As you travel your path you come to whatever condition it is that obstructs you, mist, or mud, or boulder, or narrowness, or crumble, whatever it is.

Sink down deeply within to the deepest level of your being, so that the moonlight becomes more vivid, more real, more sliver gold and call in your heart to the Lady of the Moon. The Moon Goddess goes by many names. You may see her in the moon, or materialising before you in the moonlight, or just imagine her coming down a shaft of moonlight. Feel her presence, see the radiance of her face shining in the darkness .... And as her light intensifies, see the obstacle in your path, how you can progress, how you can move forward. Let come into your mind what it is you need to do ....

Hear her deep wisdom within your mind. Feel her blessing .... And the Lady of the Moon points to a little path that you are to go along as a little digression, a path that leads to her place. You are walking along this path to this special place of spiritual nourishment. These little places near your path are very important, very useful, rich places to visit to replenish yourself, to cool your irritations and anxieties, to give you solace and inner nourishment.

You find you are coming to a circular place surrounded by cypress trees and in the centre is a little pool and somehow magically that place is this room and we can now rise and stand around the altar, imagining that the chalice of water is the little pool. So gently arise and stand .... Now take each other's hands and let us reach up to the Lady of the Moon, gathering her power, taking it into a beautiful beam of moonlight and bringing it down into the chalice, into the little pool .... The little pool, the chalice, is filled with her magic. Take her guidance, her empowerment into your hearts.

Now we will take the little chalice which is full of moon energy. See how the light shows us the energy and glory of the moon in it. So each dip our fingers in it and pass the blessing to the next person. Just say, 'May the Lady of the Moon empower you on your path' ....

[Each person does this and blesses their neighbour, going round in a circle. You could touch their forehead with your finger.]

Let us thank the Goddess of the Moon for her presence, her glory, her empowerment, her guidance. May her light shine ever in our hearts and illuminate our paths, showing us a new perspective based on love, our emotional natures, our intuition. She brings us all these gifts and now her presence withdraws and our image of her special place beside our path dims and fades.

Optional circle closing: We are back here in this room, within our circle of blue fire and we thank the mighty ones of the Element of Air for their presence that has kept us balanced because we do value our intellects, but our intellect cannot solve everything. Sometimes we have to give due hearing and listening to our hearts, our intuitions. The powers of the East withdraw.

We thank the Mighty Ones of Fire for guarding our southern portal, knowing that their presence has kept the fire of our own wills alight because without will we will not properly pursue our path and follow it and deal with those difficulties. So we thank the Powers of Fire as they depart.

We thank the Powers of Water for being part of our work this evening, welling up within us, swirling through us, awakening our hearts, our imaginations. We thank them for their protection and their influence as they depart.

We thank the Element of Earth, the great Powers of Earth; earth in which we have to manifest the results of following our path. We may have travelled our path in our imagination in symbolic form, but in earth we have to go out into the world and make our decisions and do our thing. So Powers of Earth we thank you for your gifts of strength and for supporting us, preserving us and teaching us to persevere. We thank you as you depart.

Now we let the blue fire die down into the ground. This room is no longer a special magical place, but the sitting room. The rite has ended.

AUTO-SUGGESTION AND PRACTISE EXERCISE

Transcript of a talk given by Jean Williams

I'm just going to natter about auto-suggestion and put it into some sort of a context. I think that it is related to an awful lot of other things that we look at in the Pagan, occult and magical world, such as trance work, shamanic journeying, psychic work, psychic healing, healing yourself and healing others, and doing magical work to heal people at a distance, or to achieve some end, that sort of thing. Also things like changing your mood when you are down or angry and you are not enjoying it but can't do anything about it at the moment, just to get yourselves out of it, that sort of thing. It has use in divination and of course the placebo effect in medicine. I think that that is very much related to all of this. In fact every week I have to take a bone hardening drug and I have to use any placebo effect I can summon to make this drug work flat out and to really get my bones back in shape and really hard again and so on. So I have this little magic chant where I say, 'Magic pill, magic pill, make my bones grow strong', and swallow it down and drink a glass of water after it, and then I have to stand up for half an hour, you see, so I make a little ritual of it to harness that placebo effect and since it is first thing in the morning I'm in a pretty sort of dozy relaxed state at any rate.

There doesn't seem to be very much research into this sort of thing at the moment, but I must say I haven't really searched into it. Back in the 1970s and '80s there was a lot of research on trance work and healing work and so on, and what they mainly looked at then was brain wave patterns. Now that they have this brain imaging technique, they seem to have given up looking at brain waves, but there is some very interesting stuff about the different brain wave states you get into when you are getting into a trance and it is the alpha waves that come particularly strongly. People who did psychic healing, who had a good reputation at that, were found to be able to keep the normal waves of social interaction, the beta waves, going, but also get a strong alpha rhythm going. Maxwell Cade, who did a lot of research on this, found that when he had wired up this middle aged lady who had a very good reputation as a psychic healer, and also the person she was working on, time and again she would natter away at a beta wave level, just little inconsequential chatter and so on, very soothing; but she also would get a strong alpha rhythm going and somehow this would transfer to the person she was working on. The getting into that alpha rhythm state is when there is access to the deeper levels of the mind, to your self-healing and so on.

What I want to do is to see if we can develop some triggers that will help us to get into this sort of trancey state. I'm afraid I haven't got a mind mirror for measuring your brain waves. Unfortunately they do cost rather a lot of money. You can still get them, they are around. I had an experience with one once and when I finally got these alpha rhythms going I found my mind was rather different from normal. I was very relaxed, but very alert, and somebody asked a question and the answer came just like that. There was no memory searching, it just went 'boing' into my head. I don't think I could have thought of it that quickly normally, so it does seem that it sharpens up the connections between the different parts of the brain, the sort of emotional and the lower levels and the intellectual levels, so that you can bring up into awareness things that you want to find out about, like you are tapping your own inner wisdom.

A lot of stuff we do in PP with these archetypal images, like wise old women in caves with lovely cauldrons of sweet smelling liquid and so on, are ways of tapping your own inner wisdom. It is an archetypal energy inside you and without you. That is what I think is happening. My opinion of what is happening is that it is connecting up the different levels of the brain.

What I want to do today is to look particularly at auto-suggestion and maybe in a couple of weeks' time we'll do something more on divination, trying it then. We will also do a little bit of healing so you are tuning into somebody else, do a little shoulder massage, hopefully in this lightly trancey state.

The way that I learnt it and I tend to pass on is to do relaxation exercises first and then to do five breaths and counting down, getting deeper and deeper into a level of relaxation, and then going to the psychic plane, whatever that might mean to you. People use all sorts of different images. I tend to use going down ten steps out of doors and then through an archway and into a beautiful garden, and that garden is the psychic plane for me and I can sit there and do whatever it is I want to do in the way of auto-suggestion, but the imagery is a trigger. You don't have to keep that image in front of your mind all the time, but it is something you can go back to if you find yourself slipping out of it. You make your own image. Some people do frightfully mundane things like seeing a television set, or a cinema screen and projecting onto that. That never attracted me at all. Maybe there is a particular place, or a lovely lake, or a river, or some other image that to you would mean the psychic plane, or it might be just a dark place with some coloured lights around.

Another thing that I find is often a very good trigger is a particular piece of music and this can be particularly good for changing your mood, or something of that sort, taking you down into this level. There are some very trancey bits of music, but I think each person finds their own. Finding a piece of music for yourself that really works for you would be a very good trigger. Finding some particular image would be a really good trigger.

We will start now by doing our usual preliminary relaxation and then doing a countdown, one to five, with these five breaths and getting as deeply relaxed as you can. Then we will go to the psychic plane and I will count from one to ten there. You may find an image has already come into your mind that you want to use that would mean going to the psychic plane for you, or you might discover one, or you might do it in some other way, it is up to you. You might think of music in your mind.

Sit yourselves comfortably, your back reasonably straight and close your eyes and breathe .... Now put your awareness on your out breath and let each out breath carry away any remaining tensions, any tensions anywhere in your body. Just feel them ebbing away. Don't forget those favourite places for tensions at the solar plexus area, the throat and shoulders, or around the eyes .... Now feel your out breath carry away any tensions in your mind, any preoccupations with what has happened today, or in the recent past, or any concerns about the future, what you have to do tomorrow. Just let them all go .... Now imagine that you are surrounded by a bubble of beautiful golden light, shot through with sparkling effervescent energy. Put your awareness on your in breath and draw that sparkling energy in with your in breath, into your lungs and feel it travelling into your blood stream, all around your body, right down to your toes and your fingertips, zinging along your nerve fibres. Feel it cleansing you, vitalising you .... Now feel it surging up your spinal column, into your brain, into your mind; your mind becoming clear and bright and relaxed and focused .... If there is any part of your body that has any residual ache or pain, imagine that golden sparkling light gathering there, breathe into that part and feel the pain being washed away, healing coming to that place .... Now imagine that sparkling golden light swirling through your aura, the colours of your aura becoming brighter and sparkly, your aura expanding as your subtle emotional body is cleansed .... Then let the golden light sink back into the floor, leaving you relaxed, refreshed, cleansed and vitalised.

Now as I count from one to five, take five deep breaths and with each breath discover that you can become yet more deeply relaxed. One .... two .... three .... four .... five .... Just say to yourself: deeper, deeper relaxation, deeper. Now as I count from one to ten, let yourself sink to the psychic plane, the everyday mind closing down and your psychic mind waking up. One .... two .... three .... four .... five .... six .... seven .... eight .... nine .... ten .... Just rest there in that state, notice any thoughts or images that arise ....

Now as I count from ten to one you are going to come back from the psychic plane to the state of deep relaxation. Ten .... nine .... eight .... seven

.... six .... five .... four .... three .... two .... one .... Notice any differences between the state of being at the psychic plane and being in the state of deep relaxation ....

Now I'm going to count from five to one and come back from that state of deep relaxation to the here and now and open your eyes. Five .... four .... three .... two .... one .... and open your eyes.

I have done it that way on purpose, so you are not going to do anything at the psychic plane because I think what you need to do first is just to practise going to the psychic plane and coming back out of it, getting familiar with it.

What I want you to do now is to do that again on your own, just yourselves; just the counting one to five, going to the state of deep relaxation and then one to ten and going to the psychic plane, staying there for a few moments and then coming back up again. Off you go then ....

AUTO-SUGGESTION PATHWORKING

Spoken by the Guide:

Get yourself sitting comfortably again. Get yourself centred and relaxed. Now we take five deep breaths and with each breath seek a deeper level of relaxation. One .... two .... three .... four .... five ....

Now let come into your mind what it is you want to change or achieve. Formulate it as a positive statement that will happen and when you want to achieve it by ....

Now just say to yourself: deeper, deeper relaxation. Now I will count from one to ten and take yourself down to the psychic plane. One .... two .... three .... four .... five .... six .... seven .... eight .... nine .... ten .... When you are ready, repeat your positive statement, slowly and clearly, three times ....

Now see a little green feather or a leaf floating down and as it floats down, your instruction sinks deeply, deeply into your unconscious mind. Just rest there in a still peaceful place, confident that that instruction or intent will happen ....

Now, in the darkness, you see stars appearing. You float within the starry sky, feeling yourself connected to the whole universe; the huge web of life and wonder and potential. We know so little about it. We know so little about the universe. We know so little about our own inner universe, but we sense the life and the potential and the promise, the promise of ever-increasing marvelousness. So feel yourself one with the creative life force, connected to all that is, and who knows what magic can be performed through that web, that connectedness. Feel yourself blessed and welcomed and loved and strengthened by that contact with the web of creation .... Feel yourself connected particularly strongly to this planet; the wonderful web of life, the living biosphere of earth. What an extraordinary and marvellous place it is ....

Let come into your mind an image or sense of presence of a God or Goddess that you feel a particular affinity with and listen, that God or Goddess may have a particular message for you at this time to guide you and strengthen you .... Then the presence and the image fades.

Visualise once more whatever you visualise for the psychic plane .... Now as I count from ten to one, return from the psychic plane to that place of relaxation. Ten .... nine .... eight .... seven .... six .... five .... four .... three .... two .... one .... Be aware of this room around you and your body, your weight on your seat or the floor, and as I count from five to one, you come back from that place of deep relaxation, open your eyes and move around. Five .... four .... three .... two .... one .... Wiggle your toes, your fingers, take some deep breaths and open your eyes.

MOON CYCLES PATHWORKING

Best done close to a full moon.

Spoken by the Guide:

Now imagine that you are on the way to your own special secret place, that place that is just as you want it, it may be an outside place or an indoors place, but it is a private place that nobody else can get to. Only you know the way and only you know the magical key that opens the way into it. You are coming to your special place and make the gesture, or say the word, or whatever it is that opens the entrance. You go into your special place and feel the peace and security of it wrap you around. Here you can be entirely yourself. Here you can look within, without fear, knowing that you will find your own inner strength and wisdom.

Sit down in your favourite place in your favourite seat and visualise the full moon and the lunar cycles, the frequency with which it changes. It will soon be full and only a week ago it was a half moon, two weeks ago a crescent. The moon power is strong at full moon, a time for looking at ourselves by that silvery light where everything looks strange and mystical. You get a new perspective on things by the moonlight and you realise that, like the moon, your life has its own cycles. Some cycles are very short, like breathing in and out, or hunger and eating and being satiated, and sleeping and waking, work and rest and work and play. Similarly our emotional nature has its cycles, cycles that are particularly governed by the moon, cycles of feeling sociable, or wanting to be alone, to be talking and chatting and laughing, or to be quiet, to be energetic or to be resting, and cycles of optimism and pessimism, happiness and unhappiness, excitement and quiet contentment. All these changes and cycles and moods are part of our search for equilibrium as we dance through life. But we don't seek perfect, still equilibrium; we seek moving equilibrium like a dancer around our centre, so we value all these moods and swings of feeling. Life would become so dull and weird if we were just in one mental state all the time.

So look now at your current situation, your current emotional state. Where is it? In what sort of cycle? If you were to put a label to the state you feel in at present, what do you contrast it with? What are you measuring it against? ....

Now see if you can look at that from a bit more distance as though you take a few steps back away from it and see this current state you're in, this current situation, as part of an overall pattern, part of your pattern, one of your cycles, and accept it and value it as part of your life dance .... Remember what it is you have looked at in this bit of inner exploration as we shall come back to it later.

Now it is time to leave your special place, so take a last look around, enjoying its peace and tranquillity. Leave by that special doorway, closing it behind you and magically sealing it. Make your way back along that secret way and then take some deep breaths and when you are ready, open your eyes and have a stretch.

BENEFICENCE IN THE JEWEL PATHWORKING

Spoken by the Guide:

Imagine you are in your room. You go to the cupboard and find at the back of it another door, a door that is not always there, but it is there now and as you touch it, it swings open revealing a flight of old stone steps leading down a spiral staircase, and you step through and go down the steps.

As you go down and round, and down, with each step you become more deeply relaxed, but staying very alert, listening to my voice .... The staircase becomes more real, the steps slightly worn beneath your feet, the touch of the rough stone walls and the smell of old stone. Your way is lit by guttering sconces in the walls, lights which flutter and flicker in the faint draft. You go on down and round, and down, and down, and down, until you come to a landing and see there an ancient door set in a stone arch and you remember that this is the door to your own private magical temple.

You open the door and find your temple just as you remember it. In the centre is a small waist high altar on which burns a beautiful lamp. To the east are two tall pillars, one black and one white, and against one of the walls is a large chest in which you keep your magical tools and robes. You close the door and go to your chest and find within it a robe of your choice and put it on. Then you find your talisman and put it around your neck. This talisman is a powerful protection on your journey. Whenever you feel a bit overwhelmed, or lost, you can take hold of your talisman and be back in your temple. So look now at your talisman, note what it is made of and what its design is, feel the comforting feel of it in your hands ....

Then look again in your chest and find a small box of beautifully inlaid wood and take it with you to your altar and open the box and find within it your collection of magical jewels. Select from it one jewel of whatever colour you feel drawn to, that you feel you need. Take it in your hand.

Now you look towards the two pillars and there seems to be a shimmering veil of many colours between the two pillars, shimmering in a slight breeze. You walk around the altar and go towards the pillars and find that you can just walk through this shimmering veil. It touches your face lightly as you pass, like strands of silk. You pass through into a bright, sunlit landscape and there is a path in front of your feet leading up a rocky hillside. The air is fresh and invigorating.

Take some deep breaths and walk up the path, striding comfortably up the slight incline. Now it is a little steeper, but the light is so beautiful, the air and the sun are so lovely. Breathe deeply and find you have plenty of puff to take you up to the top of the hill. There is a little flat plateau and before you is a marvellous view, a view of rolling hills and woods, meandering rivers, rocky outcrops, cultivated fields, raging torrents and waterfalls, maybe towns, villages, buildings, temples, houses, a wonderful panorama ....

This panorama, all that you can see there, is a symbol of your life. You can see the difficult places, you can see the barriers, the challenges, the frightening areas, the unknown territory. You can see the lovely, calm, peaceful places. You can see the busy things, busy activities. You can see your work, your home, your friends, your relationships, your problems, your joys, all spread out within this view, but from this high point you have a different perspective. It is all just a wonderful pattern, a beautiful, interesting, intricate pattern of your life, the landscape of your life through which you are travelling ....

Now you have become aware that clutched in your hand you have this beautiful jewel. You drag your eyes away from the landscape and look down at the jewel which seems to be tingling with some inner life. You look at it and it is glowing and sparkling within. The beautiful colour of the jewel starts to expand and grow, so the whole jewel is expanding and glowing. You place it on the ground and step back to watch it. Within the jewel, in the heart of the jewel, there is an intense shimmering and now the jewel is growing, the light of the jewel is expanding, so it is much higher than you and that shimmering within the centre becomes a beautiful being .... This beautiful entity reaches towards you, drawing you forward, and you step into the jewel, bathed in that beautiful, translucent light. This entity greets you with great beneficence and love. You feel healing flowing into you, strengthening you, filling you with happiness and confidence. You open your mind to this entity, this entity that is from within yourself, is beautiful, powerful and wise and loving, and let the entity speak within your mind, bringing you perhaps a special message, or just some words of comfort, or just a sense of healing. Take a few moments to commune with this entity, the spirit of the jewel ....

The entity can show you how your life can become more beautiful, more rewarding and more fulfilling. Perhaps you may become aware of things you can change, things you need to do and things you need to let go of. Listen some more to this beautiful being ....

Now simply open yourself fully to the light and colour of the jewel and the beneficence of the life force within it because it is your own inner beauty, your own wonderful life force, your own wisdom ....

Now the image and the light, the colour, starts to fade and pale .... Send thanks from your heart to that entity and then you find yourself back on the plateau, and the jewel is a small jewel at your feet which you pick up and you can still see a little sparkle within its heart. You place that jewel with your body. Let it be absorbed into yourself. You turn and make your way back down the path, the sun is sinking towards the west and for a moment you see the colours of your jewel in the colours of the sunset, and then you find yourself back outside the pillars of your temple, pass through the veil and you are within your temple. Stand before the altar for a moment and just absorb all that communing with the entity and the jewel, the beauty and the love, the wisdom and the healing ....

Then it is time to leave your temple, so you take off your talisman and put it back in your chest. Put your jewel box in the chest, take off your robe and leave your temple, closing the door behind you. As you make your way up the spiral staircase you are returning to the here and now as I count from twenty to one. Twenty .... nineteen .... eighteen .... seventeen .... sixteen .... fifteen .... fourteen .... thirteen .... twelve .... eleven .... ten .... half way back now .... nine .... eight .... seven .... six .... five .... feel your feet on the ground, feel your hands, take some deep breaths .... four .... three .... two .... one .... More deep breaths and open your eyes.

OUTLINE FOR AN ELEMENTAL SESSION

As discussed previously in this book, in the section contemplating the elements as metaphors, we often worked with the elemental archetypes in Pagan Pathfinders, using that element as a focal point for drawing energy into, and exploring, the qualities it represents. For example, water is often seen as connected to emotions (love, pleasure, empathy, compassion, fear, sadness), as well as dreams and imagination. Using water as an example, but obviously it is interchangeable for any of the other elements, below is an outline of such a session.

- Stretch and centre yourselves. Perhaps do a movement exercise, for example imagine floating in the sea.
- Golden Bubble meditation.
- Discuss the qualities of water as a group.
- Meditate and sink into your own secret place. Review the good and bad, strong and weak aspects of the element of water: emotions getting out of hand, fear, anger; but also pleasure, love, happiness, dreams and imagination. Are you too changeable, or too rigid? What would you like strengthened or changed? How do you maintain emotional equilibrium? Take a moment to acknowledge how our common need for water connects us to all animals and plants.
- As a group, discuss this.
- Prepare for a ritual by lighting candles and creating the sacred space, creating the circle and calling the quarters.
- Sink down into inner stillness, into your inner depths. The group leader could do a pathworking, transporting the group in their minds to a watery place, evoking the magic and wonder of water.
- All compose an invocation to water.

- The group opens their eyes and writes down their invocations.
- All stand and take it in turn to read the invocations.
- In a circle, begin to focus on the power of water and all its aspects. Feel the power building. Call to mind, or speak out loud watery places: springs, slow and placid rivers, babbling brooks, surging ocean, deep still depths. Ask the group to feel themselves sinking down into the power of water, submerged.
- Pass around a goblet of water and all take a sip, drinking in the magic of water, absorbing its healing, its insight and wisdom. Feel refreshed and blessed.
- Close the circle.

THE GODDESS PERSEPHONE PATHWORKING

Editor's Note: This is an example of a pathworking ritual, where the Goddess Persephone is invoked and encountered during a pathworking. At all times the group remains silent in a meditative state, seated or lying down, eyes closed, while being led through the ritual by the spoken words of the Guide.

Spoken by the Guide:

This is a trip to meet the Goddess Persephone as she returns to the earth above after her sojourn in the Underworld. We can regard the Underworld as being the equivalent of the unconscious mind, the land of dreams, but also the land of potential.

So imagine that you are in your room and you go to your cupboard and you find at the back of it a door. It is not always there, but it is there now and it opens for you, revealing a flight of old stone steps leading down. Eager to explore, quite unafraid, you step through and start to go down the steps, finding it is a spiral staircase of ancient stones lit by flaming torches in sconces in the walls, and you go down and down becoming more deeply relaxed, the steps becoming more real and you feel the rough stone walls with your hands. You smell the slightly musty old smell of the place as you go down and round and down and round ....

Until you come to a landing and find there an ancient door set in a stone arch. You remember that this is the door to your own private magical temple and you open the door and go in and see the little square waist high altar in the centre. On the other side are two great tall pillars, one black and one white, and against the wall is a chest in which you keep your magical weapons, your robes and your talisman.

You go to your chest and take out of it your talisman, putting it around your neck, knowing that this will keep you safe and to get back to your temple in a magical instant all you have to do is get hold of your talisman in your hand and visualise your temple.

Now you take from the chest your four magical weapons of the elements. You take your short sharp dagger of air and place it on the east side of the altar. You take your magical wand and place it on the south side of the altar. You take your beautiful chalice cup, the element of water, and place it on the west side and you take a beautiful shiny stone, symbol of the element of earth, and place it on the north side.

You stand before your altar and each of the weapons glows with its elemental colour. The dagger glows with yellow, the wand with fiery red, the chalice is filled with blue light and the stone glows green. You absorb the power of your elemental weapons, giving you a wonderful sense of equilibrium, inner balance and harmony.

Between the pillars you notice that there is a dark veil and it is blowing gently with a mysterious wind. You go around your altar to the pillars and pass through the veil into the twilight world of early dawn. Beneath your feet is dew wet grass and poppies and narcissi grow around your feet. Ahead of you is a beautiful little Grecian temple of white marble, the circle of pillars holding up the little domed roof. Beyond the temple you see the entrance to a great dark cavern, the gate to the Underworld, the place of death, the realm of the unconscious mind. In there dwell our deepest fears, our angers, our hurts, but also our loves and joys and our deepest most mysterious dreams; the magical seeds of our potential. It is the realm of the dark Lord Hades, he who fell in love with the daughter of the Earth Mother. He took her down into his kingdom and gave her to eat a pomegranate, the fruit of death, but also symbolic of the seeds of life and such was the union of life and death, of light and dark, and from that union life returns to this world, to the realm of consciousness, bringing great wisdom and inner light, the seeds of creativity, and this now is the spring time when Persephone returns to us.

So let us invoke her to take her seat in her temple:

> Hail Persephone, Goddess of the gates of death and life, who art throned in the midst of a spring garden in the shadows of the Underworld. In thy right hand is the deadly fruit of Hades, the pomegranate whereof all creatures must eat at the last. Thou art crowned with palm leaves and with poppies and corn. Thy voice is a low call heard at evening, luring the hearer to deep dreams. Wait then eternally at the gate between the worlds that there might be a sweet, grave welcome for life as it passes into death and a light swift welcome for death as it passes into life, for at every spring shalt thou return to us and gladden the earth with birdsong and cleanse eye and mind to innocence, that a new tale may be told. Wherever sleep follows waking and waking follows sleep, wherever the rhythm of days and seasons call forth and echo from the souls of creatures, wherever life passes from flesh to earth to flower to flesh, it is thy garland that is worn, thy sarabande that is danced. By the brevity and the eternity of life, by the pulse of light and darkness, by the seed hidden under the ice, by the shed skin of the serpent, by the hope that is beyond hope and despair, we call upon thee to be with us in body and in spirit.

We see Persephone come forth from the Underworld and as she comes her face lightens with joy as the sun falls upon her beauty. She flings open her arms to accept the sun and the fresh air and the birdsong, the grass and the flowers, and steps into her temple .... Feel her wisdom flowing into us, firing up your creativity that this spring may bring you new ideas, new ventures, new hope, new joy. Her blessing flows into us. Open your heart to Persephone. She brings the treasures of the dark into the light of day, into the fecundity of spring. She brings your own treasures up from deep within you. The seeds within you are starting to sprout. There is a glory of possibilities ahead of you ....

Now Persephone steps down from her temple. She doesn't return to the Underworld but goes onwards back into the live earth above and flowers spring around her feet. A flock of little birds dart and sing around her head. Rabbits and squirrels appear and wild deer peek shyly from the trees. All of life rejoices at the return of Persephone. Her mother, the Earth, welcomes her back. Now is the time for growth ....

We must now return to our everyday lives, but blessed and enriched, full of new spring energy. So we turn back along the path we came and find, as we pass between two trees, it is as though a veil touches our faces and we find we have passed through a magical gateway back into our temple. We stand for a moment at our altar and feel within us the blessing of Persephone, the seeds of new life .... Then we must put away our magical weapons. The elemental glow has faded from them and we take them one by one and put them back in the chest. We put our talisman back in the chest and then make our way out through the door, closing it behind us, up the staircase, up and round and up and up and up and up, back to the everyday world ....

We find that door back into our cupboard and we are back in the here and now. Take some deep breaths. Feel the earth, the ground, the floor, your hands, and open your eyes.

RITE OF EQUILIBRIUM AND PATHWORKING

Requirements

- Dish or goblet of water

You could begin by calling to mind the protective circle of blue flame and the elements in the four quarters.

Spoken by the Guide:

At this time the powers of light and dark are also in balance and the sun and the moon are opposite each other in balance, and the moon has entered the sign of Libra, so the powers of the moon are in balance and can aid us in the immediate future, just over the next couple of days particularly, to maintain balance.

The sun is growing in strength, growing in light and warmth, bringing us clarity and energy, longer days in which to do things. The sun warms the air so that we love to breathe and enjoy the perfumes that the sun releases from the spring flowers and the green, growing things of the earth. The sun warms the birds of the air and excites them, switching on their instincts for mating and nest building. They are everywhere, flying, singing, bringing delight. So the element of air is enhanced by the spring sun, the gathering warmth, to bring us extra clarity and mental energy, inspiration.

And the sun ignites our fires, the element of fire burns yet more brightly. The sun, as it warms, encourages our inner fires to burn more brightly so that we use the energies of fire more productively, we are more focused, more directed into our true purpose, our real inner will.

The sun warms the waters. The element of water flows as the ice melts. The water circulates so that we get the spring rains moistening the soil and helping things to grow. The sun warms the water, the warmer waters warm our hearts. Our emotions are more open, warmer, more generous, more receptive, more giving, more loving.

And the sun warms the earth, it warms the element of earth. The ground of our being becomes fertile so that all that we undertake comes into manifestation. We put our work to good purpose and persevere, we focus, we build, we plant, in the warmed earth. The warmed earth draws us into action.

So we welcome the spring sun, the longer days, the increasing warmth and feel that in every way, every aspect of our lives is enriched and enhanced by the powers of the sun.

But now it is night time, the time of the moon. The sun is hidden behind the earth and the moon shines clear and bright and by the light of the moon we see a different perspective. The light of the moon shines upon the element of air and it puts us in touch with alternative ways of looking at things, alternative ways of thinking. The moon sharpens our imagination and our intuition. Everything looks different and slightly unfamiliar and thus we look anew with fresh eyes and we breathe the night air and our minds take flight in new directions, a new sort of clarity. Old habits of perception and interpretation shift and slide and glide and reform as new ideas, new evaluations, new perspectives.

The moon shines on the element of fire and by the light of the moon we see the sparks rising from the fire. We see new, bright beauty. We formulate our goals, we formulate our purpose and at night the fire is more visible. By the light of the moon we see a candle flame which might be invisible in the sunlight. We see the little fires, many of which may be very important to us, the little fires of will and purpose, of energy and action, those little things we put off doing, or haven't yet thought about doing, and in the light of the moon we see new possibilities, new ways of forging ahead, following our life's purpose.

And the moon shines on the element of water. The moon influences the ebb and flow of water and our inner tides. By the light of the moon we can perceive the flows and eddies and currents that are invisible in daylight and we can feel them, feel them flowing deep within us, new depths coming to the surface, new depths we can dive into and discover within ourselves. By the light of the moon we see raindrops sparkle, we see the foam of the waterfall. The moonlight turns the water to silver and by the light of the moon we see the earth, the familiar looking, strange and unknown. We see new possibilities. We feel the rocks, we feel the earth. All our senses come alive by the light of the moon. And by the light of the moon the powers of the earth are strong. Now is the time to plant our seeds and all is in balance, the moon in the sign of Libra ....

Let us stand and join hands and be aware of the powers of the elements, the moon above in opposition to the sun, in balance, the moon in Libra. Let us reach up and imagine the moon right above us. Focus the light of the moon down through the circle made by our hands and we bring it slowly down into the blue goblet of water ....

Now we will pass the cup around and each person just anoint the forehead of the person next to them and say something like, 'May the powers of the moon in Libra guide you and give you your heart's desire', or 'May the power of the moon in Libra guide you and care for you' ....

[Pause to allow this to happen.]

Now is this moment of balance, the balance of the powers of the elements, the balance of light and dark, the balance of sun and moon and the balance of the moon in Libra. All shall be well if you trust these powers of balance and seek always your own equilibrium. Draw in the strength of this time when the moon is all too briefly in Libra for just two days. Use this moment well, use these powers. They are there for us to use, for us to draw into ourselves and to give of ourselves. We give to them and they give to us. We are in them and they are in us ....

We thank the powers of sun and moon for their special gifts tonight. We thank the powers of the elements for their special gifts and their equilibrium. We thank the sun and the moon for showing us different aspects of the elements and we thank the circle of blue fire for holding us in this magical space. We feel the powers of the elements withdrawing to the edges of the circle, the moon powers becoming remote overhead, the sun powers on the other side of the earth.

Let us turn to the east and let the powers of air withdraw with our thanks.
Hail and farewell.

Turn to the south and let the powers of fire withdraw with our thanks.
Hail and farewell.

We let the powers of water withdraw into the west with our thanks.
Hail and farewell.

Then we let the powers of earth withdraw back deep into the earth with our thanks and we say hail and farewell.

The blue fire sinks down into the earth. The room returns around us, the sacred space melts away. We take it within ourselves.

Merry meet, merry part and merry meet again!

SPRING EQUINOX FESTIVAL

For a Pagan Federation Open Ritual

Editor's note: Jean was very involved and committed to the Pagan Federation so it was common for Pagan Pathfinders to do rituals at Pagan Federation events. This is one example. Doing a ritual for a large group has its own challenges and good preparation is crucial. We always rehearsed and there was the usual mix of volunteering and cajoling that Jean was so good at. Any of these rituals for larger events can be adapted to be used in a smaller group.

Requirements:

- Altar with candles, incense, optional Goddess figure and flowers, cakes and wine
- Quarter candles
- Elemental symbols (eg wand, pentacle)
- Sun God's wand, sistrum (or other percussion instrument), green cloak, crown of flowers
- Optional music for meditation, elemental journey and joyful music for the final dance
- Hand fans, red candles, small bowls of water, some kind of tunnel – all placed near the altar

Roles:

- Circle caster
- Elemental Quarter Officers
- Narrator
- Elemental Gifts Officers (Quarter Officers with extra people)
- Sun God
- Spring Goddess

The Narrator begins by describing the themes of the Spring Equinox: balancing the elemental forces of dark and light, cold and warmth, winter and summer, finding balance within ourselves, equilibrium; growth and new life in nature and uncovering our own growth and potential.

The circle is cast.

Quarter Officers stand at their Quarter and call upon each Elemental Power to be present:

EAST: I call upon the Powers of the Element of Air,
At this time of the Spring Equinox.
We welcome you in all your capricious variety -
The relentless Spring gales
That blow away the debris of Winter;
Your sudden cold Easterly winds that refresh our minds;
Your sweet warm breezes that bring us the song of birds
And the promise of Summer.
Come, Powers of Air, Powers of the East,
Grant us your gifts and your protection.
Hail and Welcome!

SOUTH: I call upon the Powers of the Element of Fire,
At this time of the Spring Equinox.
We welcome you in all your guises -
The hearth fire that warms our hearts in the evening chill;
The fierce blaze that burns away the deadwood
And releases our energies;
The inner flame that illumines our path and our purpose.
Come, Powers of Fire, Powers of the South;
Grant us your gifts and your protection.
Hail and Welcome!

WEST: I call upon the Powers of the Element of Water,
At this time of the Spring Equinox.
We welcome you in your myriad forms -
The mist and dew of a Spring morning
That brings the dreams of night into the waking day;
The gentle rain that germinates the seed within the soil;
The deep, still pools of mystery and magic;
The great sea, ocean source of life, ebbing and flowing,
Now calm, now wild and billowing, never still.
Come Powers of Water, Powers of the West;
Grant us your gifts and your protection.
Hail and Welcome!

NORTH: I call upon the Powers of the Element of Earth,
At this time of the Spring Equinox.
We welcome you in all your aspects -
The hard rocks and deep caves that endure the ages;
The gems and minerals that are the Earth's treasures;
The soaring mountains that reach for the heights,
Yet give of themselves to form the fertile valleys;
The sweet soil, ground of being, in which life is rooted.
Come, Powers of Earth, Powers of the North;
Grant us your gifts and your protection.
Hail and Welcome!

The group sing (encouraging all to join in) this chant or similar:

Earth my body, Water my blood,
Air my breath and Fire my spirit.

The Narrator asks everyone to take a moment to centre themselves and guides them through a simple meditation with a Spring theme, for example the 'Seed Meditation' at the beginning of Part 2 of this book, with optional background music.

NARRATOR: We will now go on a journey, a journey that will take us through each of the Elemental Kingdoms, seeking the gifts that we need to achieve inner harmony and balance. (Optional): On this journey, it is good to have a companion, so find a partner, hold hands and journey together through the elements.

During the following, fans are collected from nearby the altar by the ritual group and the gateway of air is formed in the east for people to walk through.

NARRATOR: Now imagine that you are on a steep path that leads to a high plateau. A playful wind buffets you as you walk; breathe deeply of fresh air; as you climb you feel yourself becoming lighter - light of heart, clear of mind, nimble footed. And now, ahead of you, you see tall slender trees on either side of the path; they bend and sway gracefully in the wind, and beyond them you see the high plateau. This is the gateway to the Kingdom of Air. Pass through the gateway and receive the gifts of the Element of Air.

Suitable music played.

As people pass through the gateway created by the ritual group, officers fan them and utter words with intent to give a quality of air as a gift, for example: clarity, lightness, laughter, intelligence, communication, wit, joy.

When all have passed through:

NARRATOR: Close your eyes. Feel the Winds of Air all around you and through you. Accept these gifts into your innermost being .... Now thank the Elemental Beings of the Kingdom of Air for their gifts.

During the following the fans are returned and red candles are taken up and lit, forming the gateway of fire.

NARRATOR: It is time to continue our journey. We leave the high plateau by a stony path leading down. The wind has dropped; the sun is strong and it becomes hot. Now a red haze fills the sky and ahead we see flames on either side of the path - the portal to the Elemental Kingdom of Fire. We realise that these are no ordinary flames but Elemental Fire. If we have courage and a burning desire to receive the gifts of this Element, we can go into the Fire without harm. So with the courage of True Will, pass through the gate into the Kingdom of Fire and receive its gifts.

Suitable music played.

As people pass through the gateway, officers gently wave the candles and utter qualities of fire as gifts, for example: warmth, energy, passion, will, purpose, excitement, transmutation.

When all have passed through:

NARRATOR: Close your eyes. See the purifying flames of the Element of Fire around and within you. Accept its gifts into your innermost being .... Now thank the Elemental Beings of the Kingdom of Fire for their gifts.

During the following, the candles are returned and bowls of water taken up. The gateway of water is formed.

NARRATOR: It is time to continue our journey. As we pass on, the flames die down and we find lush plants and trees around us. A light cooling rain falls, refreshing us and the land. As we journey on, we see drops of water sparkling on the leaves like brilliant diamonds. We find we are walking along the banks of a river; the water chuckles noisily over stones and rocks. Now we see ahead of us a rocky height and the noise of the water increases to a roar. We see a spectacular waterfall leaping down the cliff. A shimmer of rainbow light plays about it and a fine spray reaches us. As we draw closer, we see that behind the fall of water the cliff face curves inward, leaving a space between cliff and water; and there is a ledge, just wide enough for two people to walk along. Here is the gateway to the Kingdom of the Element of Water. Let the exhilaration of the leaping foaming water enter you as you dare this perilous and exciting path. Pass now through the gateway and receive the gifts of the Element of Water.

Suitable music played.

As people pass through the gateway, officers sprinkle everyone with water and utter the qualities of water as a gift, for example: dreams, creativity, compassion, empathy, love, vision, friendship.

When all have passed through:

NARRATOR: Close your eyes and feel the swirling of Water all around you and within you. Accept its gifts into your innermost being .... And thank the Elemental Beings of the Kingdom of Water for their gifts.

During the following, the bowls of water are returned and the tunnel is erected.

Editor's Note:

This became infamous in PP and many jokes were had at its expense. It was some kind of children's play tunnel, but you could use sheets, or anything you can find to make a darker space to crawl or walk through. We were 'cajoled' into crawling inside and tickling people as they went through. Some were less than keen on this idea and if it causes unease, perhaps just ask the participants to crawl through and utter the qualities of Earth to them as they go through.

NARRATOR: Now it is time once more to continue our journey and our path leads into an ancient forest. Great trees send gnarled roots deep into the Earth, their spreading branches hiding the sky. Under our feet is the rich leaf mould of years, and where the sunlight breaks through, there are primroses and great drifts of bluebells. Our path is rising now and becoming more difficult, strewn with boulders over which we have to clamber. The trees are becoming sparse, giving way to hardy bushes that have pushed their roots into crevasses in the rocks. We look ahead to see where our path leads and see the dark mouth of a cave in the hillside, and we know that this is our goal, the gateway to the Kingdom of the Element of Earth. We must enter it if we would receive its gifts. Pass now through the gateway and go down into the Kingdom of Earth.

Suitable music played.

As the people pass through the tunnel, they are touched (optional) and officers utter the qualities of earth as a gift, for example: strength, endurance, health, plenty, growth, fertility, rebirth.

When all have passed through:

NARRATOR: Close your eyes and feel the Kingdom of Earth around you and within you, the ground beneath your feet, your body, your strength. Accept its gifts into your innermost being .... And thank the beings of the Element of Earth for their gifts.

During the following, the Sun God takes up position in front of the altar, carrying a wand and sistrum (or other percussion instrument) and holding or having available nearby a green cloak and a crown of flowers. The Goddess of Spring also takes up position on the floor in front of altar, behind the Sun God, covered with a black cloak.

NARRATOR: We have come to the end of our journey and have come full circle. Join hands now in a circle .... Feel the Elemental Powers all around us. Visualise a swirl of colours, yellow and red and blue and green, the elemental colours. They swirl around us faster and faster, until they coalesce into brilliant white light that incandesces all around and over us. Absorb that brilliant white light as the gifts of all the elements come into perfect balance and harmony within us .... (Gesturing to the Sun God) .... And behold, from that synthesis of all the elements comes the Lord of Light - the young God of the Springtime, virile, beautiful, full of energy and gladness!

The Sun God steps forward in front of the Goddess, facing away from her to the congregation. He holds the wand and percussion instrument which he shakes.

SUN GOD: I am the golden Sun at this time of balance;
I am the wind that blows through your mind,
And the rain that falls on your fertile Earth;
I am the fire in your heart,
And the health and strength and lustiness of your body.
I am in all of you!
And I seek to awaken my beloved,
For I am incomplete without her.
We are all incomplete without her!

He turns to face the Goddess who is curled up on the floor.

SUN GOD: Come, Goddess of Springtime -
Awaken, my beloved, *[He removes her black cloak]*
Open your lovely eyes, arise! *[He raises her up]*
Let me clothe you in green. *[He puts the green cloak on her]*
I crown you with flowers *[Does so]*
Bring us the joy and rapture of Spring!

He kisses her and gives her the percussion instrument which she shakes.

GODDESS: I am the awakening Earth at this time of balance;
I am the quickening within each one of you.
I am growth and laughter and joy!
I and my beloved are one -
One in the joy of Springtime;
One with each of you.
Come! Join my dance,
The joyous dance of dynamic balance.

She shakes the percussion instrument and joins hands with the Sun God. Now all join hands. She leads everyone in a spiral dance to joyful music, ending back in front of the altar.

The Goddess and God stand before the altar with the percussion instrument and wand. The Elemental Officers collect cakes and wine from the altar and kneel before them in a semi-circle.

SUN GOD: I bless this wine which is the transmutation of all the Elements. May it bring to fruition the gifts of the Elements within you.

(Touches each container with the wand.)

GODDESS: I bless these cakes which are of the essence of my being. May they nourish your deepest centre and bring you to a rich harvest.

(Touches each container with the percussion instrument.)

Suitable music played while cakes and wine are passed around.

When this is completed, all join hands.

SUN GOD: It is time to end our rite. Let us thank the Elemental Powers and close the Quarters.

The Elemental Officers close their Quarters, starting with the East and continuing round:

OFFICER: We thank you, mighty Powers of the Element of Air/Fire/Water/Earth for your protection and your gifts, and we now say Hail and Farewell!

NARRATOR: Now let the circle of blue fire die down as we close our sacred space. The rite is ended.

ALL: Merry Meet and Merry Part and Merry Meet Again!!

STONE CIRCLE INNER PRIESTESS/PRIEST MEDITATION

Spoken by the Guide:

As you stand, relaxed and centered within yourself, breathe slowly .... And deeply .... And imagine yourself slipping back in time many hundreds of years to a time when great stone circles were being erected for the worship of the solar god, for the celebration of the union of the Earth Mother with the god and for the marking of the seasons. Feel the wonder and excitement as the great stones, transported from far away, are moved laboriously into position .... And the circle finally takes shape and is ready for use.
Imagine that you are a priest or priestess of that ancient time. Feel that priest or priestess emerging from within you. You have undergone training and initiation and are deeply in tune with forces within the Earth that are focused by the stone circle and with the powers of the sun and its season. Let that priest or priestess emerge now ....
Imagine that it is the time of the Spring Equinox and you are gathered within the stone circle to participate in a great ritual. This rite will take place at midday, when the sun reaches its height. When the music starts you will take part in a ritual dance to celebrate this point when the light equals the darkness, but the light is waxing and the darkness is waning; the Earth is fructified and everyone's heart is filled with new hope and joy. As the music starts, let your spontaneous ritual dance to the Spring Sun emerge as naturally as the green leaves on the trees ....

Allow time for people to dance to the music, if possible with their eyes still closed in a meditative state. When the music ends:

Be aware of that priest or priestess within you, that aspect of you that is in tune with the seasons and that has a wisdom, both of the Earth and of the long eons and let it become more accessible to your present day self .... Now the stone circle fades and take three deep breaths and open your eyes.

EGYPTIAN SPRING RITUAL

Credited in Jean's notes to the late Chris Moroz, a regular Pagan Pathfinders attendee.

Requirements:

- Altar with candles, incense, optional Goddess figure and flowers, cakes and wine
- Quarter candles
- Elemental symbols – feather, candle, bowl of water, pentacle

Roles:

- Circle caster
- Elemental Quarter Officers
- Priestess 1 & 2
- Priest
- Horus
- Isis

Circle cast and Quarters opened.

PRIESTESS 1: We have come to a time in the wheel of the year where it sometimes still feels like winter, and yet the spring is on its way. We celebrate the strength of the growing Sun and the response of new life springing up from the Earth. But also we celebrate the Moon powers, for if there were no moon, there would be no life. The Moon rules the Waters of Life. On the inner, we are the Earth that responds to the differentiating and energising powers of the Sun and the integrating receptive powers of the Moon. Thus we celebrate the sacred marriage within of Sun and Moon.

Horus stands East of altar, Isis West of altar.

Priestess 2 invokes Horus:

PRIESTESS 2: Awaken thou Priest of Horus;
Come into life, for thy strength is needed.
Homage to thee, O Ra, when thou risest,
And to thee, O Temu, in the rising of beauty.
Thou risest, thou shinest, at dawn of day.
Thou art crowned king of the gods,
And the goddess Maat performs an act of homage unto thee.
The company of the gods praise thee,
From the places of sunrise and sunset.
Great Hawk that flies with the flying Sun,
Thou passest over the height of heaven
And thy heart is filled with gladness.
The Sektet boat draweth on,
And Ra advanceth in the Atet boat with fair winds.
Ra rejoiceth, Ra rejoiceth.
Oh thou who art Ra-Heru-Khuti,
Thy divine boat advanceth in peace.
Spread thy golden beams over the palm trees
and green fields,
Lord of the Horizon, Lord of the Two Lands.

HORUS: I come forth and am born each day as a child
Seated on a lotus flower, in the sign of silence.
My Mother is Nu, the starry night.
I fly as a Hawk out of the brilliance of the dawn sky.
I bring new birth, new life.
Before my face the Two Lands awaken.
Victorious in battles, I triumph like the bull.
I am the winged disk, Lord of the Horizon.
See with my hawk-eyes the unfolding of your destiny;
Fly with my wings into the golden blaze of your future.
Receive my Blessing. *[Raises arms in blessing.]*

Priestess 2 leads Horus to each of the four quarters, and the Elements reply:

EAST: The Eastern Heavens bear witness to thy passing in the glory of Light and in Breath. *[East draws whistling breath and waves feather]*

SOUTH: The Southern Heavens bear witness to thy passing in the blaze of fire, the heat of noon, and in action! *[South raises candle aloft]*

WEST: The Western Heavens bear witness to thy passing; the Waters of Nu rejoice with feeling and depth. *[West sprinkles water]*

NORTH: The Northern Heavens bear witness to thy passing in strength, endurance and balance. *[North raises pentacle]*

Horus returns to position East of altar.

Priest invokes Isis:

PRIEST: Isis, Heavenly Mother, Queen of all the world,
Thou art crowned in the heavens.
Oh Lady of right and truth, Oh Circle of Stars,
Thou who art all things to all men.
Veiled in earthly form with the beauty of nature,
Unveiled in the Heavens and crowned with stars.
Pour forth thy healing magic and thy love,
And bring us to growth and regeneration,
For without thee we are lost in the mists of time and space.

ISIS: I who am the Great Mother of all,
Answer your call.
On Earth, I am the Isis of Nature,
Clad in the beauty of Spring time.

In the Heavens, I am the white moon and the starry sky.
I bring you the healing of the harmony of the spheres.
All who travel my path shall be enfolded
In the ecstasy of my being.
I call out to your soul, arise!
And walk in the mysteries of my temple;
There shall you find within you the seeds of regeneration.
Go forth with my love in your hearts,
And know I am with you always.
Receive my Blessing. *[Raises arms in blessing]*

Priest leads Isis to each Element in turn:

The Elements speak:

EAST: Behold now the Element of Air has been transformed. Where the mists lay over the ground, now the air is filled with light and joy, and fragrant breezes blow away the shadows. *[Waves feather and makes whistling breath]*

SOUTH: Behold now the Element of Fire has been transformed. Where cold and darkness dwelt, the Sun God Ra now shines his golden beams, bringing energy, new life and the will to grow." *[Raises candle]*

WEST: Behold now the Element of Water has been transformed. The dark and turgid depths now sparkle with light. The Waters of Life are giving birth to a new spirit of love and joyous creativity." *[Sprinkles water]*

NORTH: Behold now the Element of Earth has been transformed. Where the ground was hard with frost, the soil is now warm and receptive and gives forth new life and regeneration. Rejoice in life renewed. *[Raises pentacle]*

Horus and Isis go to the altar.

Priestess 2 and Priest present cakes and wine to Horus and Isis for blessing. All partake.

PRIESTESS 1: Oh Unseen Powers that are active all around us, nourish us, and shape our destiny in the ebb and flow of our lives. Awaken in us the sacred marriage of lunar conjoining and solar differentiating energies, in this season of balance. Hail Horus! Hail Isis!

PRIESTESS 2: Horus, Lord of the Horizon, Lord of the Two Lands,
We thank thee for thy presence at our rite
And bid thee now to depart from thy priest
And to soar once more as the mighty Hawk of Ra.

PRIEST: Lady Isis, Mother of all and Queen of the Heavens,
We thank thee for thy presence at our rite,
And bid thee now to depart from thy priestess.
We see thee veiled in the beauty of Spring
and in serene majesty as the Moon."

Thank the Elements and close the Quarters.

Close the circle.

Editor's Note: We often used Ancient Egyptian mythology or imagery in Pagan Pathfinders, both in pathworking and ritual. Jean drew on words from occult writer Dion Fortune to create a beautiful ritual to Isis, for example, and here Chris has drawn on genuine Egyptian texts.

AIR PATHWORKING AND RITUAL

This pathworking and ritual could be preceded by a small talk about the qualities associated with the element of Air if needed. These include communication, wit, intellect, concentration, inspiration, psychic work, ideas and wishes, travel and freedom.

Requirements:

- Candles at the quarters and on the altar as required
- Optional incense
- Feather
- Other elemental symbols (optional)
- Music (optional)
- Pens and paper

Roles:

- Guide/narrator
- Quarter Officers

GUIDE: Let yourselves become even more deeply relaxed and let your mind contemplate the qualities of the element of Air .... Which are you most attracted by? What are your strengths in this element? What are you skilled at? What do you enjoy doing in exercising the qualities of Air? .... What qualities of Air do you admire in others and wish you were able to excel more at? .... Which qualities do you have to excess so that they perhaps show aspects of Air that you would rather not have quite so much of? ....

Now imagine that you are becoming lighter and lighter and floating up into the sky. You see the world flooded with sunlight beneath you, beautiful blue sky and clouds and you feel the presence of strange ethereal beings, beings made of wisps of cloud. These are the sylphs of the Air, the creatures of the elemental kingdom of Air, gently holding you and guiding you, taking you to a high, high place, the top of a beautiful mountain, or the top of a cliff, the top of a tree, some high place where you can see for miles around you and below you you can see the landscape of your being, a wonderful pattern of light and dark and strengths and weaknesses. Let your eye rove over this fascinating landscape until it comes to rest on a particularly intriguing feature that claims your attention and, as you look at it, you realise that it is something of importance to you. It may be a quality that you need to develop, or to enhance, a quality that you may have but haven't yet expressed and developed, or it may be a quality that shows negative aspects that you want to transmute into its positive aspect. You feel the wind blowing around you. Feel it on your face, breathe it, hear its sound as you examine this feature in your landscape that has caught your attention, demands that you pay attention to it, that speaks to some yearning within your soul ....

Let that yearning become a call to the element of Air to bring the change or development, transmutation, that you require, that you yearn for. Let words form in your mind to express that yearning. The element of Air gives you the gift of eloquence to express that yearning within you and when you are ready take your pen and write whatever seems to be coming to your mind, or just formulate it within your mind ....

At this point the Guide invites the group to stand in a circle.

GUIDE: Now let us cast our circle .... See around us a circle of blue fire forming deep within the earth and rising up and up, flaming up and curving over our heads to enclose us in a globe of blue fire creating a sacred space within which we can safely go on a journey. Make that circle of blue fire really vivid around us and then let us ask the mighty ones of the quarters to guard our circle and support us in our work.

EAST: Oh mighty ones of the East, Lords of Air, we ask you to come to our circle, to guard us and protect us as we do our rite and to bring to us your gifts of inspiration and the quickness of thought. We bid you hail and welcome!

ALL: Hail and welcome!

SOUTH: Spirits of Fire, we ask you to be here with us to guide and guard our circle and our workings. Come to us in your gentler aspects of warmth and understanding, inspiration and gentle passion. We bid you hail and welcome!

ALL: Hail and welcome!

WEST: Elements of the West, Water, we welcome your gifts of understanding and compassion, your ebb and flow. We bid you to join us tonight in our circle and we bid you hail and welcome!

ALL: Hail and welcome!

NORTH: Spirits of the North and of Earth, we ask you to come to our circle, to guard us and protect us tonight at our rite and to bless us with your gifts of growth, prosperity, gratitude and deep wisdom. We bid you hail and welcome!

ALL: Hail and welcome!

GUIDE: Let us just be aware of the elemental powers in perfect balance at the quarters, guarding us, protecting us and keeping that balance that allows us to work safely, to go adventuring in other realms .... Let us now in the eastern quarter create in our minds a great portal as we ask the element of Air to fill our circle with its power.

EAST: Air, sweet breath of life, invisible, intangible, yet we see your passing and we feel your touch. We know you in soft breezes and quiet thoughtfulness. We know you in the icy winds of logic and clarity that cuts us like a sword from cosy self-delusion. We know you in the great gales that blow away the cobwebs, the deadwood, the rickety structures of our lives.

We know you in exuberant laughter and ready wit, in the joy of dialectic and in eloquence. Oh, Powers of Air, we invoke you in all your aspects that we may use our minds and our intellects fully to the enrichment of our lives.

GUIDE: Feel the Powers of Air coming into the circle, feel it surrounding us .... (Music) ....Feel the wind on our faces, the sweet smell of flowers .... Feel that lightness and joy and clarity of mind .... Let us each in turn, starting with the Officer of Air, make our own particular plea or invocation to the element of air. Take the feather and read your invocation.

Individual invocations read out in turn, passing the feather to the next person when complete.

GUIDE: Now we feel the presence of the great gods of Air, of Jupiter and Nuit, Zeus and Hera in all their majesty, those that give the law and keep the peace and set the bounds, and Hermes, swift messenger of the gods. He whose wit and tricksiness bring laughter to the gods. He who teaches science, the basis of medicine, exploration and knowledge. He who is articulation, articulateness personified, golden-tongued, persuasive and full of laughter. Feel the presences of these great ones, feel their blessing and feel their gift, feel that they grant what you yearn for. They empower you and enhance those aspects that you wish to enhance .... Their blessing flows into this wine like golden rain. As their presences withdraw, we thank them for their gifts .... Let us now drink the wine that they have blessed, being aware that the circle is still filled with the element of Air. We drink this wine in honour of the gods of Air and in gratitude for their gifts. In taking into us the nourishment we need, feel that wine going straight to the part of us that we want to enhance and develop.

Wine passed around the circle.

GUIDE: Let us thank the powers of Air. We let them depart through that portal back to their station in the eastern quarter, knowing that we can invite them to aid us whenever we wish. We can draw them in with our breath, invoke them with dance and music and song, ride with the sylphs through the airy firmament. The element of Air drains away and we become aware of Fire in the South and Water in the West and Earth in the North as all the elements come into balance. So let us close the circle.

Quarters closed and circle opened.

ALL: Merry meet, merry part and merry meet again!

AN INTRODUCTION TO EARTH DAY

Earth Day occurs every year on 22 April. It was an event that was close to Jean's heart and she began organising a day in the woods involving litter picking, celebration and eco ritual. Earth Day marks the anniversary of the modern environmental movement in 1970[4].

It goes without saying that followers of a nature based religion such as Paganism should have concerns about the environment and try to protect it as best we can. This is often hard in modern society, where facilities may not exist, or environmentally friendly options may be more costly, but Earth Day gives us all a chance to do something positive for the environment, however small, to raise awareness and to come together in celebration of the beautiful world we share with each other and many other creatures. It offers many opportunities for a group such as Pagan Pathfinders to organise a day trip out and about in nature, to litter pick, to take part in a beach clean, or to send healing energy out to Planet Earth (embodied in the Goddess Gaia) through group ritual. The website earthday.org says this:

"Today, the fight for a clean environment continues with increasing urgency, as the ravages of climate change become more manifest every day. We invite you to be a part of Earth Day and help write many more chapters—struggles and victories—into the Earth Day book."

Jean's blurb for her Earth Day event is reproduced here:

"EARTH DAY - NORTH LONDON – Each year, an Earth Day event is held in Queen's Wood, Highgate. Litter is picked up and a ritual held to change hearts and minds to stop the desecration of the Earth through greed, ignorance and lethargy. We also pledge to do more ourselves to protect the Earth. One year, London Pagans raised £300 to contribute towards the planting of a circle of 12

---

[4] For more information see www.earthday.org

young oak trees in a very run-down and treeless North London park. Our £300 paid for 4 trees; the rest were paid for by Trees for London and Trees Trust for Haringey. The participation of Pagans in this work was appreciated by Haringey Council and the other contributing organisations."

Below is a brief outline of an Earth Day Ritual. With a clear theme like this, it lends itself to adaptation and embellishment by the individual group and writing the ritual yourselves could help increase people's confidence. Perhaps devote one or two sessions before the day itself to creating the ritual as a group.

Earth Day Ritual Summary

1. Tuning in and opening prayer.
2. Creating the Circle - all participating, stamping/walking it out.
3. Leader calls upon the Gods.
4. Invocation of the Quarters.
5. Dance to raise power, possibly singing the well-known chant[5] "We all come from the Goddess..." or similar.
6. Visualisation to raise awareness of injury to the Earth, each officer doing their own Quarter, expanding upon these themes:

    AIR: Factory chimneys, car exhausts, smog, greenhouse effect, acid rain, etc.
    FIRE: Creeping desert wastes, forest fires, radioactive waste, nuclear plant accidents, the ozone layer, etc.
    WATER: Factory effluent into rivers and seas, over-fishing, coral reef destruction, killing of whales and dolphins, etc.
    EARTH: Destruction of the rain forests, erosion, pesticides, battery farming, hunting of rare animals to extinction, scars of mining, fracking.

[5] There are many Pagan/New Age/Environmental Movement chants to be found online.

7. **LEADER:** "It is humanity that has caused this desecration of the body of the Mother ...." *[Expand]*

8. **ALL** will humanity to change and the Earth to be healed.

9. **ALL CHANT:** "She changes everything She touches, and everything She touches changes [6] ...."

10. Visualisation at each Quarter, seeing the damage and sickness as healed.

11. **ALL CHANT**: "The Earth is our Mother, we will take care of her ...."

12. **ALL CHANT:** "Earth my body, Water my blood ...."

13. Blessing and sharing of bread.

14. Leader gives thanks.

15. Each officer closes their Quarter in turn.

16. **ALL:** "Thanks to the Powers of Air/Fire/Water/Earth .... Hail and farewell." *[Expand]*

17. Share food and drink in celebration.

---

[6] See online for complete words of the chants.

ENDORPHINS – GAIA PATHWORKING

The next three pathworkings develop our work with endorphins, as explained in the transcripts of Jean's talks on the subject in Chapter 5.

Spoken by the Guide:

Breathe and relax and think of your favourite strawberry and feel it bringing a little smile and relaxing you even more .... Be aware of your body, notice how it is feeling. Again notice your mood ....

Be aware of your aura all around your body and, as you breathe, get that sense of your aura having expanded and let your awareness flow out. Be aware of the group of us sitting here in this room and of Tigger [the cat] on his cushion. Take a moment to let your awareness flow to Tigger in particular, getting a sense of the relaxed, still and contented cat consciousness ....

As you relax even more deeply, let your consciousness flow out beyond this room. Be aware of our connections. Be aware first of your own personal connections, as though you are the centre of a circle of your friends and family and acquaintances, workmates and so on .... and be aware of the connection of your circle with other circles, forming a web. You are part of a network of connections. Feel the sense of flow and harmony with all humanity, sharing our hopes and our fears ....

Let your awareness flow out to the other life forms on the planet, feeling that sense of connectedness. We are all part of a wonderful web of connections, a wonderful whole, interdependent .... Let your awareness flow out to the plants, the trees, wonderful trees, the air we breathe, the oceans, the mysterious depths of the oceans. We are only just beginning to realise how immense they are and what treasures and wonders and terrors they hold within their depths. Let your awareness flow to the mountains, their mighty crests covered in snow and the volcanoes with the great inner powers of earth that comes spewing forth with great energy and force. The air we breathe, the winds that blow, the gentle breezes, the gales, the tornadoes, the trade winds and the jet stream ....

Gaia herself, a wonderful living planet, always changing, giving birth to new creatures, new species, new individuals, new tiny things and new huge things, all evolving, changing, growing, dying. Gaia, our mother, the earth, all her wonder, all her beauty, all her terrors. Here is a translation of a Homeric hymn from Ancient Greece showing her that the sense of wonder has called to the soul of humanity:

> I will sing of well-founded Gaia, mother of all, eldest of all being.
> She feeds all creatures that are in the world
> All that go upon the goodly land
> And all that are in the paths of the sea
> And all that fly.
> These are all fed at her store.

Feel part of the body of Gaia, part of her life energy, part of the changing, flowing, ebbing and flowing again, life of the planet ....

Here is an ancient song from Wales in which Gaia speaks and we are part of Gaia:

> I am the wind that breathes upon the sea
> I am the wave on the ocean
> I am the murmur of the leaves rustling
> I am the rays of the sun
> I am the beam of the moon and stars
> I am the power of trees growing
> I am the bud breaking into blossom

I am the movement of the salmon swimming
I am the courage of the wild boar fighting
I am the speed of the stag running
I am the strength of the ox pulling the plough
I am the size of the mighty oak tree
And I am the thoughts of all the people
who praise my beauty and grace.

Gaia is one jewel among many, so let your awareness flow out to the solar system: the sun, the dance of the planets and asteroids around it, the sun that powers life on earth, and the moon, our near neighbour that dances with earth as our partner in the dance around the sun. Let your consciousness flow out to the stars, to the immensity of the galaxy, all those bright jewels dancing and whirling in the immensity of space, Nuit, the goddess of infinite possibility. We can barely count ourselves as specks in that immensity and yet we are part of it and our awareness flows out. We share the life of the stars, the sun and the earth .... Feel the joy of that immense dance of the universe. Feel its beauty, its wonder, its mystery ....

Gradually detach from that immensity and come back to our galaxy, to our solar system, to our planet, to our own circles of people and to this room and the group of us sitting here .... Gradually return to the here and now, becoming more aware of your body, your breathing, your weight upon whatever you are sitting on, aware of your hands and your feet ....

This is one of my strawberries: connectedness and companionship with all of you who come to PP .... Now take some deep breaths and open your eyes.

ENDORPHINS – THE CURLED DEER PATHWORKING

Spoken by the Guide:

If you would like to get yourselves comfortable and lie down if you want to, but as long as you don't go off into a deep sleep.

Let yourselves relax. Find that still point within yourself .... Don't forget to breathe. Let your breathing be slow and easy ....

Now think of one of your strawberries, something that gives you pleasure, and let that inner smile develop and your eyes soften. Focus down into your body, noticing where you are feeling, what you are feeling, regarding your bodily sensations with affection, appreciating all it does for you .... Take a few breaths down into your lower stomach. If it feels appropriate, you can put your hands on your lower abdomen ....

Feel like a deer curled in upon itself, nose on tail, completely relaxed and comfortable and stay with that inner smile, keeping your focus down deep within yourself. Allow yourself to sink into the sensations of the curled deer, enjoying the kinaesthetic experience ....

Become aware of this micro-cosmic circuit just in the flesh under the skin, the loop that runs over the top of your head, down your face, neck and chest, down your abdomen, under your groin and up your back, over the top of your head. Allow the muscles of your neck and chest and abdomen to relax and sense your spine relaxing .... Place the tip of your tongue on the roof of your mouth and just visualise that energy as you breathe. As you breathe out it travels down your front and as you breathe in it travels up your back, up your spine, over the head. So find your own rhythm to continue that breathing ....

Now be aware of that circling energy. It is drawing to it the energies around you. First imagine golden sunlight shining down upon you, gentle and light, delicate, the sunlight of early spring .... Stirring beneath you is the body of Gaia, the earth, ready to awaken from her winter sleep.

Imagine now that the golden sunlight intensifies and takes form, the form of the beautiful Sun God Apollo as the young spring sun; beautiful, golden, virile, eager, touching the earth, eager to awaken Gaia from her sleep. Gradually the Goddess awakens, responding to the touch of the golden sun. See her arise as a beautiful maiden, flowers in her hair, a robe of delicate floating green .... You see the energy that passes between them, the love, the giving and receiving, and they include you in their circle of giving and receiving, of loving and blessing.

Feel your consciousness rising up in response to their presence, enriching you, expanding you, making you aware that you are part of a wondrous whole, a wondrous circuit of energies, the cosmic energies of sun and earth, nourishing you and nurturing you. You may feel it flowing into a particular part of your body, or a particular aspect of your mind, or touching your aura, your emotional nature .... You have become part of their cycle of giving and receiving, of loving and being loved, of blessing and being blessed ....

Then the images of the God and the Goddess fade, leaving you feeling comfortable resting on the earth in the spring sunshine, a little curled deer. But the little curled deer cannot sleep forever. It is time to waken, to play and to feed, to grow, to explore all the joys of loving and living. So imagine that the little deer is awakening and you too are awakening. Feel yourself gradually returning to this room. The sense of being on the earth under the sun fades away ....

As I count from ten to one, feel yourself rising back up to the here and now. Ten .... nine .... eight .... seven .... six .... five .... four .... three .... two .... one ....

ENDORPHINS – FULL MOON PATHWORKING

Spoken by the Guide:

Sit comfortably and close your eyes. Today was a beautiful sunny day. You could actually at last begin to feel there was some warmth in the sun.

I want you to imagine that you are walking up a fairly steep path on a hillside, short grass around you and a few shrubs and bushes, little trees of one sort and another, and there is warm sunlight, early spring sunshine, just like today. By the light of day you feel active, you feel you have clarity of purpose. The sun makes us active, energises us, makes us feel we want to be up and doing things, but it is also the time of the full moon. The sun and the moon are opposite each other in the sky, so we are caught between these two very different powers and yet they are complementary. They hold a balance in our own natures.

As you are walking up this path you are feeling the warmth of the sun and the brightness of the sun, looking around you, breathing deeply, feeling active and energetic, full of plans, thinking of the things you are going to do in the coming month, thinking of it with pleasure and joy and anticipation ....

The sun is sinking towards the west and the sky in the west is beginning to take on wondrous sunset hues, apricot and pink merging to purple in a glorious sunset. Now the path is about to wind through a small woodland and immediately the light of the sun is dimmed as you find your way, but it is still beautiful. The warmth hasn't faded altogether. You still catch glimpses of that wonderful coloured sky to the east, but it is fading as the sun sinks and now you emerge from the trees, the sun just below the horizon.

Twilight is gathering and you are coming to the brow of the hill, and there before you is the sea and over the sea you see the full moon starting to rise.

As the sun sinks lower, the darkness becomes more intense. The moon is rising higher and the quality of the light has changed. It is a different sort of light. Everything starts to look different. Your mood changes. There is a sense of magic and mystery, lurking possibilities, things just below the surface of your mind, ideas, images, visions. By the moonlight you can see that there are some steps leading down to the beach. In this strange moonlight the colours are almost invisible. It feels a bit hazardous, but you pick your way down the steps, drawn to go down, down to the sea ....

Now there is actually a little handrail that some thoughtful people have put there and you are able to get down a little more quickly, feeling a little more secure. As you go down to the realm of water and moonlight you can feel and hear the surge of the sea power, the ebb and flow, the restless wavelets breaking on the shore and beneath that restless surface, the deep flowing currents, the currents of the tide and the deep ocean currents that swirl in mysterious patterns. The moon now is climbing higher and becoming brighter as it gets higher in the sky and there is less atmosphere to penetrate. There is something so magical about this light and you feel a sense of mystery and magic building up. You let yourself open to the magic of the sea and the magic of the moon ....

Now the moonlight and the moon itself seem to turn into silver sparkles and now they form the body of the lady of the moon. Feel her presence bringing a sense of awe and exaltation. Her beauty and her perfume are indescribable. Her voice is like silver bells in your inner ear .... (Option to play music) .... You feel yourself drawn up, drawn up into her heart. Feel yourself loved and cherished and blessed .... She imparts to you a secret, a word, or an image, a key to open up your inspiration and your creativity. Receive that key, that word, that image, that little gift. Then rest in the bliss of her presence ....

Now feel the Goddess withdraw to her silvery realm, leaving you with the treasure for you to discover, to develop, to use.

Now it is time to find your way back up that staircase, the steps quite brightly lit now by the moonlight, feeling blessed and touched and somehow cleansed by the touch of the Goddess of the Moon .... You reach the top and as you set off back down the path in the darkness of the wood, the moonlight doesn't penetrate. You feel the spell of the Moon Goddess's presence fading away, but leaving you with that inner treasure.

The whole astral place starts to fade. Feel yourself coming back to this place. Feel the floor beneath you. Be aware of your body sitting here. Be aware of your feet, and your hands, and your heart, and your head. Take some deep breaths, stretch, more deep breaths and it is a good idea just to put your awareness briefly on your solar plexus centre and just let it close down, then your heart centre .... Take some more deep breaths and open your eyes.

SUMMER

MOON GODDESS PATHWORKING AND RITUAL

Requirements:

- Usual candles
- Altar with chalice of water

Spoken by the Guide:

Relax and breathe, close your eyes and go into yourself. Before we begin our journey, let us just call to mind the circle of blue fire all around us. Feel it encircling us and protecting us .... Now sink down deep within yourself and then within that inner space see a doorway form before you and you step through it and find yourself in a green meadow. As you walk across the grass, all lush with spring growth, you crest a small rise in the ground that falls away before you and you see it leads down to a lake and in the lake, at the edge, you see a little boat. You go down and climb into the boat and because this is a magical boat it immediately starts to move gently through the water. Somehow you can't see very far ahead. There seems to be a mistiness, but the movement of the boat through the water is relaxing and somehow comforting. Now the mistiness envelops you. You can still feel the boat moving and the chuckle of the water against the bow. You seem to hear sweet voices singing and these are the elemental spirits of the kingdom of water, singing their song of welcome as you pass through their realm ....

Now the mist seems to be becoming radiant with silvery blue light and you realise that it is beginning to thin, and now you are through the mist and see that the boat is nearing a little island in the lake. You see in the dim light that it is fringed with white sand .... Now your little magical boat is coming to the shore. It stops at a convenient place for stepping out onto a convenient rock and onto the lovely white sand. This beautiful radiance is the full moon and you see a little white path leading inland and you follow it. The ground is rising, not very steeply, but it is quite rocky. The few small trees and shrubs give off a smell of rosemary and thyme as you pass.

You hear the tinkling of water, splashing of water, and the pleasant noise of a little stream. You find that you have reached the summit of this island and there amongst the rocks and stones is a natural little fountain. Impressions of the underground water and the spring rains lead this water to gush up in little spouts that fall back with a beautiful splashing noise and they sparkle, silver and blue in the moonlight. This water fills a natural hollow and then flows down the other side of the island into the lake as a little stream. You stand there fascinated, watching this little natural fountain as it ebbs and flows and spurts up, and then almost dies down completely to just a little bubbling water, and then up it comes again and falls back sparkling in the moonlight. You know that you are in a really magical place. You feel the magic enfolding around you, comforting and healing, touching the deep inner wells.

You feel the presence of the Goddess of the Moon, lady of healing and of magic. Mistress of the imagination, the deep wells of creativity. Mistress of the waters, the inner waters and the outer waters. You let her presence bring you deep blessing and healing and let her speak within your inner ear, giving you her wisdom. Ask her whatever you wish to ask her, or just listen ....

Now the sense of a presence begins to fade, but you can feel her magic all around you. You see that there is, beside the little pool where the little fountain gathers its waters, a chalice. The chalice is filled full of water from the fountain.

Now, without losing the sense of the place or the magic, stand and gather round the altar .... The magic is all around us and we have the chalice of spring water, the waters of the moon. So let us raise up our hands, gather up that beautiful silver blue light of the moon and bring it down into the chalice

.... Now let us each take a sip .... We ask the Lady of the Moon to send her blessing to us (or insert something/someone that the group would like to direct this energy at, for example for healing). So mote it be.

Now let us imagine that we are leaving that sacred space, saluting the magical fountain, travelling down that little path, finding our magical boat and crossing back to the everyday world, thanking the spirits of the realm of water as we pass through the mist for their protection and for letting us pass through their realm .... We each go back through our doorway and find ourselves back in this room. We thank the elemental beings for their protection and for being here to guard us and let the circle of blue fire fade away, sink back into the earth and we are back here in the everyday world, our feet on the ground, ready to have something to eat and a cup of tea.

BELTANE RITUAL

Requirements:

- Altar with flowers, God and Goddess images, incense, candles.
- Bell/gong
- Green scarf (not needed if God role pre-allocated)
- Green robe
- Cauldron with candles inside to represent the Bel Fire
- Dish of flowers and leaves if unable to visit a garden
- Paper and pens
- Cakes and wine
- Maypole (optional)

Roles:

- Narrator
- Quarter officers
- Circle caster
- May Queen
- Green Man (to be chosen during ritual, or if you prefer this role can be allocated beforehand)
- Two Servers for cakes and wine

Editor's note: At Pagan Pathfinders we were lucky enough to have a maypole which just about fitted in Jean's lounge, although I seem to remember it was a bit wobbly! You could craft your own as a group, or just dance freely around the space.

Preparation

If possible, begin with a garden meditation. Take the group out into the garden, or even a nearby park, and sit or stand with a tree or plant, tuning into its energy. Listen to the birds, feel the vibrant growth all around. Wonder at it. Do this for about ten minutes, or however long feels right.

The Narrator rings a bell or gong. At this point, all pick a leaf or flower from the garden and return to the room. If it is rainy or there is no access to a garden, open a window and spend time listening to the sounds outdoors, then pick a leaf or flower from a bowl already prepared in the room.

The Ritual

Begin by invoking the elements at each quarter and casting the circle.

NARRATOR: Everyone *[including the May Queen]* should sit comfortably, focus on your breathing, keeping it relaxed and slow. Feel yourself grounded and centred .... Now close your eyes.

Visualise a circle of golden light around us. Sink down. We feel our life force quickening, it is the greening of the land, the waking of the earth. Young shoots have become vibrant, healthy plants. Flowers are bursting into colour and their new scent fills the air. Birds are singing joyously and all the animals are awakening to the vital spirit of May ....

This is the time of the Green Man, also known as Robin, Jack-in-the-Green, the Wild Man, or Puck. He is elusive, mischievous, lusty, the wild and rebellious part of ourselves, the renegade. He is the source of new ideas, the source of energy to break old patterns. He is also Bel, the Fire God, the fire that burns the debris, bringing purification. He is the bright, golden sun, gathering strength.

Our Lady of the Earth responds to his energy. She is Queen of the Greenwood, Lady Marian, Queen of the May, Lady of Fertility. She responds with warmth and generosity, giving of herself gladly. The Wild Woman – she lights the Bel Fire! She channels the force of the Wild Man.

This polarity translates in our inner life: the transcendence of opposites through love, the unity of complementary forces to bring forth new life, new ideas, the power to change and to bring about growth.

Contact their forces within you – that yearning to release the Green Man within you, to find your inner Wild Woman, to let go of some of the inhibitions, self-consciousness and self-doubt that restricts you .... Feel this change, this new freedom and confidence growing inside you ....

Pour your yearning, your image of your change and growth into your flower or leaf. Let it arise from your centre .... Now open your eyes and place your flower or leaf on the altar. Then return to your place and on a piece of paper, write an invocation to the Goddess of the May.

Pause for writing, during which time the May Queen dons her green robe and stands by the altar.

Then all stand in a circle and each take it in turn to invoke the Queen of the May. She manifests, the person taking on the role of the May Queen becoming a representation of the Goddess in the ritual, channeling those energies and qualities.

The May Queen speaks of her gifts and her longing for her lover, the Lord of the Greenwood. This can be improvised or as below:

MAY QUEEN: I am the Queen of the Greenwood, Lady of Fertility, consort of the Sun. I am the mystery of Birth and Death. I am the fecund Earth that receives the love and light of the Sun. My love is poured out to all beings. I also receive you into my arms that you may rest and be renewed. Always I promise growth, renewal and inspiration.

She seeks and selects her lover[1], the Green Man, in the group, capturing him with a green scarf while everyone sings or chants:

ALL: The Greenwood is calling
Chalice calls to sword
Come to the wedding
Of the Lady and the Lord.

[1] Optional. The role of the Green Man could be allocated before the ritual commences.

NARRATOR: Spirit of the Greenwood, Robin, Lord of Light, Bel, Lugh, Bright Sun. You are the vital, desiring, fertilising force. Be with us, Spirit of the Greenwood.

The chosen Green Man speaks of his gifts and his love for his consort, the Queen of the Wild Wood. This can be spontaneous or prepared. Together they light the Bel Fire saying:

GODDESS AND GOD: We light for you the Bel Fire, the fire of purification, that you may receive the blessing of the Lord and Lady of the Greenwood. Jump the fire and be purified and blessed! Join our dance!

All dance and jump the Bel Fire. Be wild and free, let go of inhibitions.

After a suitable time, the Servers present cakes and wine to the God and Goddess saying together:

SERVERS: Lord of Light, Lady of Earth
Bless our land.
Bless our crops and our cattle
That they may be wholesome, fruitful
And in harmony with thy love.
Bless these cakes and wine
That they may symbolise your love
And in this sharing may we be blessed
And fruitful and at peace.

GODDESS: *[Stretching hands over cakes and wine]*
These gifts are of me
I do bless them
And give them to nourish you
That you may be beautiful as the fruits of the Earth.

GOD: *[Stretching hands over cakes and wine]*
These gifts are also of me.
I bless them
And give them to inspire you
That your light may shine forth as the sun in the sky.

The Servers take the dish of cakes and goblet of wine around the circle for each person to partake. You may wish to say "Blessed be" to each other as you give and receive the food and wine.

The Narrator thanks and dismisses the God and Goddess so they may return to the circle.

NARRATOR: Dancing around the Maypole is a representation of weaving the web of mystery and celebrating the intricate dance of the Lord and the Lady. We celebrate and invoke the principle of fertility and creativity.

Maypole dancing or free dancing, followed by more wine shared among the group. There is the option for chanting here, such as:

The Earth, the Air, the Fire, the Water
Return, return, return, return.

Close the circle.

INVOCATIONS TO THE MAY QUEEN

Written by Attendees of Pagan Pathfinders

In the Beltane Ritual preceding this, there is time given for participants to write their own invocations to the Goddess, the Queen of the May. We often did this in Pagan Pathfinders as Jean wanted to encourage our creativity and confidence. She felt strongly that we all have hidden potential within ourselves and tasks like this helped us to access it. Often beautiful words were written, with very little preparation. Even if people only managed a few lines, what mattered was the feeling behind it. Here are some examples I found collected in Jean's notes. They were all anonymous.

Come Great Goddess, Queen of the May
Come, Great Goddess, Mother of All
Clothed in Spring Beauty and Flowers
Come to thy people who wait for thee.
Come, Lady, dressed in green.
Come on the wind in the trees
Come to us in the flowers
And in the showers of rain that feed the Earth
Be in the seed that sleeps deep in the soil
Be present with us this day.

Come Lady in your green robe.
Come Queen of the May
We call upon you to honour
And bless us with your presence.
May you find your Wild Lord here
So that your union will fertilise the land.

Lady of the Greenwood
Queen of the May
Goddess of Spring time
We yearn for your warmth
Your love, your wildness.
We yearn to join your dance of joy and life.
Be present here tonight and always.

Come to us Queen of the Wild Wood
With the beauty of your green mantle
To carpet the land.
Bring us joy at your power of creativity
As you bring new life to our world.
Come to us Queen of the May.

May Queen come and be with us tonight.
Embolden us with your wildness and
Encourage us with your determination
May Queen, come and grace us with your joy
And lust for life.

Bright Maiden of Beltane,
Your beauty lights up the earth with the summer sun.
Kindle the fire within us,
The fire of passion, freedom and spontaneity,
That we so often bury.
Light that well-spring of joy within us all.
Earth mother, your fertility brings life and sustenance to us;
May it be so for all the lands of this earth.
As you dance round the great Bel fire with your Wild Man,
Lord of the Greenwood,
Bless us all with your love and joy.

Hail to the Queen of May
In whose footsteps summer quickly follows.
The dark time of winter is behind us,
We rejoice as the earth is alive!
The Green Goddess garlanded in flowers gifts light and laughter,
Warming the earth and cheering hearts.
Trees and fields are verdant green again,
Woodlands are full of patches of vibrant blue.
The soil is fertile,
Animals breed and plants pollinate,
Bees hum and the geese fly overhead.
We gather together as in times past and ask:
May the light of the Beltane fire
Bring joy, vitality and love,
As the May Queen and Green Man are united
So are we all to each other and to all things.

BELTANE RITUAL

For a Pagan Federation Open Ritual

Requirements:

Altar in the North
Cauldron in the centre containing four candles, unlit, and tapers nearby
Bowl of water and incense for the Greeters
Music/drums
Four wands for the Elemental Officers
Copy of 'Walpurgis Night' poem by Doreen Valiente, or similar
Green robe and flower crown for the Goddess
Robe for the God
Bell/gong

Roles:

Narrator
Greeters
Circle Caster
Four Elemental Officers
Goddess
God
Reader of poem

The action takes place in the centre of the hall. There is music and/or drumming as people enter. Have some people to greet the congregation – sprinkle them with water and waft incense as they enter the space.

RITUAL

All stand and hold hands (making two circles if necessary).
Elemental Officers stand with wands in a circle around the cauldron in the centre.

NARRATOR: The purpose of the rite is to celebrate the primordial powers of life, to bring forth that energy for the healing of the Earth and for our own regeneration. *[Expand]*

CIRCLE CASTER: I cast this circle to contain and protect this ritual and this hall, to create a sacred space in which we will celebrate this Beltane rite. As I walk around the circle, picture a blue flame flickering on the ground, rising up to the height of your ankles, rising higher and higher .... blue flames all around ... rising higher and higher .... up to your waist, and higher and higher .... blue flames rising up over our heads to create a sphere. We have formed sphere, glowing with blue flame, a circle of power, a gateway between the world of men and the world of the Old Ones. The Circle is cast!

ALL CHANT: Lady, spin your circle bright
Weave your web of dark and light
Earth, air, fire and water
Bind us as one.

Each Elemental Officer turns to face their Quarter as they invoke:

AIR: Powers of the East, Powers of Air,
We call to you at this time of Beltane.
As the dawn sun rises earlier each day,
Awakening us to new possibilities,
Let your fresh breezes bring us clarity of mind,
An eagerness to start new ventures and endeavours.
Breath of Freedom, great Force of Intelligence.
Spirit of Joy and Laughter,
Come at our call and bless our rite and all who are here.
Powers of Air, Hail and Welcome! *[Raising wand in salute]*

FIRE: Powers of the South, Element of Fire,
We call to you at this time of Beltane.
As the noonday sun increases in brilliance and warmth,
Bring your light and heat and energy into our hearts,
That we may blossom as the summer flowers.
Flame of True Purpose, Great Force of action,
Spirit of Creativity and Strength,
Come at our call and bless our rite and all who are here,
Powers of Fire, Hail and Welcome! *[Raising wand in salute]*

WATER: Powers of the West, Element of Water,
We call to you at this time of Beltane.
As the evening sun sets later each day,
The falling dew cleanses and refreshes our spirits.
Ever changing, ever renewing,
Let your deep currents stir within us
That we may be renewed in love and friendship and inner harmony.
Ocean Source of life, Great Force of Emotion.
Spirit of Love and Compassion,
Come at our call and bless our rite and all who are here.
Powers of Water, Hail and Welcome!" *[Raising wand in salute]*

EARTH: Powers of the North, Element of Earth,
We call to you at this time of Beltane.
As the time of darkness grows shorter each night,
We send our roots deeper into the Earth to find nourishment.
Help us to find within ourselves your strength and stability.
Empower us to ground our intentions in joyous action.
Enduring Ground of Being,
Great Force of Evolution and Action.
Spirit of mystery and wisdom,

Come to our call and bless our rite and all who are here.
Powers of Earth, Hail and Welcome!" *[Raising wand in salute]*

ALL CHANT: Earth my body, Water my blood
Air my breath and Fire my spirit ....

Elemental Officers retire to the altar area and place their wands upon it.

All are invited to sit for a pathworking led by the Narrator.

NARRATOR: Now take some deep breaths and close your eyes. We are walking in the Greenwood. You can see the new spring leaves; beautiful wild flowers are dotted about by your feet. You can feel the warm sun on your skin. Nearby you can hear a little melodious stream babbling gently. There is the sound of busy birdsong all around. We pass between two trees - a magical gateway into the realm of Faerie. It is the same wood, the same stream, but now we see the spirits of the trees, the stream, the dryads, sprites and faerie folk. There is a magical golden light filtering through the leaves. Breathe in the magical air, feeling it refreshing you, cleansing, healing .... Now you feel beside you a presence. You meet a magical being of this place - perhaps a bird or woodland creature, or a dryad, or water sprite, or flower fairy. Welcome that being's offer of friendship, listen to its special wisdom .... Feel the presence of the Goddess permeating this place, all the creatures in it, the plants and trees, the stream, and the very soil and rocks. They are all her body and her garment. She is the burgeoning life-force of the Spring time. But she is incomplete without her gentle lover, the Lord of the bright Sun, who sheds his light and warmth over and through her ....

We wander through this enchanted wood and find we have come full circle and the two great trees that formed the gateway to this place are before us. Once more we pass through; but this time we find that we are no longer in the wood, but here in this Hall. Somehow, we have brought the magic with us and before you open your eyes, feel the magic around you; each person is a wonderful embodiment of the life force - of the Goddess and the God, of the beings of Faerie .... And now open your eyes and see the magic of this gathering, each person enveloped and overshadowed by a flame of glowing colours - their True Selves, the spirit that burns within. So, let us call into our midst the Lady of the Woods.

During the pathworking, the Goddess has donned the green robe and flower crown but is still hidden and in a closed position near the altar, gradually being revealed and emerging into a 'Goddess' stance as the invocation proceeds. Each Elemental Officer comes forward and walks around the circle, speaking their invocation, ending near the cauldron facing the Goddess.

AIR: I see the fresh leaves
Upon the trees of the wild wood.
The quickening of Mother Earth,
A new year's growth.
O Queen of the Green Wood,
Come to us!

FIRE: I smell the lush scent
Of flowers just in bloom.
The heavy aroma of fertility hangs across the fields
Like a lover, ready for her mate.
O Lady of the Flowers, Maid Marian,
Come to us!

WATER: I hear the song of the birds,
The lark calling.
The buzz of the bees,
The bleat of the new-born lamb.
Great Goddess, Lady of the beasts,
Come to us!

EARTH: I feel your smooth skin
Like a lover in a leafy bower,
I taste your passion;
Lady of Love, Come!

The Elemental Officers bow to the Lady and move to the sides and towards the altar, as the Goddess comes forward. She walks around the circle as she delivers her charge, ending at the cauldron facing North.

GODDESS: I am Marian, Queen of the Greenwood. This is my time!
I rise from the Earth veiled in the tiny hawthorn blossoms
And clothed in new green leaves.
I am the fertile womb of life, Lady of the Wild Wood.
I am the breathy excitement of the summer breezes,
The song of the swallow, playful and bent on life.
I bring joy and life, song and laughter.
Join your voice with mine! Wrap your limbs with mine!
Lay your skin on the emerald grass!
Flow with the merry tide of life in the Greenwood.

And give me your promise to protect me:
Protect my fields, my waterways, my trees and my herds,
Protect my forests and seas,
And keep clean the sweet air we breathe.
For these are my womb, the Cauldron of Life.

I am the Eternal She.
Where is my He? Where is my Jack-in-the-Green?
Where is my Bel, the Golden Sun?
Without his warmth and light,
My own fire will pale and my spirit languish.
Where is my naughty Jack?
Where is my Lord of Light and Song?

Each Elemental officer delivers their invocation to the God with verve, walking or dancing at a good pace around the circle, ending facing the altar. The God has donned his cloak but is hanging back. At the end of all the invocations, the Elemental Officers grab the God and pull him into the circle.

AIR: Puck and Pan and Robin Hood,
Lord of the Wild and Greenwood.
Herne, Cernunnos, Jack in the Green,
Tis time to come and take your Queen.

FIRE: As warming sunshine wakes the land
Tis time to take the maiden's hand.
Arise, arise from slumbers deep
Tis time to waken from your sleep.

WATER: Bring your laughter, bring desire,
Bring your lusty heart of fire.
Bring your strength and sing your song
As we invoke you to our throng.

EARTH: So come and take your maiden's hand
That fertile be, our sacred land.
Herne, Cernunnos, Jack-in-the-Green,
Come and claim your Beltane Queen.

ALL: Herne, Cernunnos, Jack-in-the-Green,
Come and claim your Beltane Queen!

The Elemental Officers bow to the God and retire to the North. The God walks around the circle, ending at the centre. As the mood takes him, he might be a bit naughty towards members of the congregation!

GOD: I come as Bel, the Flaming Sun.
O'er boundless sky and silver oceans, I seek my love.

I am Cernunnos, the horned one of the forest,
And Robin Hood, Wild Man of the woods,
And naughty Jack-in-the-Green,
Chasing the maidens through the trees,
Celebrating the greening of the land.

As the golden light of Spring shimmers, I reveal my glory.
Sweet sap rises at the call of my Lady of all Life.
Blazing Beltane stirs Earth's sleeping Dragon,
And in the sacred grove of Greenwood,
My Lady and I quicken May Eve with our perfect love.
My Lady and my Love!

GODDESS: My Love and my Lord!

They embrace.

GOD: Together we will light the Bel Fire,
And bring light and warmth and healing
To the land and to all beings.

Lighted tapers are handed to the God and Goddess who alternate in lighting one of the four Bel candles in the cauldron while saying:

GOD: *[Lights candle]* This is the Cleansing Fire; it shall cleanse the land of sickness and pollution.

GODDESS: *[Lights candle]* This is the Fire of Light: it shall drive away the shadows of fear and intolerance.

GOD: *[Lights candle]* This is the Fire of Warmth: it shall bring harmony and love and good fellowship.

GODDESS: *[Lights candle]* This is the Flaming Fire: it shall bring inspiration and energy and inflame your Wills.

GODDESS: Dance with us around the Beltane fire; celebrate our union and receive our fiery gifts.

The God and Goddess lead all in a spiral dance and song.

ALL: The Greenwood is calling
Chalice calls to Sword,
Come to the wedding
Of the Lady and the Lord.

The Greenwood is calling
Chalice calls to Sword,
Come to the wedding
Of the Lady and the Lord.

The God and Goddess position themselves in front of the altar at the end of the dance.

GOD: Now is the time of growth, the time to be bold, the time of adventure! Jump the Fire and make a wish!

All jump the cauldron. Narrator rings a bell/gong.

NARRATOR: The lord of the Greenwood has found his Bride,
The May Queen has received her lover.

The woods are filled with the green and gold of their passion.
Love and warmth and joyous life return to the Earth.

[Raising hands over cakes and wine]
In their names we bless this wine
That we may be one with the joy of their union.
In the names of the Lord and the Lady we bless these cakes,
The fruit of their union, that we may all be nourished.

Alternatively, the cakes and wine are presented by the Elemental Officers to the God and Goddess and blessed by them.

READER: Walpurgis Night, the time is right,
The ancient powers awake.
So dance and sing, around the ring,
And Beltane magic make.

Walpurgis Night, Walpurgis Night,
Upon the eve of May,
We'll merry meet, and summer greet,
For ever and a day.

New life we see, in flower and tree,
And summer comes again.
Be free and fair, like earth and air,
The sunshine and the rain.

As magic fire be our desire
To tread the pagan way,
And our true will find and fulfil,
As dawns a brighter day.

The pagan powers this night be ours,
Let all the world be free,
And sorrow cast into the past,
And future blessed be!

Close the Quarters:

AIR: Great Powers of Air,
We thank you for your presence at our rite,
And we ask that you continue to watch over us.
Bestow upon all here your gifts of clarity of mind,
Lightness of heart and joy and laughter,
That all here may be filled with your essence.
Powers of Air, Hail and farewell! *[Raising wand in salute]*

FIRE: Great Powers of Fire,
We thank you for your presence at our rite,
And ask that you continue to watch over us.
Bestow upon all here your gifts of inner light and warmth,
Energy, passion and enthusiasm,
That all here may be inspired by your flame.
Powers of Fire, Hail and farewell! *[Raising wand in salute]*

WATER: Great Powers of Water,
We thank you for your presence at our rite,
And ask that you continue to watch over us.
Bestow upon us your gifts of love and harmony,
Generosity of spirit and good fellowship,
That all here may feel the fluidity of your power.
Powers of Water, Hail and farewell! *[Raising wand in salute]*

EARTH: Great Powers of Earth,
We thank you for your presence at our rite,
And ask that you continue to watch over us.
Bestow upon all here your gifts of strength and stability,
And of intentions grounded in action,
That all here may be nourished by your power.
Powers of Earth, Hail and farewell! *[Raising wand in salute]*

CIRCLE CASTER: I do not now close the circle but extend and transform it to create an atmosphere of magic which will last throughout our Beltane festival. As I move around the circle, see again the blue flames of the sphere, changing, expanding and rising to encompass the whole festival and the physical and spiritual spaces in which it takes place ....The circle of blue fire is expanding, expanding to encompass the festival, creating a magical atmosphere, encircling the hall .... The circle is now porous so that people can come and go, but always find within it the magic of Beltane. May this circle protect our festivities and provide a vessel for the nurturing of new friendships and new discoveries, and for the magic which we will create. The circle is open but unbroken .... Merry Meet, Merry Part and Merry Meet Again!

Allow time for socialising and feasting.

QUINTESSENCE AT BELTANE

This could be added into a Beltane ritual, just after the four elements have been invoked by the Quarter Officers, or you could build a ritual around the concept. There are some beautiful words here, written by Jean, which could complement many celebrations.

Spoken by the Narrator or Guide:

O ye mighty Powers of the Elements,
Of Air
Of Fire
Of Water
And of Earth
Be ye all about us and within us.
Weave the magic of your dance,
In perfect balance and harmony.
Through your quintessential unity do we become whole,
Unique, empowered, a boundless source of love.

Gather now the powers of the Elemental forces in mystic union into your heart centre. Their colours swirl and become pure white light. Place your hand on your heart chakra. Hold the magic of the Quintessence within your heart ....

This is the Dragon time of the year, when we light the Beltane Fire. On 1st of May the sun rises on the Dragon leyline that runs from Suffolk to St Michael's Mount in Cornwall; it passes through many ancient sites and many St Michael's churches; churches built where ancient temples stood. St Michael, the slayer of dragons. But the Dragons are not dead! They are merely sleeping! We awaken them with our Beltane Fire.

Dragon of Air, I fly you high,
Master and Mistress of the limitless sky.
Scream on the wind as you beat your wings,
'I hold the wisdom that knowledge brings!'

Dragon of Fire, I fly you with flame.
Scarlet your breath as you call my true name,
And gathering power, roar to the Sun
'I am the will and it shall be done!'

Dragon of Water, Serpent of Sea,
Together we bathe in the Mystery
And soar aloft with a scatter of dew;
Your cry is the rainbow's transient hue.

Dragon of Earth, I fly you deep,
Into the caverns where the fires sleep;
Your song wakes the Flame in the Jewel of Love
That there may be flowers on the earth above.

Dragons of grace, Dragons of power,
You are whole, you are one, unique in this hour.
O Dragon of Life, Quintessence entire,
We are sparks in the flames of your glorious fire.

Spoken by the Guide:

Get yourselves comfortable, close your eyes and relax. Breathe. Take some deep breaths to oxygenate your blood. Get back in touch with that deep inner centre .... Discover that you can relax even more deeply, staying in touch with my voice, and as the pathworking progresses, let yourself become more deeply relaxed and let your imagination free. Let the everyday conceptualising part of your mind quietly close down and your imagination, your visualisation, become more acute so that you see clear images and allow ideas and images to well up from deep within you.

So imagine now that you are on your way to your very own private, secret place. Only you know the way to this place. Only you know the magic word, or the gesture, the sign that opens the way into it. It might be a special room, or a cave, or just a little glade in a wood, or a stone circle, an ancient monument, whatever to you feels like your own special place. You are making your way there now and you come to your special place and say the word, or make the sign that opens it for you. You go into your special place, close the way behind you and feel the serenity and the security of this place. No other being of any sort can enter here unless you ask them in. Here you can be completely relaxed, you can be completely yourself, honest with yourself and at peace. There is no one here judging you, looking at you, criticising you; no one whose expectations you need to live up to, no obligations you have to meet. Here you can be relaxed, secure, at peace. Here you can look clearly at your life.

Think now, what are the uncertainties in your life? What decisions may you have to take? What problems might be looming around the corner? We all have to live with uncertainty; we don't know what tomorrow will bring. So just take a moment to pinpoint any particular areas of uncertainty that may be causing you a bit of anxiety or trepidation, or just that you wish you could see what is going to happen in the future, make the decisions now. Just let come into your mind any particular area of your life that seems to have these uncertainties ....

We are going now on a journey to seek wisdom and guidance and inner balance, so that we have all our faculties, our own inner certainty, ready to cope with whatever our lives may throw up. So now imagine that you are leaving your special place by a different way than the one you came in by and finding yourself in rural countryside. A meadow spreads before you and you follow a little path across the meadow and the ground is rising. As you come to the brow of a small hill, you are met by a strong wind which seems to be growing stronger and it is buffeting you about. It seems to be roaring through some trees nearby and they are thrashing around. It is almost as though in the noise of the trees and the wind you can hear argument, people making demands of you, voices buffeting you .... You press on against that strong wind, holding on to your inner core and the wind becomes gentler and you breathe it in. It is fresh and perfumed with the strength of flowers. You feel yourself getting lighter as you breathe it in. Suddenly this wind is exhilarating, bringing a sense of clarity, joy. You hear the birds singing and the noise of the wind is now like music ....

Now the wind is dropping altogether and the day is getting very hot. The sun is overhead. You press on on your journey, beginning to sweat rather. You come to a bonfire. Somebody is burning surplus wood, weeds and brambles. It is scorching hot. The flames are roaring up and in the noise of the flames you seem to hear angry voices and shouting, fighting, but soon the wood and brambles are consumed and the fire starts to die down. You pass on your way, feeling that you have absorbed the energy of the fire for it is filling you with enthusiasm and the will to go on to your journey's end.

Now clouds blow up and it starts to rain. The rain extinguishes the last of the fire and soaks your clothing, making you feel quite cool. The downpour becomes even heavier. The ground beneath your feet is getting muddy and slippery and you can hardly see where you are going for the rain in your face. Suddenly you feel yourself sliding in the mud and you realise that you cannot stop and you are sliding down into a river. You feel fear at first as the current seems to grab you and then you feel very angry about landing yourself in this predicament, you couldn't stop slipping. Then you realise that you are able to swim quite strongly with the current and that you are making some headway to the other bank. As you swim, you begin to feel a joyous exaltation in your strength and you remember times in the past when your emotions have threatened to drown you, but now you can swim with them, swim through them and reach the other side. You make it to the shore and climb out onto solid earth and as suddenly as the rain started, as is the way with these sudden downpours, it stops.

You make your way up the further bank, but mud is clinging to your feet and weighing you down. You feel heavy with inertia, but you press on and come to a grassy area where you can wipe the mud off your feet and stride on on a new path, enjoying the sense of physical activity, the physical act of walking. You feel your body is strong and energetic. The path is now going uphill and is quite dry here, and rocky and hard. You feel you are walking over the ancient bones of the earth, requiring determination and perseverance to press on to reach your objective. Although you did not know where you were going and feeling this urge to travel onwards, you now see ahead of you a building on the hill top and you know that that is where you have been aiming for all along.

You come finally to the building and realise it is some kind of a temple. The doors are closed. You stand outside and think back over the journey you have just taken, a journey through the elements. So which element did you find was the most daunting, the most scary, or challenging? .... Which one did you feel most comfortable with? .... Which one do you feel you would like to strengthen in your inner being? .... Which one is the most dominant? .... Is it perhaps a little too dominating? ....

Recall now those thoughts you had in your secret, private place about the uncertainties in your life, the problems or decisions you have to face .... Feel within you that yearning to tap the inner wisdom, to tap your potential, to strengthen your being. Become aware that we are all there, standing outside this temple, and above the doors to the temple are the words, 'Air, fire, water, earth'. This is the temple of the elements.

Now you hear the sound of bolts being drawn and the doors open inwards and two figures, a man and a woman, wearing white robes, stand there. They invite us all to enter the temple, the temple of the elements, and as we enter the woman sprinkles us with salt water; the element of water to which has been added the element of earth. The man wafts incense around us; the element of fire burning sweet resins, the element of air. So thus purified, we enter the temple. One wall glows with yellow light, the next one with red light, and then one with blue light and one with green light.

We know that the yellow wall represents the element of air. We all turn to face that glowing yellow wall and the light intensifies and seems to pulse with energy and we feel air blowing gently onto our faces. We breathe it in, breathing in the element of air, feeling it reaching into our minds, bringing amazing clarity, intelligence, a sense of lightness, humour, a new perspective on everything, objectivity and far-sightedness. Breathe it in, letting the element of air enhance all its qualities within you. Feel the gifts of air coming to you and the blessing of the element of air ....

Then the intense yellow light subsides again to a glow and you turn to the red wall and that starts to brighten and become more vivid and intense and to pulse with energy. You feel the heat, that energy coming from it. Feel it entering your body. Feel it strengthening your will, making your mind very focused. You feel that you can tackle all problems and make the right decisions. You feel relaxed because you are so certain of your will, your sense of destiny, your sense of being on your own true path. Draw the element of fire into you. Feel it energising you and filling you with enthusiasm and certainty and strength, knowing that your will will be focused and you can follow your own true will, your own true path. Feel that blessing of the element of fire ....

Now the brilliance of the red starts to subside and you know it is time to turn to the blue wall, the element of water. As you look at the blue wall the colour becomes more intense and brilliant and is pulsing with energy. The pulsing seems like water flowing through you. Feel the flowing within you. Feel it bringing you adaptability, flexibility, intuitive wisdom and confidence in your gut feeling. Feel it stirring the deep waters of your own inner being, your own emotional nature, your intuition and your imagination. Let the powers of the element of water flow into you, flowing through you and around you. Receive the blessing of the element of water ....

Now the intensity of blue starts to decrease and subside and it is time to turn to the green wall, the element of earth. Again the green light becomes more intense and brilliant, pulsing with energy. You feel all the powers of earth flowing towards you, flowing up through your feet. You feel it as strong, solid, positive. You know that it is the element of earth through which you bring your actions into being, your achievements. You might find come into your mind something that you can actually do physically in the world. You know that the element of earth will bring you the ability to persevere, to see things through, to actually achieve action in the world, in your own world; whether it is in your home, work, amongst your friends, in your garden, wherever you feel you need that particular strength and we all need it in all areas of our life. So feel the powers of earth strengthening you, giving you that sense of solidity and power and receive the blessing of the element of earth ....

Now the green light starts to subside back to a glow and you feel the sense within you of all the powers of the elements, like the sort of girders of your being that hold all aspects of your being in place, in harmony with each other. Imagine that as a group we are standing together in the centre of the temple and now all the walls start to glow more strongly, all become more brilliant and the light starts to swirl around us in a spiralling vortex of coloured light and as they get faster and faster and more intense, those coloured lights coalesce into brilliant white lights, the quintessential union and harmony of all the elements, enveloping us, bringing a wonderful sense of balance and integration, so that all the elements work together within us. Feel that white light all around, a wonderful vortex of energy, and then we are right in that vortex and the light is a vortex within each one of us and we are all part of that vortex. We realise that if all the elements work together within us they are much more than any one of them is individually. They enhance each other and balance each other, work together in all sorts of wonderful and intricate and harmonious ways, and that is there for us to absorb. So feel it nourishing you and strengthening you and inspiring you. Receive the quintessential blessing of the pure white light, one with the quintessence. Absorb that right into your innermost being ....

The brilliance of the white light subsides and we stand for a moment in the temple and again look at our lives, the uncertainties that the future holds, the challenges we are facing, and feel that sense of confidence and calm, particularly that deep inner calm, that confidence in your own ability to make decisions, to hold your own ground, to stand on your own two feet and yet also to reach out to those you love, those you work with, those you deal with everyday. Feel that inner sense of balance and strength ....

Now it is time to leave the temple of the elements. The priest and the priestess lead us to the door and they bow to each one of us, acknowledgment of the journey we have achieved, and raise their hands in blessing and farewell as we leave and follow the path down the hill. We find that very quickly we are on the path that leads back into our special secret place. We go and sit there in our special place just for a moment, appreciating its beauty and its serenity and security, and that it has provided the place from which you set out on this journey. You know that any time you need calm and strength, and comfort and security, you can go to this special place.

But now it is time to leave it by that doorway that leads back to the everyday world and you go out. Close the way behind you, sealing it magically, and, as I count from twenty to one, gradually make your way back, back to the everyday world and this room. Twenty .... nineteen .... eighteen .... seventeen .... sixteen .... fifteen .... fourteen .... thirteen .... twelve .... eleven .... ten .... nine .... eight .... seven .... six .... five .... take some deep breaths .... four .... feel your body, your hands, your legs .... three .... two .... one, and awake.

This pathworking would combine well with a ritual based around 'Quintessence at Beltane' (see earlier in the Workbook).

HERMES PATHWORKING

Requirements:
Feather

Spoken by the Guide:

Before we begin the pathworking, try to think of a communication problem you are experiencing. It could be a misunderstanding, a difficulty, perhaps you need to work to persuade someone of something or need to do a tricky negotiation. Take some time to bring this problem into your mind .... Now try to formulate a positive outcome, visualise yourself with the problem resolved ....

Now we will begin to sink down to the psychic plane. Breathe, breathing in the cool, fresh air, that lightness. Feel yourself filled with light and air. Imagine a lovely pale blue sky, clear of clouds, in which birds fly .... We wish to call upon Hermes to come to us and to share with us his wisdom, his insight, his intelligence and his skills of communication.

> Hail Hermes, swift jesting messenger in endless flight through the orange and violet ether. In thy right hand is the serpent wand of science, magic and healing. Thy winged feet are set upon the clouds and wings crown thee. Thy voice is laughterful as living water and clear as the stars. Divide the light from the darkness, the north from the south and flash as quicksilver through the veins of the universe, bearing the divine word.

Wherever atoms dance, or planets whirl, wherever the syntropy of life turns back times arrow, wherever form crystallises from the void, wherever the mind of man razor cuts toward truth, thy voice is heard. By the double helix of the seed of life, by the miracle of language, by the joy of swiftness and the laughter of the endless quest, we call upon thee to be with us.

We see him flashing across the sky and then turn and speed back again and we feel his presence, his touch. We hear his laughter and his music and feel his magic.

So now recall your communication problem and solution and feel Hermes' power flow into you, and all communication difficulties becoming an intriguing and soluble challenge, a game for the mind. Perhaps the solution takes on a new dimension, or a new image of you dealing with whatever it is, of you communicating clearly with humour, with persuasiveness. Let it sink into your deep mind and feel the confidence of Hermes permeate you that you can deal with it.

Hermes comes to each one and his air fans you and he gives you a token, something to remind you that the problem can be overcome ....

Now all stand and form a circle. We each fan each other with the feather of Air, remembering the power of Hermes ....

Now, remembering the solution to your communication problem, let the energy of Hermes float away on the breeze, take a few deep breaths and feel yourself back in the here and now, back in this room.

COLOUR HEALING PATHWORKING

This pathworking will have been preceded by some partner work, as described in Chapter 6. Each person in the group will work with a partner and sit facing each other, taking it in turns to see or sense the colour of the other's aura, the field of energy surrounding a person; or just simply feeling if any colour particularly associates with their partner. Try to feel the colour that is of benefit to the partner, a healing colour.

Spoken by the Guide:

If you make yourselves comfortable again and close your eyes. Again get back in touch with that deep inner calm and peace and relaxation, letting yourselves sink down to the psychic plane and focus on your physical and mental wellbeing .... You may feel you want to work in some general way for physical and mental wellbeing, or you may feel there is some specific physical or mental problem, a difficulty in your wellbeing that you would like to tackle, and you are going to be able to find some healing for that state of your wellbeing.

To start with, visualise yourself as surrounded by the colour that your partner suggested to you. Feel that colour glowing brightly around you in whatever hue of that colour feels appropriate. You may find it shifts and changes, softens or becomes more intense, becomes brighter or dimmer, but explore that colour, visualising it all around yourself, permeating within you, perhaps glowing particularly strongly in the appropriate chakra centre. Breathe it in and bathe in it, feel it concentrating wherever it is needed ....

When or if you feel you have got all the benefit you can from that colour, let other colours come into your mind, either modifying that colour, or replacing it, or replacing it in parts, forming layers, or whatever you feel. Let your own creative intelligence tell you what will heal you ....

Now think in terms of your spiritual wellbeing. What colour, or slight shift in tones of colour do you feel would enhance your spiritual wellbeing? ....

Then gradually let the colours fade away and note any particular results of this, any feeling of healing where you need to do more work, any part of you that showed up as being in need of attention, any information about the colours that you find most helpful ....

Then it is time to emerge from this deep inner psychic place, so as I count from ten to one feel yourself coming back to the here and now. Ten .... nine .... eight .... seven .... six .... five .... four .... three .... two ... one ... and when you are ready let us just stand and hold hands in a circle. Close your eyes and just be aware of how wonderful it is that we have colour vision. Not all species have colour vision. Let us think how much pleasure, how much beauty, how much information there is in colour for us .... How gifted we are. We create the colour out in the world around us all in our heads through an incredible system we have developed of being sensitive to different wavelengths of light and clever brains that translate what we see into pictures in wonderful colour and distances, and that we can also do it in our own minds; we can visualise the colour. Let us just be aware that we are part of a wonderful, intricate system of life, a great web of life and our particular bit of that web has particular virtues for us, particular rewards and pleasures and opportunities. So let us glory in colour. Let us use the colours. Let us value them.

So next time when you are out of doors in daylight, particularly if you are in a garden or park, or passing other people's gardens, just look at all the beautiful colours of the flowers and the leaves and the sky and perhaps find that the ones that cause you particular pleasure are the ones that give you the most healing.

Now be aware of the floor beneath our feet and the circle of hands. Just make a little feeling to each person, each hand, that passes around the circle. Take some deep breaths and open your eyes.

MIDSUMMER SUN AND MOON PATHWORKING

Followed by the sharing of cakes and mead

Requirements:

- Chalice of mead
- Dish of cakes to share

Spoken by the Guide:

Again, make sure you are comfortable. Close your eyes, go into yourselves, relax. Find that deep level of relaxation. Breathe slow and deep .... Let your mind be still .... Let yourself sink even more deeply into a state of complete relaxation .... Let yourself sink, a little gently, deeper towards the psychic plane where you have access to the deeper levels of your mind and your imagination, deeper levels of insight and intuition and more vivid imagery....

Imagine that it is the hour before the dawn at midsummer. We are standing within the great circle of stones at Stonehenge. We feel the power of those great stones all around us and we marvel at the vision and the ingenuity and the dedication of our ancestors who built them. We await the miracle of the midsummer sunrise. As we wait we are aware of the earth beneath our feet and that it is the body of our mother, the Earth Mother of whom we are part. A deep love arises within us for the earth and all its teeming life, a love for the beauty of the mountains, and the lakes, and the rivers, and the great oceans; a love for trees, marvellous trees, and the birds that fly in them; great elephants, tiny mice, snakes and bees, spiders, insects. What a wonder it is, the web of life, from the tiny, the invisible, the microbe; to the enormous, the great whales ....

We marvel at it and are grateful that we are part of it, part of the body of the Earth Mother, and our gift to her is our awareness, our wonder, our love and our caring. The Lady of Earth is the mother of all life. She is warmed and kissed by the sun to be fruitful and abundant, but we must remember that with life comes death and the abundance of the Earth Mother is a never-ending dance of life and death and renewal. So we must honour the Lord of Death, who is also King of the Greenwood and leader of the hunt. He is the cut corn and the crushed grape. He gives his life that we may eat. Not just us, but all life. He is the Lord of Death, but also the spirit of life and renewal. He is the Green Man, the power of evolution. Nothing is ever lost or destroyed, but is recycled. Everything is recycled into new and wondrous life. Although we are children of the Earth Mother, we are all - both the Earth Mother, the Lord of the Greenwood and all of us - children of the stars and at midsummer we honour that great star, the sun, from which we came.

Now the first ray of the sun strikes through the stone circle, straight onto our faces. The light strikes through to our centres, to each one of us, as though it was sent individually to each of us; that light piercing us, igniting our passion and our will.

As the sun rises it also becomes warmer and the fire of the sun burns through to us, kindling an answering fire within our hearts, giving us energy, power and strength and healing. Let that burning fire of the sun bring you all the energy and the healing that you need ....

After midsummer the world turns. The long days of glory begin to wane. The sun's power starts to wane, but it is still strong. The harvest is yet to come and the harvest will be bounteous. You feel that health-giving sun, that light and that warmth, bringing your own fruits to ripeness, your own harvest to fruition ....

Now the long midsummer's day comes to a close and the Sun King sinks in the west. But behold, in the east rises the Lady of the Moon in full beauty and mystery, Queen of the Night. She catches the light of the Sun King in her mirror and for a moment we are held in an embrace between the Sun King and the Lady of the Moon. We are at the focus of their powers, their powers are in perfect balance. This is a moment of deep magic because it is the interplay of the forces of the sun and the moon upon the earth that have created the conditions for life. So feel now we stand between the midsummer sun and the midsummer full moon; their powers, in perfect balance, creating and energising our inner life. So let these two powers embrace you, enrich you ....

Now the sun sinks below the horizon and the moon rises higher. We feel the full individual power of the moon, Mistress of the Waters, who rules our inner depths. From the sun we have drawn energy and passion and will, but we also need the gifts of the Lady of the Moon. She brings us love and imagination and intuition, poetry and song, and that deep wisdom that wells up from the heart. She also brings us challenges, conflicts, problems with priorities, values, stimuli to growth. So let her give you her own special gifts that she has for you .... Feel the power of the moon deep within yourself, deep within your psychic levels, deep within the depths of your mind, the depths of your heart ....

Midsummer night is the shortest night of the year and already the Moon Queen is sinking towards the horizon and behold, the eastern sky is lightening and the sun is ready to rise on a new day. Once again as the moon sinks and the sun rises, there is that magical moment of balance, just like a draught of cool, clear water ....

So without losing that contact with Stonehenge and midsummer, let us stand in a circle .... We stand between the powers of the midsummer sun and the full moon. The sun and the moon hold the earth in a net of magic. We are poised at the dawn of a new day. Now is a new beginning. Find your new beginning within you. Feel it growing like a flower, a flower that has roots in the moist earth and is warmed by the sun's fire and nourished by the waters of the moon. Feel your will and your energy empowered by the sun and your imagination fructified by the moon, so that that boulder on your path disintegrates, that obstacle is dealt with and banished ....

Since spring the Earth Mother has been flowering and with the blossom come the bees, and from ancient times people have harvested honey around midsummer and from it they have made cakes and mead, and this midsummer full moon is therefore called the Honey Moon, a symbol of love and union and fruitfulness.

Let us hold hands. We ask the blessing of the sun and the moon on this mead and on these cakes. They are the fruits of the union of the Earth Mother and the Lord of the Greenwood. These powers of earth, we also ask to give us their blessing as we give them our love and our dedication. May the Earth Mother and the Lord of the Greenwood bless this mead and as we drink let us give them our love and also strengthen our determination to care for them, to look after our planet ....

The chalice of mead is passed around the group.

The Lord and the Lady bless these cakes, remembering that the Lord of the Greenwood gives his life that we may eat, that life feeds on life, but nothing is ever lost. All is transmuted and renewed.

The dish of cakes is passed around the group.

SUMMER SOLSTICE RITUAL

For a Pagan Federation Open Ritual

Requirements:

- Altar in the North, with candles and decorations
- Bowls of water and incense for the Greeters
- Drums/percussion instruments
- Ability to play music
- Incense
- Lantern
- Mirror
- Dish of water for the Moon Goddess
- Cauldron containing unlit candles & tapers/matches
- Trays
- Sprigs of rosemary and willow
- Green twine or string
- Honey cakes and mead

Roles:

- Narrator
- Greeters
- Circle Caster
- Elemental Officers
- Sun God
- Moon Goddess
- Earth Mother
- Green Man
- Servers of cakes and mead

In the centre is the cauldron. The Elemental Officers stand around it.

Play music while the congregation enter. All are censed with incense and sprinkled with water as they enter and form a circle.

NARRATOR: Let us celebrate the Summer Solstice, the longest day, the Sun at its highest; and the Full Moon, the Honey Moon, when the night is shortest. Let us together create our sacred space. Please all stand and turn outwards. Hold hands and make one complete circle of the room, visualising a circle of blue light forming around the room .... *[Optional drumming].* Now turn to face into the circle. And let us call upon the mighty Elemental Powers to be present. We will call them with song and chant. Join your voices with ours.

These parts are intended to be sung as a chant, repeated a few times, hopefully with all present joining in:

AIR:

Breath is Air
Air so pure
Wind is air
The Breath of Heaven
Inspire me. *[Repeat]*

[Spoken by Officer] Powers of Air, hail and welcome!

FIRE:

Light is Fire
Fire so Pure
Sun is fire
The Fires of Heaven
Purify me. *[Repeat]*

[Spoken by Officer] Powers of Fire, hail and welcome!

WATER: Water's rain
Rain so pure
Sea and stream
The Blood of Heaven
Sanctify me. *[Repeat]*

[Spoken by Officer] Powers of Water, hail and welcome!

EARTH: Soil is earth
Earth so pure
Mother Earth
The Ground of Heaven
Underneath me. *[Repeat]*

[Spoken by Officer] Powers of Earth, hail and welcome!
Quarter Officers go to the Altar.

NARRATOR: Sit if you wish. Close your eyes. Relax. Breathe .... It is dark. We are standing within the circle of great stones at Stonehenge. We feel the power of the great stones around us and marvel at the vision, ingenuity and dedication of our ancestors who erected them. We await the miracle of the Midsummer sunrise. And, as we wait, we are aware of the Earth beneath our feet, the body of our Mother, of whom we are part. We feel a deep love for the Earth and all its teeming life, for the beauty of mountain and lake, for rivers and mighty oceans; for trees and birds, elephants and mice, for snakes and bees and spiders .... What a wonder it all is - from microbe to great whale. We are part of this, part of the body of the Earth Mother; and our gift to her is our awareness, our wonder and our love.

ALL CHANT: Mother, I feel your heart beating.
Where do I feel it, under my feet.[2]

---

[2] Or choose a similarly appropriate chant, see online sources.

During the chant, the Earth Mother comes to the centre and when the voices die down, she raises her arms saying:

EARTH MOTHER: I am the Lady of Earth, Mother of all Life;
Warmed and kissed by the Sun to be fruitful and abundant.
Your love and your worship have called me forth
To join you in your Solstice celebration.
But with Life comes Death.
My abundance is a never-ending dance
Of life and death and renewal.
So must you also honour the Lord of Death,
King of the Greenwood, Leader of the Hunt.
The cut corn, the crushed grape,
He who gives his life that you may eat.

ALL CHANT: Hoof and horn, hoof and horn, all that dies shall be reborn.
Vine and grain, vine and grain, all that's cut shall rise again.

During the chant, the Green Man comes to the centre and when the voices die down, he raises his arms saying:

GREEN MAN: Greetings, Lady. *[kisses her and takes her hand]*
I am the Lord of Death,
Yet am I also the Spirit of Life and Renewal.
The Green Man, the power of evolution.
Nothing is ever lost or destroyed,
But is recycled into new and wondrous life.
You are children of the Earth Mother,
Yet we all – you, I, the Earth Mother – are also
Children of the stars!
And the time of the magical Midsummer sunrise is here.
The Star from which we came!

The Earth Mother and the Green Man turn to the North East and raise their arms in salute to the Sun God. They then retire to stand in front of the Altar. The Sun God steps forward from the North East, but not yet to the centre. He carries the lantern and says:

SUN GOD: I arise in all my Majesty and Might;
This is my day of glory.
My Light strikes through to your Centre;
My Fire ignites your passion and your will.
I bring light and life and glory to the Earth.
I bestow energy, power, strength and health.

He now walks to the centre, saying:

I bring you the Magical Fire of Transmutation,
And the blinding Light of Wisdom.
It is noon, and my power is at its height.
I light the fire within the Cauldron of the Earth Mother.

The Sun God lights the candles in the cauldron, then says:

Dance around my Fire, shed what holds you back
And take my power into your hearts.

Circle dance and Sun Chant:

ALL CHANT: Sunlight, Circle bright
Spinning of the Wheel
Sunlight, Circle bright
Free and change and heal.

NARRATOR: The Elemental Powers interact and intertwine in complex ways. Let us now invoke the fire aspect of each element, that we may start the process of empowering our wills.

The Elemental Officers give the gifts of Fire:

AIR: I give you the gifts of Fire of Air:
The lightening flash of inspiration;
The eloquence of the impassioned orator;
The scintillating creative ideas that shape your future.
USE THEM WELL!

WATER: I give you the gifts of Fire of Water:
I give you the rainbow vision of hope,
See how it leads you into the future!
I give you the steam power of enthusiasm
To fuel the dynamo of your Will.
USE THEM WELL!

EARTH: I give you the gifts of Fire of Earth:
The heroic spirit that awakens the Dragon power within you.
Nought shall turn you aside from your path.
And I give you the treasures of Earth
To resource your endeavours.
USE THEM WELL!

FIRE: I give you the gifts of Fire of Fire:
The Fire of True Will, burning within you;
The bright clear flame of creativity;
The Fire of Transmutation
That burns away your fetters and sets you free!
USE THEM WELL!

NARRATOR: Take these gifts within yourself.

Pause.

SUN GOD: The world turns and my long day of glory ends.
From today, my power will start to wane;
But I am still strong,
And the harvest is yet to come –
And it will be bounteous!

The Sun God walks to the North West saying:

Now I go to my rest ....

He turns and salutes across the room, continuing:

But see! As I sink to rest,
The Lady of the Night rises in her Fullness!

The Moon Goddess steps forward in the South East but stays back from the centre. She carries the mirror and says:

MOON GODDESS: I arise in my Fullness of Beauty and Mystery,
Queen of Darkness,
And I catch the Light of the Lord of Day in my Mirror.

She salutes the Sun God across the circle and continues:

Vast and mighty Sun,
Blazing Star among a myriad blazing stars,
To you, I am but a tiny speck.
Yet you and I together have wrought a great Magic:

We have brought the gift of life to this precious Earth.
Continue now your journey below the horizon,
And I will light the Earth during this short night.

SUN GOD: Lady, I salute you. And I pass to you my Light and my Power.

The Sun God steps back and unobtrusively makes his way back to the North East.

MOON GODDESS: Behold, People of Earth, I am Mistress of the Waters,
And I rule your inner depths.
From the Sun, you have drawn energy, passion and will;
Yet without my gifts, you are incomplete.
I turn the Light of the Sun into silver magic;
I bring you the gifts of love, imagination and intuition.
I bring poetry and song,
And that deep wisdom that wells up from the heart.

The Moon Goddess moves to the central cauldron and continues:

It is midnight and my power is at its strongest.
The Cauldron of the Earth Mother is filled with my Waters.
Come, dance the spiral dance to the centre of your being
And take my Wisdom within your hearts.

Spiral dance and Moon Chant, during which the Moon Goddess sprinkles people gently with water.

ALL CHANT: Moonlight, circle bright,
Spinning of the wheel.
Moonlight, circle bright,
Let your magic heal.

The Elemental Officers give the gifts of Water:

AIR: I give you the gifts of Water of Air:
I give you the morning dew, diamond bright,
That turns the images of your dreams into poetry and song,
I give you cloud castles in the sky and the magic of words
To express your aspiration.
USE THEM WELL!

FIRE: I give you the gifts of Water of Fire:
I give you the thunderstorm –
Hot air rising, electrical charges, the mighty downpour.
I give you challenges!
I give you excitement, competition, the setting of goals.
USE THEM WELL!

EARTH: I give you the gifts of Water of Earth:
I give you – mud! Damp and fertile soil,
In which the seeds of your inspiration can germinate.
I give you the flowering of your actions,
And the seeds for future flowers therefrom.
USE THEM WELL!

WATER: I give you the gifts of Water of Water:
I give you your still and mysterious depths,
The well-spring of your capacity to love,
Source of inspiration and imagination,
Your connection to the deepest wisdom.
USE THEM WELL!

The Moon Goddess moves towards the South West saying:

MOON GODDESS: My short night is ending and I sink towards the horizon
But Lo! (Turns to face Sun) A new day dawns!
The vast and mighty Sun arises again in his glory!

The Sun God steps forward in the North East, polarising with the Moon Goddess who stays visible in the South West. The Earth Mother and the Green Man come into the centre, bearing trays of rosemary and willow and green twine.

GREEN MAN: Moon and Sun hold the Earth in a net of Magic.
We are poised at the dawn of a new day.
Now is our new beginning!

EARTH MOTHER: We bring rosemary, wherein is captured the power of the Sun; and willow, wherein resides the mystery of the Moon. Let each person take rosemary and willow and the green twine of Earth, and feel their power.

Herbs and string are distributed.

EARTH MOTHER: Find your new beginning now within you - NOW!
Feel it growing like a flower within the moist earth,
Warmed by the Fire of the Sun,
Nourished by the Waters of the Moon.
Feel your will empowered by the Sun,
And your imagination fructified by the Moon.

With full magical intention, bind together your rosemary and your willow, with the green twine of Earth. Bind the powers of Sun and Moon together within you!

The Sun God and Moon Goddess raise the lantern and mirror on high. The Earth Mother and Green Man raise their arms, gathering the powers and distributing them, while all bind their rosemary and willow together. Music is playing.

SOMEONE: [3] Since the Spring, the Earth Mother has been flowering;
And with the blossoms come the bees, gathering nectar.
From times of old, the children of the Earth Mother
Have harvested the honey at Midsummer,
And from it made cakes and mead.
From the magic of Sun and Moon,
The Earth Mother and her Consort
Have given us of their bounty.
Thus is the Midsummer Moon known as the Honey Moon.

ANOTHER: The Honey Moon! Symbol of love, union and fruitfulness!
Let us celebrate the Midsummer marriage of Moon and Sun!
And as we feast, let us give thanks for this bounty.
Let us dedicate ourselves to care for our Mother the Earth;
And let us salute the Lord of Death
Who is cut down that we may eat.

Servers of cakes and mead come forward to the Earth Mother and Green Man.

SERVER 1: Lady, we ask that you bless this honey cake and mead,
That we may eat and drink with true thankfulness.

The Earth Mother blesses the cakes and mead with her own words.

SERVER 2: Lord, we ask that you also bless this honey cake and mead,
That we may eat, acknowledging that we feast on life.

---

[3] These parts could be spoken by the Narrator, or anyone in the ritual group.

The Green Man blesses the cakes and mead with his own words.

The Servers hand round the cakes and mead. Optional music or drums in the background.

NARRATOR: Our rite is ended. Let us hold hands and affirm our comradeship, our oneness with all Life.

All hold hands; a moment's silence. The Narrator then continues:

Let us thank our Gods for their presence
And the wondrous magic that they have woven for us ....

Here the Narrator either says thanks aloud, or allows time for each person present to thank the Gods silently, in their own way. Then the Narrator says:

And let us close the circle.

The Gods withdraw.

The Elemental Officers come to the centre to sing the Quarters closed, either in the same way as at the beginning of the ritual, or with alternative words.

NARRATOR: The circle of blue flame that has protected our sacred space now fades:

The circle is open, but unbroken;
Merry Meet, and Merry Part,
And Merry Meet again!

Allow time for feasting and socialising.

SEKHMET MIDSUMMER RITUAL

For a Pagan Federation Open Ritual

Requirements:

- Altar with candles and decorations
- Sekhmet statue on Altar (if available, or an image could be used)
- Sistrum/percussion instrument
- Incense
- Bell/gong
- Ankh for Sekhmet to hold
- Black cloak for Sekhmet
- Red candle on Altar
- Four chalices and wine
- Drums/ability to play music (optional)

Roles:

- Narrator - also in charge of ringing the bell
- Circle Caster
- North/Nut - Black robe
- East/Ihy - White robe, gold tabard
- South/Horus - Red robe, orange tabard
- West/Hathor - White robe, turquoise tabard
- Priest of Ra - Blue and gold cloak/robe
- Priest of Sekhmet - Blue and gold cloak/robe
- Sekhmet - Red robe and black cloak

Note: all robes/colours are optional suggestions.

The ritual begins with the Narrator giving an explanation of the Summer Solstice Fire Festival and some introductory words about Sekhmet, the lioness-headed Goddess of Ancient Egypt referred to as "Lady of Flame" and "She Whose Essence is Fire". In 'The Gods Within'[4]*, she is described thus:*

"Her dress is red; she holds an ankh in her right hand, symbol of eternal life; in her left, she holds the papyrus sceptre of power. Her headdress is the uraeus serpent surmounted by the solar disk, both symbols of rulership .... Sekhmet represents the blazing heat of the noon-day sun in the desert .... Sekhmet represented the devouring, destroying power of the sun's heat .... She was the destroyer of the wicked and the protector of the good. Some pharaohs described themselves as 'Son of Sekhmet' .... [She] remained the fiery force of will that brings creative inspiration into manifestation .... As 'Lady of Pestilence', Sekhmet could both cause and cure plagues and sickness. We have seen the same apparently contradictory powers attributed to Apollo: the heat of the sun is a powerful force that can bring both great good and great ill. As 'Lady of Life', she was mistress of healing and the art of surgery .... She is a symbol of proud, queenly power and confidence, of high self-esteem and of the mobilisation of the fiery will to make room for improvements by destroying the out-moded and restrictive. She can help us to rid ourselves of that aspect of human nature that tends to become a slave to habit, petty obligations and inertia. She gives us the energy to change, to achieve our goals, to bring our creative inspiration to fruition. She gives us the courage and that dash of ruthlessness that is necessary to break old patterns, a process that may make others uncomfortable, even angry .... Her fiery breath energises us, rouses us from lethargy and brings a new sense of decisiveness and assertiveness. Her roar reminds us that everyone has the right to make their voice heard and to be listened to with respect .... The lioness is queen of beasts: she does not need to rage for few can threaten her. She knows how to relax, to let go and be sensuous, enjoying food and drink, play, companionship, a rest in the sun. But in a moment she can

---

[4] Jean M. Williams and Zachary Cox, 2008

become fully alert, her senses finely tuned to her environment. The strength and power of Sekhmet allows us to have the confidence to be fully in the present time, neither regretting what is past nor worrying about the future, completely ready at all times to deal with zest with whatever life may bring."

The book also recounts one of the most well-known and colourful myths about Sekhmet:

".... it was recounted that the gods learned that humans plotted to overthrow and replace them. Ra was angered by this ingratitude towards the gods who had done much for mankind, and called upon the High Gods to smite them. Hathor, the beautiful goddess of fertility and love who wore the ears and horns of a cow, changed into Sekhmet, a raging lioness, and attacked them without mercy, killing many and drinking their blood. She became so intoxicated with battle lust that human survival was endangered. When Ra saw that she could not be stopped, he became alarmed and sent for beer and certain mind-altering plants. From these a brew was made and coloured with red ochre; it was poured onto the fields where the raging lioness would pass. Sekhmet drank the brew, thinking it was blood; her rage left her and 'her heart was filled with joy'."

NARRATOR: Now it is time to prepare the ritual space and call the Guardians of the Quarters.

Bell.

CIRCLE CASTER: Let all venomous and malignant creatures be gone from this place.

The circle caster goes once around the room shaking the sistrum/percussion instrument.

NARRATOR: All stamp your feet and drive away the snakes and scorpions of the day, those niggling irritations and anxieties.

CIRCLE CASTER: Let all good and harmonious vibrations enter here.

The circle caster goes once around the room with incense.

NARRATOR: Waft those harmonious vibrations about and breathe them in to yourself.

The Quarter Officers form a circle facing their quarter.

Bell.

NORTH:

Hail Nut, Lady of the Stars,
Whose body encircles the Universe.
When the boat of Ra has departed into the West,
We see thee approach thy lover, Geb, Lord of Earth,
Thy body decked with jewels,
A perfect arch of love.
Guard thou the Northern Quarter
And sustain us in this rite.
Nut, Hail and Welcome!

Bell.

EAST:

Hail Ihy, Lord of the Dawn,
Who riseth, young forever.
Thou standest in the prow of Ra's boat,
In the glory of morning.
Thou bringest a new day, a new beginning,
Bright with promise and opportunity.
Guard thou the Eastern Quarter
And sustain us in our rite.
Ihy, Hail and Welcome!

Bell.

SOUTH: Hail Horus, Lord of the Zenith,
Warrior Hawk flying from the Eye of Ra.
Thou art the protector of peace and prosperity,
Ever vigilant to fight the Forces of Chaos.
We see thee in the fierce heat of noon
Riding the air on great wings, eyes scanning the horizon.
Guard thou the Southern Quarter
And sustain us in this rite.
Horus, Hail and Welcome!

Bell.

WEST: Hail Hathor, Lady of the Setting Sun;
Thou standest at the portal of Night,
Offering nourishment to all who pass,
Whether it be the living passing into sleep,
Or the dying passing into the Judgement Hall of Osiris,
Or the babe who passes into Life.
Guard thou the Western Quarter
And sustain us in our rite.
Hathor, Hail and welcome!

Bell.

The Quarter Officers return to the sides of the Altar.
The Priest of Ra takes up position in front of the Altar.

PRIEST OF RA: Let us give praise to the great God, Ra, Lord of the Sun.

Bell.

PRIEST OF RA: Homage to thee, O Ra, at thy tremendous rising!
Thou risest! Thou shinest! The heavens are rolled aside!
Thou art the King of Gods, thou art the All-comprising,
From thee we come, in thee are deified.

Thy priests go forth at dawn;
They wash their hearts with laughter;
Divine winds move in music across thy golden strings.
At sunset they embrace thee, as every cloudy rafter
Flames with reflected colour from thy wings.

Thou sailest over the zenith, and thy heart rejoices;
Thy morning boat and evening boat
With fair winds meet together;
Before thy face the Goddess Maat exalts her fateful feather,
And at thy name the Halls of Anu ring with voices.

O Thou Perfect! Thou Eternal! Thou Only One!
Great Hawk that fliest with the flying Sun!
Between the Turquoise Sycamores that risest, young forever,
Thine image flashing on the bright celestial river.

Thy rays are on all faces; thou art inscrutable.
Age after age thy life renews its eager prime.
Time whirls its dust beneath thee; thou art immutable,
Maker of Time, thyself beyond all Time.

Thou passeth through the portals that close behind the night,
Gladdening the souls of them that lie in sorrow.
The True of Word, the Quiet Heart, arise to drink thy Light;
Thou art Today and Yesterday, thou art Tomorrow!

Homage to thee, O Ra, who wakest life from slumber!
Thou risest! Thou shinest! Thy radiant face appears!
Millions of years have passed - we cannot count their number,
Millions of years shall come. Thou art above the years! [5]

As a bell rings, the Priest of Ra bows and retires.

NARRATOR: Now we will do a mediation focussing on the element of fire, so make yourselves comfortable. Let your mind dwell on the subject of the element of fire, how you feel about the element of fire and its qualities. Is your immediate feeling that fire is strong, or weak, or just right in your nature? ....

Imagine a really fiery person, maybe somebody you know or just an imaginary person. How do you feel when you meet a really fiery person? What tends to be your first reaction? ....

How do you feel about some aspects of your own fiery nature? If you become angry, if somebody makes you feel really angry, how does that make you feel? Do you feel exhilarated, or embarrassed, or frightened, or what? How do you feel when you are angry? Some people feel really upset when they get angry ....

How would you assess your energy levels as a whole? Sometimes we feel tired and down and sometimes we feel energetic or up. Overall do you feel you have the energy and enthusiasm you would like to have? Is it free? Do you feel it is inhibited, or what? ....

Overall do you feel that your will is weak, or strong? Do you find yourself plagued by indecision and problems with working out priorities, or do you feel that you make up your mind quickly, knowing what to do? ....

---

[5] From the Egyptian Book of the Dead.

Now that you have those thoughts in mind, sink down deep within yourself. Don't forget to breathe .... Imagine that you are sinking down deep within your own inner darkness, down and down into a state of deep relaxation, so you are gently floating down a deep hole to the bottom of your being. In the darkness, you see a tiny red glow. This is the ember of your true will and breathe deep down into that ember, letting your breath fan it into life. See that ember growing more strongly, becoming more orangey, brighter, bigger and bursting into a beautiful flame within you: the bright flame of your true will .... This is the source of your energy for action and creativity, this deep, deep place within you where you can always find, in the lowest moments, that ember and breathe into it, fan it into life and find that your energy level rises, your sense of purpose improves, priorities fall into place and you have the energy and sense of direction to move forward.

So, with that newfound energy, imagine that you are walking in the noonday sun through a desert village to a very important person who lives there, a craftsman, the blacksmith, and his forge is there and you ask him a very important request: that you yourself can fashion the spear of your will at his forge and he will show you how to do it if you need help. You choose a length of iron rod and you put the fuel of earth onto the fire of the forge and then you take the bellows of air and blow the fire into a blaze until it is really white hot in the centre. Beside you is a trough of cold water drawn from the nearby Nile. You thrust your length of iron rod into the fire and with a big set of pincers you turn it and thrust it deeper if need be, until the end of your rod is gleaming and hot, red and then brighter and brighter until it is almost at the point of melting. You take it out and hammer it into shape on the forge, then plunge it into the water to cool. Three times you do this: you heat it to incandescence, beat it into shape and temper it in the water until it is sharp and bright and strong and true ....

You thank the blacksmith for his guidance and help and the courtesy of using his forge and, taking your spear in your hand, you go forth feeling, even with it just in your hand, a sense of strength and purpose.

You see before you a path that leads amongst scattered trees, lotus flowers and papyrus bushes beside the river. With your spear held firmly in your hand, and courage and determination in your heart, you follow the path into the trees finding yourself transported into a dark, deep forest. It is so dark in there that you can hardly see anything, but you know you must press on because there is something very important here that you have to do, that your will will not be fully your own and fully aligned with your purpose and your life until you have dealt with what you have to deal with in this deep, dark forest.

You hear now a snuffling and a crashing and a roaring. There is some great beast in this forest and you know you must face this beast and the beast is searching for you. Now it is coming closer, that roaring and trampling, breaking of branches of bushes and trees, as this great snuffling, roaring, slathering beast comes for you. This is all that you fear most, all that is overwhelming and disempowering. So take your spear and, with all your will and determination, fight that creature, smite it with the spear of your will and when it rears up ready to grab you and grasp you in its jaws, you drive the spear of your will into its heart and in that instant it bursts into flame, it combusts, and that fire is all around you. Open yourself to it. Absorb the life energy of that monster. Let it flow into you, for it is your own energy that you have projected out into the monster. It is yours by right. Take that energy, feel yourself being empowered with all those qualities that you feared in other people. They are there available for you ....

The fire is fully absorbed within yourself and the darkness rolls away as the sun rises on a new day. The forest vanishes and you are strong and whole, with all those fiery powers you gave away to others back within yourself, yours to use as you need.

During the pathworking, while everyone has their eyes closed, Sekhmet takes up position in front of the Altar, shrouded in a black cloak. All will be asked to stand at the end of the pathworking.

Bell.

PRIEST OF SEKHMET: Hail, Sekhmet, Lion Queen,
Whose essence is Fire, tempestuous forever.
Thou art throned in the desert in the heat of noon,
Crowned with the Uraeus of divine power and the Sun's disk.
In thy right hand is the Ankh of eternal life,
And thy left holds the papyrus sceptre.
Thy voice is the roar of passionate will that none may gainsay.

Prowl thou the desert way of our being, O Lady of Flame;
Send the reverberations of thy roar
Into the soul's deepest canyons.
Thy breath is the hot flame
That burns away the dry brushwood of our lives,
Freeing us for new ventures.

Wherever men and women walk tall
And gaze meets gaze in fearless pride,
Wherever skill and strength unite with inspiration,
And noble aspiration blazes into action,
The heat of thy fire burns in the blood.

By the blazing Sun at noon,
By the empowerment of Will Triumphant,
By heat and flame and spitting serpent,
I call upon thee to be present in body and in spirit.

Sekhmet steps forward and removes the cloak. She holds an Ankh symbol.

SEKHMET: I am Sekhmet, Lady of Flame,
She whose colour is red, whose essence is Fire,

Mighty in Magic and Mistress of the Two Lands,
I pour as Fire from the brow of Ra.

I am the power of your Lion-nature, your inner Fire,
Your passion, your lust for life – Your True Will.
I am come to set you free, to liberate you from fear and doubt,
To empower your inner being,
Your courage and your aspiration.

Each one of you is a flame of wonder.
Each one of you is a marvel of creative wisdom –
A source of inspiration and love and joy!
Partake of my Magic!

Close your eyes, and place your hands over your solar plexus.
Feel that flame within you; and breathe into it.
And now my greater Fire surrounds you – my Goddess Fire,
The Fire of Purification that burns away all dross.
Let down your barriers and let my Fire enter you,
Let it merge with your inner flame.
And it burns away all your self doubt, your fear,
Out-moded habits of thought and action,
All unnecessary limitations.
See them turn to fine ash and whirl away
In the up-draught of my Fire.

Place now your hands upon your heart centre,
The centre from which you give out to others.
Feel the creative fire, the love, the joy,
The enthusiasm, the lust for life,
That are the birthright of your lion-nature.
Glory in your lion-nature – it is YOU!

Now open your eyes and give the lion-power out to everyone.
And give each of your neighbours a hug!

Sekhmet picks up the red candle from the Altar and walks forward to centre of the room then says:

And now celebrate my magic with a spiral dance!

Spiral Dance with drumming. Lead the dance around Sekhmet, spiralling in and then out again.

SEKHMET: Bring wine that my lion-people may drink
And their hearts be joyous.

The Four Quarter Officers bring chalices of wine to Sekhmet who says:

I bless this wine that your lion-natures may be free
And full of wisdom and courage.
Drink and rejoice!

Wine is taken round to all. Optional gentle drumming or music.

SEKHMET: Now I must return to my wild places. My blessing shall remain within you as an inner flame of strength and courage. Keep burning and ever bright the Fire of your True Will. Hail and Farewell.

Bell.

The Priest of Sekhmet places the cloak around Sekhmet and she retires.

The Quarter Officers form a circle facing out to the Quarters.

WEST: Gentle Hathor, Lady of the Portal,
We thank thee for guarding the Western Quarter,
And do now bid thee, Hail and farewell.

Bell.

SOUTH: Horus, Lord of the Zenith and Hawk of Ra,
We thank thee for guarding the Southern Quarter,
And do now bid thee, Hail and Farewell.

Bell.

EAST: Ihy, Lord of the Dawn, child of the Sun,
We thank thee for guarding the Eastern Quarter,
And do now bid thee, Hail and Farewell.

Bell.

NORTH: Nut, Lady of the Stars,
Whose body encircles the universe,
We thank thee for guarding the Northern Quarter,
And do now bid thee, Hail and Farewell.

Bell.

NARRATOR: The rite is ended.
Merry meet and merry part, and merry meet again!

Allow time for socialising and feasting.

FIRE PATHWORKING

This pathworking is also contained in the Sekhmet Midsummer Ritual, but as it is an important one in the context of using the elemental archetypes to work on psychological themes, it is reproduced here, without the added Egyptian imagery, so that it can be used purely as a pathworking exercise.

Spoken by the Guide:

Now let your mind dwell on the subject of the element of fire, how you feel about the element of fire and its qualities. Is your immediate feeling that fire is strong, or weak, or just right in your nature? ....

Imagine a really fiery person, maybe somebody you know or just an imaginary person. How do you feel when you meet a really fiery person? What tends to be your first reaction? ....

How do you feel about some aspects of your own fiery nature? If you become angry, if somebody makes you feel really angry, how does that make you feel? Do you feel exhilarated, or embarrassed, or frightened, or what? How do you feel when you are angry? Some people feel really upset when they get angry ....

How would you assess your energy levels as a whole? Sometimes we feel tired and down and sometimes we feel energetic or up. Overall do you feel you have the energy and enthusiasm you would like to have? Is it free? Do you feel it is inhibited, or what? ....

Overall do you feel that your will is weak, or strong? Do you find yourself plagued by indecision and problems with working out priorities, or do you feel that you make up your mind quickly, knowing what to do? ....

Now sink down deep within yourself. Don't forget to breathe. Imagine that you are sinking down deep within your own inner darkness, down and down into a state of deep relaxation, so you are gently floating down a deep hole to the bottom of your being. In the darkness you see a tiny red glow. This is the ember of your true will and breathe deep down into that ember, letting your breath fan it into life. See that ember growing more strongly, becoming more orangey, brighter, bigger and bursting into a beautiful flame within you: the bright flame of your true will .... This is the source of your energy for action and creativity, this deep, deep place within you where you can always find, in the lowest moments, that ember and breathe into it, fan it into life and find that your energy level rises, your sense of purpose improves, priorities fall into place and you have the energy and sense of direction to move forward.

So with that newfound energy imagine that you are coming through a village to a very important person who lives in that village, which is the blacksmith, and his forge is there and you ask him a very important request: that you yourself can fashion the spear of your will at his forge and he will show you how to do it if you need help. You choose a length of iron rod and you put the fuel of earth onto the fire of the forge and then you take the bellows of air and blow the fire into a blaze until it is really white hot in the centre. Beside you is a trough of cold water. You thrust your length of iron rod into the fire and with a big set of pincers you turn it and thrust it deeper if need be, until the end of your rod is gleaming and hot, red and then brighter and brighter until it is almost at the point of melting. You take it out and hammer it on the forge into shape, plunge it into the water to cool and three times you do this. You heat it to incandescence, beat it into shape and temper it in the water until it is sharp and bright and strong and true ....

You thank the blacksmith for his guidance and help and the courtesy of using his forge and, taking your spear in your hand, you go forth feeling, even with it just in your hand, a sense of strength and purpose.

You see before you a path that leads amongst trees. With your spear held firmly in your hand, and courage and determination in your heart, you follow the path into the trees finding yourself entering a dark, deep forest. It is so dark in there that you can hardly see anything, but you know you must press on because there is something very important here that you have to do, that your will will not be fully your own and fully aligned with your purpose and your life until you have dealt with what you have to deal with in this deep, dark forest.

You hear now a snuffling and a crashing and a roaring. There is some great beast in this forest and you know you must face this beast and the beast is searching for you. Now it is coming closer, that roaring and trampling, breaking of branches of bushes and trees, as this great snuffling, roaring, slathering beast comes for you. This is all that you fear most, all that is overwhelming and disempowering. So take your spear and with all your will and determination fight that creature, smite it with the spear of your will and when it rears up ready to grab you and grasp you in its jaws, you drive the spear of your will into its heart and in that instant it bursts into flame, it combusts, and that fire is all around you. Open yourself to it. Absorb the life energy of that monster. Let it flow into you, for it is your own energy that you have projected out into the monster. It is yours by right. Take that energy, feel yourself being empowered with all those qualities that you feared in other people. They are there available for you....

The fire is fully absorbed within yourself and the darkness rolls away as the sun rises on a new day. The forest vanishes and you are strong and whole, with all those fiery powers you gave away to others back within yourself, yours to use as you need.

SPECIAL PLACE PATHWORKING (WATER) AND TEMPLE OF APHRODITE PATHWORKING

Spoken by the Guide:

Imagine now that you're going to your own secret place. That place that only you can find. Only you know that secret pathway to it and only you know how to make the sign, or utter the word, that opens the door. So imagine now you are coming to your own secret special place .... Make the sign, or say the word, or whatever, that allows you to enter and make the place just as you want it to be. It can be a place out of doors, or a little building, or a big building, a secret room. It is your special place where you can feel completely secure, completely at peace, where you can be completely yourself. In this special place you can explore your own inner nature and today it is your watery nature that you are going to explore, your own emotional nature, thinking out what are your strengths and your weaknesses in that area, in which areas of your life is the watery element too strong, or too weak, or a bit unbalanced. Take a few minutes to explore and you may find that your weaknesses are the flipside of your strengths, that they somehow go together, that they are your strengths taken too far, or out of context ....

Be back within your own special place and imagine that in it is a source of pure spring water and beside it is a beautiful blue chalice. You fill the chalice with the spring water and slowly drink it, feeling that you are taking it in you, the pure element of water and perfect equilibrium. Feel it cleansing you and balancing your emotional nature ....

The pathworking journey now continues on to visit the Temple of Aphrodite, a Goddess who helps us understand our emotional nature. However, you could do the two pathworkings separately and develop the first one more deeply.

Temple of Aphrodite Pathworking

Spoken by the Guide:

Now imagine that you are on a seashore and a little way from the shore you see a little island ....

There seems to be a little bit of sand that runs towards it but then disappears under the waves. This little island looks very enticing and beautiful. The air is warm and you walk along the little bit of sand until your feet are covered with water and you think maybe you can just walk across to the island, but when you are about halfway there you find yourself getting out of your depth and you have to give yourself to the element of water and let yourself float. Swim gently to the island ....

Now you are reaching the shore of the little island, beautiful white sand. Feel it under your feet as you wade out from the water onto the shore. It is evening and the sun is low in the sky and golden light flows around you. The little island is covered with elegant, graceful trees and flowering shrubs and ahead of you is a little white sandy path leading into the wood and you follow this path, breathing deeply the beautiful scented air from the fragrant shrubs around ....

Now the path rises. You are going uphill, up and up and up, becoming more deeply relaxed as you go up and up. You hear the buzz of insects, the song of birds and smell the lovely scents around you, enjoying the golden dappled sunlight as it slants low through the trees.

Now you are reaching the summit. The trees and shrubs thin and as you step out from among them you see on the summit a little white temple. It is circular. It has no walls, just seven pillars on a marble floor holding up a little domed roof.

You find coming up beside you a companion, someone you know: a friend, a relative, a colleague, a child or a parent, somebody that you have dealings with, maybe problems with, even if it is only sometimes, maybe somebody you love very dearly. It is someone with whom you have a significant relationship. The sun is sinking low in the west and you sit with your companion where you can watch the sunset. Review your relationship with that person. What happens when you get angry, or when they get angry? Are there things you feel resentment about, or even fear? We always have a longing to return to peace and love and easy friendly companionship, but anger and jealousy are also part of our nature and every relationship is dynamic, moving and changing, going through different phases and different moods. So just spend a little while exploring that relationship ....

As the sun sinks and darkness gathers, we see the planet Venus rising in the western sky and we know that now is the time to enter the little temple with our companion, bringing the contradictions of our emotional nature to the Goddess of love and beauty ....

We invoke the Goddess Aphrodite to enter her temple bearing her lamp:

> Hail Aphrodite, lady of love and delight, who art throned amid the Cyprus groves on the shore of the great sea. From the lamp in thy right hand pour shafts of light, pearly and emerald green. Thou art girdled with roses and emeralds, fire opal and lapis lazuli. Thy voice is the music of doves, the breath of ecstasy. Put forth the magic and the mystery of thy beauty. Infuse all creatures with thy subtle allure to seduce, to intoxicate, to fascinate the soul. Display by concealment, initiate by mystification. Bring us through delicacy to rapture and scented sleep. Wherever nerve ends sharpen to the kiss of sense, wherever eyes flash to sudden awareness at the promise of love, wherever the soft, the warm and the fragrant seduce us from crueller paths, there falls thy light. By the marriage of spirit and flesh,

> by the breath of innocence, by the delicacy of subtlety, by the self-transcendence of wantonness, by the soft caress of the dove and the sharp caress of the serpent, I call upon thee to be with us.

The star seems to be a lamp in her hand as the Goddess appears in her temple and let the light of her wisdom help you to understand your emotional nature, to accept its contradictions, its stresses and negatives, knowing that they serve a purpose and can be understood and let go of so that we can have love and joy in our hearts and equilibrium ....

Turn to your companion and see all their good qualities. Let go of being judgmental, let go of any anger or resentment. See the divine spark within them and feel the power and wisdom of the Goddess building up, nourishing and blessing your relationships ....

Now the presence of the Goddess fades. You see a beautiful star in the western sky. Thank the Goddess for her gifts and wisdom and blessing and then, hand in hand, you and your companion leave the temple and find your way in the darkness through the wood. The little white path is just dimly visible by the light of the stars. There is a little boat to carry you back to the shore and there you say goodbye to your companion and be ready to return to this room as I count from twenty to one. Let the seashore fade away and the night sky fade away and return to the here and now. Twenty .... nineteen .... eighteen .... seventeen .... sixteen .... fifteen .... fourteen .... thirteen .... twelve .... eleven .... ten .... halfway back, take some deep breaths .... nine .... eight .... seven .... six .... feel your hands and feet .... five .... four .... three .... two .... one .... and open your eyes.

LAMMAS RITUAL

This is an example of a 'ritual by numbers'. Everyone in the group is assigned a number and then reads/performs whatever is next to that number. It is quite a simple way to organise a ritual, while making sure every part is taken. If the group is small, you may need to take more than one number. Here there are 20 spoken parts.

Requirements:

- Altar with candles and harvest decorations (corn, vegetables, fruit, etc)
- Large candle on Altar
- Incense (preferably herbs/resins to be burned on a charcoal block)
- Incense holder and charcoal
- Sheaf of corn
- Bowl of edible seeds
- Pots of earth if no access to garden
- Bell
- Cauldron or dish containing candles
- Bread and wine

Begin by casting the circle and calling the elemental powers.

1. "This is the wake of Lugh, the Sun King, who starts to fade as the year wanes. Already the days grow shorter and we know that Summer will pass."

2. "But he is still strong and warm, supporting his consort, our Mother the Earth, as she brings forth her bounty. All around us are the flowers, the fruits and the seeds that come from their love and their union."

3. "But he is also the Corn King who gives his life to nourish us and to replenish our stores. He is the sacrifice that we may live."

4. And She is also the Reaper, the implacable one, who teaches us that life feeds on life. And this truth we must accept and acknowledge.

5. "For we shall all be harvested by the reaping scythe of Time and return to the Earth to feed new life."

Pause.

6. "We stand now between hope and fear, awaiting the harvest. Light a candle to the Sun King that his strength may continue, even as his power starts to wane." *[Lights candle]*

7. "I burn sweet herbs to the Earth Mother that warm sun and sweet breezes may ripen her gifts of corn and fruit." *[Lights incense[6]]*

8. Picks up sheaf of corn and waves it gently to and fro.

ALL CHANT: "Spirits of the wind, wave gently;
The barley, the oats and the rye;
Sighing a song through the whispering wheat
Of the harvest that now draws nigh."
[Repeat]

8. The sheaf of corn is gently lowered and placed on the Altar.

Pause

9. "The Corn King dies and the harvest is gathered in. He goes willingly for he understands the Mystery that in death he re-enters the womb of the Great Mother and is reborn."

---

[6] If using incense on charcoal, it is best to light the charcoal block before beginning the ritual as it will take a while to be ready, ie when most of the block has gone grey/white.

10. "From his death, we are given nourishment of body and spirit, and also the seed of new life. Take now two seeds and hold them in your hand." *[Pass bowl of seeds.]*

11. "You hold two seeds in the palm of your hand, each one a miracle containing the germ of new life. One seed represents the first fruits of your own individual harvest. In a moment, we shall go into the garden[1] and eat that seed, being aware of what we have recently harvested in our lives, and giving thanks to our Gods of Earth and Sun."

12. "The other seed represents your future plans and goals. When you are in the garden and have eaten your first seed, meditate upon your main goal for the coming year; formulate it clearly in your mind; and then, with firm intention, plant the seed in the earth."

13. "A bell will recall you to this room. As you enter, you will pass a small fire. Put into that purifying fire all that holds you back from reaching your goals - your fear, your doubt, your anger, your rigidities, your inertia. Then shall your harvest be truly magnificent!"

14. *[Ring bell]* "Go now into the garden and be with the Gods."[7]

While the group are in the garden, or meditating on their seeds, the session leader should light candles in the cauldron or dish.

When all are reassembled:

15. "Let us now celebrate the harvest of the first fruits, sharing them in true communion with each other and with our Gods."

---

[7] If you do not have access to a garden, the group could place the seeds in pots of soil.

16. *[Takes up bread]* "The Lord and Lady bless this bread which we eat on behalf of all peoples, that all may be fed." *[Take some bread and pass it to the next person]*

17. "This is the Bread of Immortality. Though everyone must die, by this nourishment we share rebirth." *[Take some bread and pass it to next person.]*

18. "From moment to moment, from year to year, and from life to life, we die and are reborn, transformed!" *[Take some bread and pass it to next person.]*

19. "We are not separate, nor ever finally alone; for this, the Bread of Life, is the bread of communion and we are all one with the Gods." *[Take some bread and pass it to next person.]*

Each remaining person now takes some bread, saying:

"We are all one with the Gods."

20. *[Takes up the wine]* "The Lord and Lady bless this wine, made of the fruits of previous harvests, fermented and matured in a wonderful alchemical process of transmutation, that it may cheer our spirits and hearten us to new endeavours. Drink and rejoice!" *[Drink some wine and pass it to next person.]*

Each raise the cup in salutation and drink. Spontaneous words or toasts may be spoken.

ALL CHANT: "We all come from the Goddess
And to her we shall return ...."[8]

Elements thanked and circle opened.

---

[8] For full lyrics see online sources.

LUGHNASADH RITUAL

The Wake of Lugh the Sun King

Requirements:

- Altar with candles and seasonal decorations (corn, fruit, vegetables, etc)
- Incense and charcoal block
- Sickle
- Bread and goblets of beer

Roles:

- Narrator
- Circle Caster
- Four Quarter Officers
- Sun King Invoker (Invoker 1 in ritual)
- Sun King/God
- Goddess Invoker (Invoker 2 in ritual)
- Earth Mother/Goddess

Cast the circle and invoke the four Quarters.

NARRATOR: This is the wake of Lugh, the Sun King, who starts to fade as the year wanes. We know that Summer will pass yet he is still strong, and his warmth supports his consort, the Earth Mother, as she brings forth her bounty. All around us are the flowers, the fruits and the seeds that come from their love and their union. But he is also the Corn King who gives his life to nourish us and to replenish our stores. He sacrifices himself that we may live. And the Earth Mother is also the Reaper, the implacable one, who teaches us that Life feeds on Life. This is her mystery and her truth that we must accept for we shall all return to the Earth to feed new life.

The Sun King Invoker lights a candle to the Sun King, then invokes:

INVOKER 1: By the beauty of this fertile land,
By the rich dark soil of our Sacred Mother,
By seed and bud, by root and grain,
By the power of the Sun, the giver of Life,
I call to the God of the golden corn.
Come, be here, Lugh the Sun King!
Bring your presence to our ritual;
Pour your warmth and your strength
Into your priest and servant!
Bring your life to nourish us so that we may see
The magic of transformation unfold
And feel the golden pulsing of the sunlit
Wheel of Life within us!

The Goddess Invoker puts incense on the burner.

INVOKER 2: I burn sweet herbs to the Earth Mother
That warm sun and gentle breezes may ripen the corn.
[Censes Goddess]
Great Mother, by green fields and tall trees, we invoke thee;
By the golden grain and the fruit ripening on the bough, we invoke thee;
By Life and Death and Love and Liberty, we invoke thee.

The Goddess Invoker draws down the power, then takes up the sickle and kneels at the feet of the Goddess, saying:

Thou art the abundance of Life, ever renewing;
Yet art thou also the Reaper, the Implacable One,
Who teaches us that Life feeds on Life.
We must all in due time bow our necks to thy sickle.

The Goddess Invoker presents the sickle to the Goddess.
The Narrator takes up the sheaf of corn and waves it gently.

NARRATOR: We are all as plants in a field of corn;
We are all one with the Corn King
Awaiting the harvest.

ALL CHANT: Spirits of the Wind, wave gently,
The barley, the oats and the rye,
Sighing a song through the whispering wheat,
Of the harvest that now draws nigh.
[Repeat]

The Goddess raises the sickle and says:

GODDESS: I am the Great Mother of All and Goddess of Nature.
Green and gold and russet are my colours
And my bounty is poured out upon the Earth.
In me are all the creatures of Earth,
Even you, my children.
I hold in my hand the apple,
Symbol of the mystery of Life and Death.
Within it is the seed of eternal life.
Hold your hands out to me and I will give you treasure;
Hold your heart out to me and I will give you love.
Give me your innermost self,
And I will raise you to the stars.
Give me your masks and your fears,
Your anger and your tears;
Give me the dirt of your life and the death of your hopes,
And I will take your all, and your nothing.
And in return I will give you my Truth, and my Joy,

My peace, and my wisdom,
That you may find within you,
The balance of the Dark and the Light,
And dance the dance of Life in perfect equilibrium.

GOD: I am Lugh,the Shining One.
My powers now are starting to wane
And already the days grow shorter.
Yet am I still strong and bright.
I bring light and warmth and love
To my Consort, the Earth Mother,
Ripening the grain that stands so tall in the fields.
I am also the Corn King, the Life within the seed.

He kneels before the Goddess, then continues:

I give my life willingly,
That there may be abundance
For all the children of the Great Mother,
And seed for next year's harvest.

The Goddess makes a scything motion with the sickle and the God falls to the ground. The Goddess then goes around the room scything everyone down.

Now the Narrator leads a pathworking/meditation on the theme of harvest and planting new seeds. Guide the participants through thinking about what they have accomplished in the past year, what they are grateful for, which plans they had at the start of the year have come to fruition, which have not and why. Then encourage people to visualise which new ideas and plans are forming, which seeds will they plant in the coming year. When the pathworking/meditation is complete, the Goddess, as Harvest Mother, stands and says:

GODDESS: Come forward and partake of my bounty
Which I give freely to you.

The four Quarter Officers take up baskets of bread and kneel before the Goddess. The Goddess blesses the bread (use your own words) and charges us all to take in nourishment in a spirit of true fellowship and communion. She instructs people to say, as they pass the bread to the next person, "May you never know hunger." The bread is then passed around.

The four Quarter Officers then take up goblets of beer and kneel before the God. The God blesses the beer, this wonderful transmutation of last year's harvest (use your own words). He charges us to drink in the spirit of sharing and comradeship in new endeavours. He instructs people to say, as they pass the beer to the next person, "May you never thirst." The beer is then passed around.

INVOKER 2: Great Mother, we thank thee for the bounty of the harvest, and for teaching us the mystery of Life and Death and Renewal. And we ask thee now to depart from thy priestess that she may resume her human life.

INVOKER 1: Lugh, the Sun King, we honour you,
For by giving your life to us we are renewed deep within,
Inspired by your golden light,
Open to the magic of transformation.
We honour your sacrifice and thank you for your gifts,
And we ask you now to depart from your priest
That he may resume his human life."

The Quarters are thanked and closed. The circle is opened, finishing with the words:

Merry Meet, Merry Part and Merry Meet Again!

Allow time for socialising and feasting.

FULL MOON PATHWORKING, INVOCATION WRITING AND RITUAL

Requirements:

- Candles and incense
- Chalice of water
- Paper and pens
- Wine to share

Spoken by the Guide:

Close your eyes and relax .... Become aware of the earth beneath us and of gravity, our connectedness to and reliance on it .... Become aware of earth's connectedness to and reliance on the sun .... Now remember that a large proportion of the earth and of our own bodies is made up of water. Water and the moon are inextricably linked through the tides. For us the moon represents the ebb and flow of life, our emotions and deep wisdom. It is said that the influence of the moon has been vital in allowing life to endure so magnificently on our planet. Feel the power of the moon at its fullest, aligned with the earth and sun, balancing and focusing powerful forces onto the earth and to us. Take time to dwell on these forces, feeling their power enhancing your magical nature, your inner energy ....

Now imagine you are on your way to your secret place, following a moonlit path, you feel the night all around you .... Sit in the light of the full moon. The full moon illumines the darkness when the sun's light is absent, but it is as though it reveals a different aspect of reality: there are no colours, it is a magical and mysterious world, unfamiliar yet fascinating. It enables us to see things in a different light from the everyday; a more magical way ....

We can think of our lives as a journey; the path we are following is sometimes difficult, sometimes easy. Sometimes the way ahead is obscured by obstacles or shrouded in mist, or there are bewildering divisions of the way. Sometimes the path we are on seems to suddenly crumble beneath our feet, or disappear into a morass, or become too narrow to continue on. We have to change direction, or find another way, or simply push on through.

So now see your path, your current life in the moonlight. Find out what is blocked, or what is the difficulty – is it too steep, crumbly, muddy, rocky, misty ....? Pinpoint the nature of your difficulty – this can be as an image or a realisation of something specific .... Sitting in the moonlight feel intensely your desire to find your way through and write an invocation to the Moon Goddess asking for her help in moving along your path.

Instruct the attendees to open their eyes when they are ready and write down their invocations. Allow some time for this. When all are ready, ask the group to stand in a circle. If you wish, open the circle and call on the quarters.

Now let us hold hands and tune into the power of the full moon .... Let us take turns in reading out our invocations. When you are done, place it on the altar.

Allow time for invocations to be read aloud.

Now sit comfortably and close your eyes. Relax deeper and deeper but remain mentally focused on your path .... You are each one alone, on your individual path and you come to the condition that obstructs you, whether it be mist, boulders, steepness or mud. Sink down deeply within, to the deepest level of being, seek the Moon Goddess .... Feel her presence, see the radiance of her face shining in the darkness. And as her light intensifies, see your path, see how you can progress, how you can move forward; see it as an image and let come into your mind what you need to do .... You have been alone. Now come to a place bathed in moonlight, surrounded by cypress trees. In the centre there is a small pool of water. Magically this place is this room. Now all stand

and formulate in your minds the strong intention to overcome obstruction, obscurity and difficulty on your path and to progress. Draw down the power of the moon into the chalice of water ....

Here the Guide either holds the chalice of water out or places it in the centre of the circle while the group focuses on drawing the moon's energy down into it. After a pause, touch water from the chalice to the forehead of each attendee saying:

> May the Lady of the Moon guide and empower you
> on your path.

Bless the wine and pass it around saying:

> Receive the gift of inspiration and courage.

Hold hands in a circle and allow the energy to sink back into the earth. Then, when ready, close the circle.

WILD MAN PATHWORKING

Spoken by the Guide:

Imagine you are sitting in your special temple, feeling very calm and relaxed. Breathe deeply and allow your mind to become calm .... You become aware that you are wearing a beautiful warm cloak, embroidered with Celtic knotwork designs. You wrap it close around yourself and feel comforted. See before you a bowl with a flat base of shiny, polished bronze. Take this and step out through the gates of your temple ....

You find yourself on the outskirts of a forest. The forest is made up of ancient oaks, mighty beeches, yew trees, silver birch, holly, elder and elm. You feel the ancient power of the trees all around you. A homing woodsman warns us not to go into the forest; it is the haunt of Cerridwen, as well as boar, bears and wolves. But we have an inner restlessness that seeks the wild places. You begin to follow a path into the forest. As you walk deeper in, the light becomes dimmer, the trees pressing more closely around you. It is bewildering, you begin to lose your sense of direction and are unsettled by distracting and alarming noises, the source of which you cannot trace. You lose any companions you were with and sit down under a tree.

You begin to have an unsettling feeling that you are being watched. Take the bowl and turn it over, looking into your own face in the polished bronze mirror base. You see glimpses of leaves and eyes. You turn but see nothing. Place the bowl on the ground and take some time to tune into the forest, the trees, the ground, the wonder of the place so full of life, from the majestic stag, to the tiny beetles in the tree bark .... Begin to dance, aware that you are not alone, another is dancing, a whirling being of leaves and energy, life force of the forest, life force of nature, wild and free. A great wind roars through the forest as you dance, all inhibitions forgotten. Feel the life of this forest over the centuries – it experiences storms that devastate, floods, snows and blazing sun. Feel the timelessness of the ancient forest and dance until you feel truly at one with it .... When your whirling dance has ended, you fall forward and see a Wild Man dancing with a Wild Woman, swirling in the leaves and fading sunlight, dancing in endless love. They look at you, smiling, and then she leaps onto her mare and he onto a stag. With one united, wild cry, they ride off into the forest. You look around you and see your bowl is full of gifts: herbs for healing, berries for nourishment, mushrooms that bring visions.

Send out a silent thanks to the Wild Lovers for your gifts and begin to walk back down the path. As you get closer and closer to the edge of the forest, take some deep breaths and become more and more aware of your body, making some little movements to bring yourself back. Become aware of the room we are in. Take some more deep breaths and slowly open your eyes and return to the here and now.

AUTUMN

PSYCHIC PLANE DIVINATION AND PATHWORKING

For this pathworking you will need a deck of Tarot cards, shuffled and spread out in the centre of the room. Begin with the usual relaxation exercises.

Spoken by the Guide:

So keeping yourself firmly at the psychic level, let feelings arise within you about your life. What is it you yearn for? What change or development would you like in your life? It might be an inner change, or a change within your circumstances, or relationships, or whatever. Whatever you yearn for, let it arise in your mind ....

Staying firmly at that psychic level, you are going to take a Tarot card from the floor; a card that is going to represent for you the blocks, or binds, or attitudes, or things in your life that prevent or hold you back from what it is you are trying to reach, that inner yearning. When you are ready, take a Tarot card with the intention that it will reveal to you the blocks, or binds, whatever it is that holds you back .... Now look at that card, take in its image. If necessary take yourself further down to the psychic level ....

Then with your eyes closed let an entity emerge, an entity that may be a figure in the card, or an object that is somehow alive, or it might be a mythical beast, or an animal, or even somebody you know. That person, or that entity, represents something within you, or within your life that holds you back .... Imagine that you are that person, that entity, and tell yourself what it is that holds you back, in what way this entity holds you back .... See it as separate from you and put that card down beside you somewhere.

Now take another card and this card will represent the forces that can help you bring about change. Again look at the card, let its image sink into your mind, knowing that this will give you insight into where you can find the power and energy you need, or the action you need to take ....

Then let your eyes close, make sure you are deep at the psychic level and let an entity emerge from that card, and become that entity, feel yourself strong and wise, harnessing the power of that entity. Speak to yourself as that entity; as that entity that is your empowering entity, speak to the entity that holds you back and see how the other entity replies and feel those two forces within you, the one that is reaching forward and the one that holds you back, force and counter-force, both aspects of you, complementary inner forces which both have their point of view, their value, but which need to reach some sort of compromise, some sort of collaboration ....

Concentrate now again on that yearning to change, that yearning for growth, development, a change in circumstances, or whatever it is ....

Call in your heart on the Goddess of wisdom and transformation; Isis, Sophia or Brigid, whatever is your favourite Goddess who represents wisdom and transformation. Let her speak within your inner mind, showing you how to move forward, how to bring into harmony these two forces within you, how to reconcile them .... Feel her transformative power within you, feel the bonds that bind you and hold you back falling away. Feel yourself knowing the value and the limitations of that aspect of you. See the entity that opposes you withering, changing, transforming .... Let the Goddess of wisdom and transformation and the entity which shows you the way forward tell you some practical things that you can do to grow and expand your life and feel the blessing of the Goddess filling you with power and wisdom and love. Feel the innermost part of your being changing, rearranging itself, transforming, reconciling the conflicting forces, finding ways to give each their due, but to find that pathway that your feet tread in your own life ....

Then thank the Goddess for her wisdom and the entities of the cards for revealing themselves to you and let them sink back within your inner mind, your inner heart, as they are part of you ....

Then as I count from ten to six, come up from the psychic plane. Ten .... nine .... eight .... seven .... six .... And as I count from five to one, return from that deep relaxation, five .... four .... three .... two .... one .... Have a stretch, wiggle your toes about, rub your hands, feel the ground beneath you, stamp your feet.

VIRGO-LIBRA ASTROLOGY SESSION

This is a session written and conducted by Lisa Stockley, long-term attendee of Pagan Pathfinders. It is an excellent example of a session which begins with a talk, followed by a pathworking. This was a common format in PP.
Lisa began with some Yoga to start, to bring body and mind together, a key goal for Virgo, and to bring the self into Libran balance. The poses practised were: standing stretch, tree pose, cross-legged twist and forward bend. The group held each pose for several breaths.

Spoken by the Guide:

The autumn equinox marks the cusp between Virgo and Libra, when the sun moves from the sign of Virgo to the sign of Libra. The two signs mark the turning point of the zodiac. As the wheel of the year moves from light to dark at the autumn equinox, the wheel of the zodiac moves from the development of the individual to the meeting with the other and the outside world. Virgo is the last sign relating to individual development and growth, and in Libra we meet the other for the first time and seek relationships and partnerships. In Virgo we refine the ego self, and in Libra we move beyond it. The cusp of Virgo and Libra is where we move beyond our individual reality to become part of the wider social order, part of a relationship. Whilst superficially these two signs are very different - Virgo discriminates between and understands all parts of the self and of the world, whereas Libra focuses on the harmonious relationship between them – both are concerned with synthesis, but Virgo is realistic whereas Libra is idealistic.

Virgo is ruled by Mercury and is the sign of mutable earth. This means that Virgo energy doesn't have the solidity of other earth signs, the earth influence is more subtle. Being Mercury ruled and mutable makes Virgo the airy part of earth, so a strong practical sense (earth) is applied to information (air). Virgo gathers information and seeks a way to use it. Virgo keywords are perfection, analysis, detail, critical sense. Virgo always asks, is this knowledge relevant, is it useful – unlike Mercury-ruled Gemini which likes knowledge for the sake of knowledge. Virgo can be seen as the introverted form of Mercury: classifying, discriminating, seeking inner order rather than looking outwards for knowledge. Virgo can come across as perfectionist, over-critical, usually because they are very critical of themselves. Virgo's opposite sign is Pisces, and those with strong Virgo energy often fear the chaos and loss of control of that sign so seek order, structure, a system, so that they know where they are.

Virgoans often have a preoccupation with health and physical body, wanting to refine and perfect it through diet and exercise. This is the body (earth) in service of mind (Mercury, air), and for many Virgoans the mind body spirit balance is key to their wellbeing. Virgo rules the bowels and digestive system, the process by which valuable matter is separated from waste matter. On a deeper level, this means a process of healing and synthesis, of knowing what is useful and what needs to be released (emotionally, physically, and spiritually).

Virgoans often have a gift for ritual, as ritual is really just sacred routine. Earth signs like routine, and the mutability gives flexibility and the ability to see the bigger picture. Indeed, Virgo may rely on ritual to keep emotional order, to keep the chaos and sensitivity of Pisces at bay.

For Virgo, work is a sacred practice, and the giving of unconditional service, of making a contribution to community. Virgo needs to be needed, to know their role within the group. The ecology movement often resonates strongly for Virgoans and indeed much of the modern ecology movement first came into being under the transformative Uranus-Pluto conjunction in Virgo in the 1960s.

The ideal for Virgo is discrimination combined with realism. Then we can work with Virgo energy towards the synthesis and integration of the individual self. Virgo refines and orders the experiences of the first five signs, in a process of alchemical transmutation and purification.

Libra is ruled by Venus and is the sign of cardinal air, symbolising the urge to initiate airy connections, with ideas and with other people. Libra is concerned with truth, beauty and goodness; indeed Libra is more perfectionist than Virgo in many ways, being idealistic air instead of realistic earth. Planets in Libra gain affinity for beauty and harmony, a grace in their form of expression. Indeed, Libra can be very surface aware, focused on image, appearance and style, which can sometimes lead to a superficial approach or a tendency to judge on appearances.

As the first sign of the second half of the zodiac, the meeting with the other, connection and relationship are crucial for Libra. Relationship is the first step out of individual ego, the connection we make with one another, individual/ego. Relationship can also be defined as the art of comparison, of differentiation, of making balanced and symmetrical patterns, and both Libra and Virgo are concerned with the making of patterns in different ways. Libra is the only zodiac sign not represented by an animal, reflecting Libran concerns with abstract ideas and aesthetics, and those with strong Libra energy may be more concerned with an ideal of love and relationship than the day to day reality of sharing life with another person. Libra is probably the most sociable sign of the zodiac, or rather the least comfortable with solitary life. Librans will often choose an unsatisfactory relationship over no relationship at all, and a key lesson for those with strong Libra energy is a process of accepting and knowing self through the accepting and knowing of others. In relationship we often find the shadow or projection of the unacceptable aspects of ourselves, and we need to seek inner union in order for the outer union to be genuine.

On a broader level, Libra has the power to create harmonious relationships between all disparate groups and all kinds of people, and they are the diplomats of the zodiac. They often have the art of persuading people to do what Libra wants to do whilst making them think that they wanted it all along, or that it was their idea. At times they may defer to others just to keep parity or express a point of view they disagree with simply so that there is a different view to balance if everyone agrees, as Libra is constantly searching for equilibrium and balance. They like to please and want to be liked and may get upset by arguments or conflict. Libra's strength is seeing other points of view, but they may find it difficult to make decisions because they can see both sides. Librans often take social injustice personally and will use their inner core of determination and resolve (Aries again) in their deep commitment to partnership and fair play.

Even if you don't have planets in either of these signs, they are part of your natal chart just as all the signs are, and we can work with these energies for personal growth as well as to navigate the seasonal transition.

Pathworking

Focus on your breath, without trying to change it, simply allowing it to settle into a quiet rhythm. See before you a door, picture it clearly in your mind .... Go through the door and you find yourself at the top of a spiral staircase. Go down the stairs and at the bottom you find another wooden door. Going through this second door, you come out in a long room, wood-paneled, with shelves and storage all around. Out of the many windows you can see gardens and fields, where corn and vegetables grow, and an orchard, with trees ripe with all kinds of fruit. In the middle of the room are lots of boxes, all piled up.

There's a box for each individual in the group, so first you need to find yours. Then find a quiet corner to see what's inside. Opening the box, you find aspects of yourself, the things that make you you. Take some time to examine them, to see what they are and how you connect to them. What state are they in – do they need tidying or finishing? What parts of you do the objects symbolise? Take time to make sure they are clean, complete. Arrange them so that related aspects of yourself or objects that symbolise them are close by. See how the different parts of you fit together ....

Next, you need to find out how these parts fit into the greater whole. Take your box around the room – are there spaces on shelves or in drawers where some of the objects should be filed? They are still yours, but now also part of a greater whole. Use these objects and your knowledge of what they symbolise to find out what service you need to give to the collective – maybe your role is to connect people, or to convey information, or to make or grow things for others to use. Walk around, inside or outside, talk to people you meet, until you figure out what your role is in the 'great work', how you fit into the bigger picture ....

Now it's time to leave. Thank any beings you have met for their help and make sure that your box is put away in its correct place ....

Leave through a door at the opposite end of the room to where you came in. Walking past the garden, orchard and fields, you find yourself walking through a wood. The leaves on the trees are starting to turn golden and red, and some have already fallen. You can feel an autumnal chill in the air as you walk ....

After a while you emerge into open countryside and in the distance you can see a large house. You walk towards it and as you do so, you realise that the area has been landscaped so that nature has been enhanced to look more harmonious. Getting closer to the house, you see soft honey-coloured stone and classical architecture. Going inside, you find that all the rooms are tastefully decorated and there is an atmosphere of peace. Somewhere you can hear a piano playing softly. You wander from room to room until you meet another being, someone that you don't immediately feel comfortable with. The person tells you that the two of you need to find common ground. Take some time to focus on your connection with that being, to try to understand the source of your discomfort. Make sure that you are honest and are not just agreeing with what they say to keep the peace ....

Work through your differences until you find the point where you can find agreement, or compromise, or at least agree to differ ....

And now it's time to come back. You find a spiral staircase in the corner of the house, climb back up until you come to the first door you stepped through. Come back through the door and into this room, to your body. Take some deep breaths to come fully back to the body .... And open your eyes when you are ready.

Discuss your experience and any insights received with a partner, or the rest of the group, or write about them in your journal.

AUTUMN EQUINOX RITUAL OUTLINE

This is an outline for a ritual to celebrate the Autumn Equinox, a time of balance, harvest, and also a time to mark the beginning of darker, more wintery days. The group could spend a session or two creating a ritual based around this outline. Perhaps do a pathworking on the God/Goddess in order to inspire invocation writing.

Requirements:

- Altar with candles and seasonal decoration, including apples
- Bell
- Wine and apples

Roles:

- Circle Caster
- Quarter Officers
- Priestess
- Priest
- Invokers
- Goddess
- God

1. The circle is cast and the Quarters called.

Bell.

2. PRIESTESS: Now is the time of balance
When Night and Day are equal.
Yet is this a time of change;
The great Wheel of the seasons

Turns and turns, and turns again.
The Lord of Light has lain long
With our Mother, the Earth,
And she has brought forth her bounty.

3. PRIEST: But now in this season
The power of Light begins to wane
And the Night waxes longer.
The Earth Mother clothes her limbs
In a glory of russet and gold
And the pale Sun kisses her tenderly.

4. PRIESTESS: At this time, the time of balance,
We rest from the labours of harvest.
Let us meditate on all that we have harvested;
All that we have achieved through our efforts,
Our dedication and our love;
And also the good fortune we have received
Through the grace of the Lady and the Lord.

5. Pathworking or meditation on harvest, our achievements in the year, gratitude.

Bell.

6. Invocation(s) of the Goddess – this could be one invocation, or many, preferably written and spoken by the group members, or use the following:

Lady of russet and gold,
Keeper of the mystery of life and death and rebirth,
Lady of apples and all fruitfulness –
Yet are you also the Reaper, Mistress of shadows.
We who are the children of the Great Mother

Call upon you to be with us tonight,
That we may receive your wisdom
and your blessing on our harvest.

7. Invocation(s) of the God – this could be one invocation, or many, preferably written and spoken by the group members, or use the following:

Lord of the Sun, Corn King,
Your heat is waning, your light diminishing.
Yet are you also still the consort of the Great Mother,
Lord of beasts and of the autumn storms.
We feel your power and strength in the rutting stag,
The wild wind, the tempestuous waves.
We call upon you to be with us tonight,
That we may receive your wisdom
and your blessing on our harvest.

8. The Goddess speaks.

9. The God speaks.

Bell.

10. The Priest presents the goblet of wine to the Goddess and God and asks for their blessing.

11. The Goddess and God each bless the wine with appropriate words.

12. PRIEST: Drink and give thanks. *[All drink]*

13. The Priestess presents the apples to the Goddess and God and asks for their blessing.

14. The Goddess and God each bless the apples with appropriate words.

15. PRIESTESS: Behold the mystery of Life and Death, and Renewal.
Eat and marvel!

16. The Priestess gives a piece of apple to each person.

17. All form a circle around the Goddess and the God, giving thanks and communing with them.

Bell.

18. The Priest and Priestess thank the Gods and ask them to depart.

19. Close the circle.

THE SLEEPER AWAKES PATHWORKING

Spoken by the Guide:

Imagine that you are going down a stone staircase and as you go down, step by step, you are becoming more deeply relaxed, and as you go down your sense of smell becomes more acute because you can smell the smell of damp stone and you can hear the noise of water. You go on down, the noise of water getting louder and you realise that you are coming down to the bottom step on the edge of a river ....

There is a boat moored and, eager to see where the boat takes you, you climb in and seat yourself and untie the rope that is keeping it moored, and the current takes the boat and carries it along the river. The river is overhung with willow trees so it is like you are in a green tunnel. It is very peaceful and relaxing. You don't feel at all afraid. The air is fresh ....

Now the trees are thinning out and you get a wider view of countryside, fields with big oak trees standing in them .... And now the countryside is getting wilder. There are no cultivated fields and any dwellings you see are of an ancient unfamiliar style, small, rough stones, fastened together with mud for mortar and thatched roofs with reeds.

Now the river is getting shallower and the current is taking you over to the far side, and the boat comes to rest and you find that you can climb out and tie the boat to a tree stump. You are in an ancient land, rolling hills around you. In the valleys you can see woods, but you are drawn to climb the hill before you.

You climb up and up. The sun is warm. You hear a lark singing and then you come to the top of the hill and it opens out to a flat area, and in the centre you see what look like some ancient standing stones. You walk over to them and find there four great standing stones that you pass between and find before you an ancient portal. It is a portal into an ancient megalithic tomb. You pause on the threshold because you can feel that this is a magical place and you look at the great stone to your right that forms the portal and you see strange patterns on it. Your gaze travels upwards. It is much taller than you are and you see above you, carved long ago into the stone, a face, and you see breasts below and realise that this is an ancient Goddess figure, that this is a sacred and holy place. You look at the pillar to the left and see there, high up, an antlered head and a bearded face, an ancient God.

You are drawn to enter and you feel your way in the gathering gloom inside. As you pass down what seems like a very narrow and rather low passageway, you can feel the roof just above your head. You see ahead of you a very faint glow. You are drawn towards that glow. As you walk along you notice that there are small chambers on either side, feel the entrances .... You can't see, it is all dark within, but you want to get to the end to where that glow is. You go on along the passage and now you enter the end chamber. It is circular in shape with a vaulted roof and in the centre is a long slab of stone, and on the slab lies a figure. Is this a burial chamber? Is this the body of some ancient chieftain?

You come closer and realise that this is a live body, it is someone who is asleep. You hold your breath looking at this person, this sleeper, in what seems to be a magical sleep. There is a nobility about this figure. Is it a male body asleep there, or a female? How are they dressed? You feel a great yearning for this person to awake. You feel you need to talk to this person to know more about them, who they are, where they come from. You know that this person is very important to you.

As you gaze at the person's face, their eyelids flicker and the eyes open. You look into those eyes and there is somehow instant recognition between you both. Now you recognise that this person is an important part of you, a part of you that has been asleep, and the person sits up, takes your hands and gazes deep into your eyes as you greet each other and smile at each other. There is great joy in this meeting. Now you must ask this person, this person that is part of you, to tell you about themselves, what part of you has been asleep and why, and what will this person bring to you when you join together and have that person with you as part of you? What new possibilities will there be for you? So take a few minutes to converse with that person, that being, that part of you. Just let come into your mind the conversation, the words, the images, the ideas ....

Then, when you are ready thank the person for their wisdom and let them sink back within your inner mind, your inner heart, as they are part of you ....

Then as I count from ten to one, come up from the psychic plane. Ten .... nine .... eight .... seven .... six .... As I count from five to one, return from that deep relaxation. Five .... four .... three .... two .... one .... Have a stretch, wiggle your toes about, rub your hands, feel the ground beneath you, stamp your feet and open your eyes.

SAMHAIN RITUAL

Requirements:

- Candles and incense
- Altar with seasonal decorations
- Bell
- Pomegranate
- Apple
- Knife
- Goblet of wine and food to share, such as bread or cakes

Roles:

- Narrator
- Quarter Officers
- Circle Caster
- Priest
- Priestess
- Alternatively, double up narrator/priest, or narrator/priestess

Begin by invoking the Elements at each Quarter and casting the circle.

NARRATOR: This is the night when the veil that divides the worlds is thin. It is the New Year in the time of the year's death, when the harvest is gathered in and the fields lie fallow. For tonight the king of the waning year has sailed over the sunless sea that is the womb of the Mother, and steps ashore on the Shining Isle, the Land of Youth. The gates of life and death are opened, the dead are near us, and to the living is revealed the Mystery: that every ending is but a new beginning. We meet out of time, between the worlds, to greet the Lord of Death, who is Lord of Life. We will go on a journey to meet him.

ALL: It is the great cold of the night; it is the dark.

One by one participants are taken from the circle to board an imaginary boat; the first is the prow and others form a triangular wedge behind. Each person is given one of these phrases to repeat in a chant:

Sailing the waves/Weaving/Silver ship/Sunless sea

NARRATOR: *[Chanting over group chant]*
Weaving the silver ship's thread of the milk-white sail,
The waves of the sunless sea are weaving ....
[Changing chant]
Pale grey warrior, ghostly quest;
Prince of Twilight, sailing west ....

All take up this chant for a suitable period, then the Narrator says:

NARRATOR: We are in sight of the far shore
See the light on the waves, a track to follow.
Step into the surf, step ashore.
Cast off your bonds and be free!
For here there is no binding.
Cast off the veils that cloud your sight!
For here all eyes are opened!
You warriors, here your battles are over.
You workers, here your tasks are done.
You who have been hurt, here find healing.
You who are weary, here find rest.
You who are old, here grow young again.
For this is the Land of Youth, the Shining Land.
Here woods never fail,
Here there is a tree, the heart of light.

Here there is a well of silence.
Sink down, sink to sleep beside that deep green well.
Sink down .... sleep deep .... sink deeper ....
And follow him.

All sink down into meditation.

He is here!
The comforter, the consoler.
Heart's ease and sorrow's end.
He is the guide, the gate is open.
He is the guide, the way is clear.
He is the guide, death is no barrier.
For he is the Lord of the Dance of Shadows,
King of the Realm of Dreams.
Offer your life, your strengths and weaknesses.
Offer your hopes and your fears to the Great Lord of Death.
Let die all restriction.
Let the leaves of the past fall to earth to nourish
your future growth.
That growth which even now takes root in the
secret dark of your being."

All meditate on this.

After a suitable period, the Narrator rings a bell.

PRIEST: I am the Great Lord of Death
Welcome to my Kingdom and to my feast.
The Great Mother of All
Who hath created both life and death,
Hath given me my Domain.

She hath decreed that the Game of Life
Shall be 'Eat one another!'
As ye eat to live, so shall ye die to feed another.
So be not greedy, but respect all life.
Thus shall your life be a glory and a blessing,
And your death a release into greater life.
For I am the Lord of Life Eternal
And the Consort of the Great Mother.

This night ye shall drink my bitter wine and die!
Not the great death of the body,
But the little death of petty concerns,
The death of the ego, the death of restriction.
And ye shall be reborn to freedom,
To strength, joy and greater life.

The Narrator rings a bell and asks the group to stand.

PRIEST: Come, drink my wine.
Die, that ye may truly live.

The Priest holds a goblet of wine and offers it to each person in turn to take a sip, saying:

PRIEST: Die, that ye may truly live.

The Priest takes the pomegranate from the altar.

PRIEST: Behold the pomegranate, the fruit of Death,
But which holds the seeds of Life.

The Priest takes a knife and cuts the pomegranate, feeding some to each person.

PRIEST: Taste the fruit of Death,
And let go of all that is ready to die.

The Priestess takes an apple.

PRIESTESS: Behold the apple, the fruit of Life,
Which holds the secret of Rebirth.

The Priestess cuts the apple transversely (ie not from top to bottom but across the middle) and holds it up to show the inside, saying:

PRIESTESS: Behold the five-fold star of Rebirth!

The Priestess cuts the apple into pieces and feeds some to each person:

PRIESTESS: Taste the fruit of Rebirth,
And be ready for your new life.

All join hands in a circle.

NARRATOR: Here is the Circle of Rebirth.
Through the Lord of Death, all pass out of Life,
But through the Goddess, all may be born again.
Everything passes, changes:
Seed becomes shoot, becomes flower,
Becomes fruit, becomes seed.
In birth we die; on death we feed.
Know the Lord and the Lady:
He is the Giver of Life; She is the Cauldron of Rebirth.
In them, the circle is ever turning.
Now let us pass through the Gate of Rebirth
Into the New Year and a New Beginning!

The Priest and Priestess form an arch through which all pass.

Bless then share cakes and wine.

Thank and bid farewell to the Elements.

The Circle Caster closes the circle with the words:

CIRCLE CASTER: The circle of blue flame that has protected our sacred space now fades. The circle is open, but unbroken.

ALL: Merry Meet, and Merry Part, and Merry Meet again!

SAMHAIN SESSION

Firstly get the group to relax, ground and centre.

Spoken by the Guide:

Samhain, or Halloween, trick or treat, is a time of naughty, mischievous spirits. Let's be silly! Let your mischievous inner goblin out to play. As I play this music, allow your inner goblin to roam free in the room; dance about, hop around, twitch and scuttle around, whatever feels right. Pull faces, stick out your tongue. You might feel an urge to tickle people, or flick hair, or other such trickery.

Play music such as 'Night on a Bare Mountain' and allow for at least five minutes of goblin prancing.

Now it is time to return to our grown-up selves, our elegant, gracious and considerate, more elf-like inner being. As I play this music, let your body move in a courtly way around the room, be charming.

Play music, for example an elegant classical piece, and allow at least five minutes of courtly, elf-like dancing.[1]

Now all sit comfortably. Samhain is the Celtic New Year, the end of the old year. It is the time of final harvest, the culling of animals and the storage of food to last the dark days of winter.

But it is also the time of new beginnings: planting the winter wheat, planting autumn berries and new trees. It is the mating time of animals whose young are born in spring, such as deer.

---

[1] Alternatively, use the full 'Goblin and Courtier Movement Meditation', found in the first part of this Workbook.

It is the time of the Crone. She cuts away the rubbish and the weakness. We die to our old selves and enter the realm of the dark land to await rebirth.

Close your eyes and imagine we are in a wood, following a path into the depths .... There is a rocky outcrop ahead and you can see the mouth of a huge, dark cave. There are great gates at its entrance. These are the gates to the Shadowlands, the realm of the Dark Lord. They are closed. In front of the gates you see a dark, hooded figure with a sickle.

Dark Mother, Hecate, Cerridwen
Who hath created both birth and death
We are of you and accept your sickle.

Let her cut away all that is used up, unnecessary, all that weighs you down and impedes or restricts you ....

What have you shed? Let go of anything that is still held ....

But she also enables you to harvest the experiences of the year. Think on these, what you have achieved and what you have learned ....

Feeling light and unencumbered we approach the gates. They swing open. See the Great Lord of Death, his antlered head towering above us. Before rebirth we must fully enter his realm and confront our mortality. Follow him now into his realm ....

Here, on this night, the veil between the worlds is thin: life and death, past and future, inner and outer. A time for scrying. Look deep within. What inner wisdom do you find there? Let it speak to you and guide you ....

Now pass on, following the Dark Lord through his realm, deeper ....

The great ones who have gone before draw nigh: your own dear ones, your ancestors who by their fight for survival gave you the gift of life, ancient wise ones, the pioneers of Paganism, the great inventors and champions. Feel their blessing and love ....

He leads you now to the Gates of Rebirth. Beside them stands his Queen, Persephone, Goddess of both death and life, the Spring Maiden and the Queen of the Underworld. She blesses you and puts into your mouth a pomegranate seed. You take this with you that you may be truly fruitful in the coming year ....

The Gates of Rebirth swing open. You give thanks to the Lord of Death and the Lady of Rebirth and pass through into a new day, a new year, a new life! Feel the boundless possibilities before you and your freedom from the restrictions of the past and go forward into the coming year with confidence, courage, trust and joy.

Now holding that joyous feeling of freedom and possibility within you, as I count slowly from ten to one, return to the here and now. Ten .... nine .... eight .... seven .... six .... five .... four .... three .... two .... one .... Take some deep breaths and have a stretch.

SAMHAIN RITUAL OUTLINE

Here is another example of an outline ritual. You could use this as the basis for creating your own ritual, perhaps using a prior session to prepare and write the invocations as a group.

Requirements:

Candles and incense
Altar with seasonal decorations
Paper and pens
Means of burning pieces of paper – fireplace, cauldron, pot
Tarot cards
Pomegranate
Cakes and wine

Roles:

Circle caster
Quarter Officers
Narrator
Invokers (if not done by Narrator)
Crone
Lord of Death
Lady of Rebirth

1. Draw Circle and open Quarters.
2. Invocation of the Crone, the Dark Mother, the Ancient One, Hecate, Cerridwen.
3. Crone replies and invites us to write down what we need to get rid of, all our rubbish.

4. Crone invites us to burn our rubbish on her Fire. *[All take turns to burn their list in the fireplace/cauldron/pot.]*
5. Narrator sets scene for invocation of the Lord of Death, eg:

> Before rebirth, we must fully enter the realm of
> death and confront our own mortality. Only then
> shall we be ready to live fully ..." *[Expand]*

6. Invocation of Lord of Death.
7. Invocation of the Lady of Rebirth, Persephone.
8. The Lord of Death and the Lady of Rebirth both reply. They then invite us to enter their realm.
9. Lord and Lady form an arch through which all pass into their realm. Group is guided through by the Crone.
10. Lord of Death asks all to sit & to greet their friends and ancestors.
11. Lord of Death offers a Tarot card to each one to guide us in the coming year.

Short period of meditation on Tarot card.

12. Lady of Rebirth offers pomegranate seed to each to make us fruitful in the new year.
13. Lord and Lady bless the Wine of Life and pass it round.
14. Lord and Lady invite us to pass through the Gate of Rebirth into new life.
15. All chant:

> The Earth, the Air, the Fire, the Water,
> Return, return, return, return ....[2]

16. Close Quarters and Circle. Share food and wine.

---

2 See online sources for full lyrics and tune.

AUTUMN CRONE PATHWORKING

Requirements:

- Fruits and seeds
- Wine

Spoken by the Guide:

Relax. Find that deep, quiet spot within and breathe. Imagine that you are going down some old stone steps to a door that you see at the bottom. As you go down the steps, you are becoming more deeply relaxed and the imagery is becoming more real and you can feel the stone steps beneath your feet and the rough wall beside you ....

Now you are reaching the door. You lift the latch and the door swings open and you step out into a golden autumn afternoon. Before you is a field and a path that runs along beside the hedgerow. You start to follow the path and your attention is attracted to all the lovely plants that are growing in the hedgerow. You see the hips of the briar rose, the red berries of the hawthorn bush, old man's beard, hazel trees with some nuts still on them; a really lovely mixed hedgerow, and occasional trees, bushes and a mass of plants growing beneath the bushes. You see the dried seed heads of foxgloves, honesty and poppies.

Now your attention is caught by a figure ahead of you. It seems to be an elderly woman clad in black, with a shawl over her head. On her arm she has a basket and she is very busy collecting things, plants, flowers, berries, leaves, from the hedgerow. Curious to see what she is doing and maybe to ask her what she is collecting, you hasten along the path. But somehow, old and bent though she is, she always seems to be the same distance ahead of you.

The shadows are lengthening. The golden sunlight slants low across the field. The old woman is reaching the end of the pathway by the hedgerow and turns aside into a small wood. You follow her and find that the track way leads upwards. You see silver birch turning golden around you, occasional oak trees all bronze and you feel the acorns crunching under your feet. Beech trees are also turning bronze, squirrels eating the beech mast.

As the shadows grow within the wood, you have difficulty seeing where the old woman has gone to. Panting up the hill, you strive to catch her up and are just in time to see her vanish into the mouth of a cave. You hasten after her, even more curious to know who she is and what she is up to. When you enter the cave, at the moment of a sudden change to the darkness, it is hard to see. You cannot see where she has disappeared to, but then a shaft of evening sunlight strikes through the cave and you see that there is an opening at the back and this is the only way the old woman must have gone. So you go to the opening and squeeze in. It is very narrow and you find yourself in a very narrow, rocky passage, totally dark now, just feeling your way along, feeling with your feet, feeling with your hands, hoping that the passage will be big enough for you to get through ....

Suddenly the passage opens out and you find that you have entered a great rock chamber, deep within the earth and, far down below you, you see a flicker of fire and you spot a movement and you see it must be the old woman. She is putting more logs on the fire, over which hangs a great cauldron and into the cauldron, which is steaming, she starts to throw things from her basket: berries and leaves and roots. You have an urge to climb down and get closer to see what is happening. Your eyes are now accustomed to the darkness and you are just able, with the aid of the firelight below, to make your way down, clambering from rock to rock in what seems to be a very crude staircase, perhaps worn by many feet over the centuries.

Now you reach the bottom and quietly draw near to the old lady. She is very busy stirring her cauldron. She gestures for you to sit on a seat of rock close to the fire and now she too sits. She pushes back her shawl and turns her face towards you. You look into her eyes, ready to ask her all sorts of questions, but somehow, when she holds your gaze, the questions all vanish from your head and all you can do is to submit to her gaze. She seems to see right into the depths of your soul, stripping away all pretence, all self-deception. She sees everything about you and all you can do is to humbly present who you are to her. Her gaze is merciless and yet there is infinite understanding and compassion. She calls to your innermost being to be fruitful, to discard the weeds and clutter that choke the garden of your soul …

She withdraws her gaze and turns back to her cauldron and you are able to gaze into her fire, mentally throwing into it all the weeds and clutter that you need to discard. Her gaze has been like a farmer's plough preparing the field for sowing. So throw into her fire all you need to get rid of ….

Now she takes an earthenware cup and pours into it, with her ladle, some of the brew from her cauldron and passes it to you. You smell the perfume of the fruits and berries and herbs within it as the steam rises. Even the very perfume of it seems to lift your spirits. Now you take a sip, and another one, with each sip taking in nourishment, that nourishment of the spirit that leads on to true fruitfulness ….

When you have emptied the cup, she takes it from you and gently lays her frail old hands on your head in blessing, blessing your harvest so that it may be fruitful in the future, an even better harvest in the coming year …. She puts her shawl over her head and closes her eyes and you know it is time to leave.

You climb up that rocky staircase, up and up until you find that narrow passageway and squeeze back through it and into the cave at the top and back into the wood.

You see in the wood a herd of deer and you hear a rather frightening bellowing noise and clashing, and you see two stags in a trial of strength, for this is the rutting season. You watch their combat and feel the exuberant, lusty strength with which they engage. Finally one retreats. The victor, snorting triumphantly, is now free to choose his first mate from amongst the does. Feel the life force of the stag and the deer, for you are both the stag and the doe. Feel within you the virile lustiness of the stag and the eager, excited receptiveness of the doe and the ecstasy of their union that will bring forth new life.

But the sun is now almost set and it is time to return down the hill, back across the field, through the door and climb the staircase back to the here and now. But the magic of the Earth Crone's cave is still around us, and the magic of the wood and the herd of deer. We can feel within ourselves the seeds of our future and the coming harvest. So take three big, deep breaths, slowly, and when you are ready just stand in a circle around the little altar and place on it our fruits or seeds ....

We will drink the Earth Mother's drink. This is blessed by the Great Mother in her crone aspect as we pass into the dark season of the year. We take in the nourishment and strength to make full use of our harvest and to prepare our ground and plant our seeds for future harvests .... *[Wine shared].*

Spoken by the Guide:

Let yourselves relax. Let all thoughts of the day fade away. Let your mind become still and clear and sharp and focused .... Let your breathing become slow and deep .... Be aware of the circle of blue fire around us and this magical space in which we sit ....

Be aware of the presence of the great elemental powers around us and within us. As you breathe, feel the element of air within you, your mind becoming clear and focused and feel the warmth within your body and a warmth particularly, like a fire, in the solar plexus area and be aware of the power of the element of fire. Feel its energy, its heat and feel the strength of your true will that is founded within the depths of your nature, the depths of your being .... Be aware of the blood coursing in your veins and the fluid within your tissues and the flowing and fluidity of your emotions that ebb and flow like the great sea, ranging from great pleasure, to pain, to sadness, to happiness, to joy, to disappointment, to love and to loss, but all founded upon the depths within of joy and peace and boundless love. Be aware of your weight upon your sitting bones, your body, your strength, your health, your ability to persevere, to achieve things in the world. You are the master of these elemental powers, but also they are the master of you. They provide a framework for empowering you, for inner exploration, for development, for learning, for reaching a state of equilibrium, that dynamic equilibrium that is the dance of life.

Now think in what area of your life you need the guidance of your spirit, you need to bring your spirit through into it, to harness your true will and to make use of all your elemental weapons and let this area of your life, your current situation, or future situation, let that come into your mind ....

Now visualise a representation of your choice of the magus or magician and enter that image and let the magus/magician speak to you, let him tell you about his power in your life and his relevance to your life .... And now ask him what does he need from you in order for you to work with him and have his guidance, what does he need from you? .... And now ask him what gift he has for you that will enable you to work with him, what gift does he have for you? .... If his gift is a bit obscure, you don't understand how you use it, ask him to tell you how to use your gift ....

Then thank the magus/magician for his or her wisdom and let them sink back within your inner mind, your inner heart, as they are part of you ....

Then as I count from ten to one, come up from the psychic plane. Ten .... nine .... eight .... seven .... six .... five .... four .... three .... two .... one .... Have a stretch, wiggle your toes about, rub your hands, feel the ground beneath you, stamp your feet and open your eyes.

CLOSED DOOR, HIDDEN ROOM PATHWORKING

Requirements:

- Paper and pens

Spoken by the Guide:

Now imagine that you can sink down deep within yourself, become even more relaxed in mind and body, deep within your inner being, letting your deep intuitive nature come awake as your every day mind quietens down ....

Imagine that you are in your own home and suddenly you notice a door that you have never noticed before and, intrigued, you go to open the door. You find that it is very stiff as though it has not been opened for a very long time. It is very difficult to open. The handle doesn't turn easily and it seems to resist you pushing. You are very intrigued to see what is behind this door. As you push against it, let come into your mind the sorts of things in your life, or in yourself, that tend to prevent you going into new places, new areas of knowledge about yourself, that prevent you changing and hold you back ....

But now the door has opened wide enough for you to get inside and you find there a room that seems to be full of all sorts of things. You can see that there is a little window encrusted with cobwebs and you manage, again with some difficulty, to push it open and let in more light and fresh air. Then you are able to look around the room and you see that it has all sorts of things in it that you maybe thought you had got rid of and things that you had forgotten you ever had, or things you had intended to get rid of but not got around to. Each one of those things represents some piece of baggage in your life, or in your past, that weighs you down and holds you back, so wander around this room and identify some of these objects. You may just see them as objects, you don't know at the moment what they mean, but the meaning may become clear ....

Now you find something that is particularly intriguing. It may be something rather beautiful, it may be a dusty old box which when you open it you find contains something beautiful, something wonderful, some treasure, some precious object. Take this object and examine it. It represents some unrecognised talent within you, some creative spark that has been hidden away for too long ....

Now taking your treasure with you it is time to leave this room, go away and think about it, so close the window and then go back through the door with your treasure. Close the door and then find yourself not in your own home, but back in this room thinking about that experience.

I want you gradually to come back sufficiently to take your pens and paper and to write down some notes under three headings:

What is it that makes the door so stiff?
What is causing it to be difficult to get into that room and what is hidden in that room that you want to get rid of?
What is your treasure?

You may not find it comes yet as insights and meanings, but it might. It may come as objects that become clearer later on. I will just repeat the three headings:

What makes that door so stiff and difficult to open?
What in the room do you need to get rid of?
What treasure did you find, or unexpected treasure?

Allow time for this exercise.

Now sit comfortably again and close your eyes. Take some deep breaths and feel yourself relaxing deeper, tune back into your inner being .... The image of this room fades and you find yourself again standing by that door, holding your treasure, sensing that the door is still stiff and difficult to open. And you become aware of a presence beside you, an entity of some kind. You may be able to visualise them, or just feel their energy beside you .... Ask it what you can do to make that door easier to open and then ask it to advise you what to do about all the things that are in the room. Should you be throwing them out, cleaning them up, turning them to use, refurbishing? What should you be doing? ....

Now ask the being how you can make use of your treasure. How can you make that treasure manifest in your life? ....

Now thank the being for the advice and guidance and, as you do so, you see behind this entity great gates of brass and iron and through them shines a beautiful golden light. The being gestures that you should go towards these gates and as you approach they open and you pass through into a place of light and beauty and peace ....

[Play music] You feel a presence forming, a tall form of a beautiful woman. It is the Goddess Sophia, goddess of wisdom, and she radiates peace and inner strength, love and beauty. You draw near and feel her power and blessing permeate you. Feel yourself grow in stature. Feel your own inner power vitalised and directed, directed into the channel of your will. Feel with certainty that your treasure is part of you and your treasure is filled with light and life and potential .... Take your treasure into your heart and know that it is part of you that has been released and empowered by your own higher wisdom ....

Then when you are ready, thank the Goddess for her wisdom and love and, carrying that sense of peace and inner strength with you, let her sink back within your inner mind, your inner heart, as she is part of you ....

Then as I count from ten to one, begin to return to the here and now. Ten .... nine .... eight .... seven .... six .... five .... four .... three .... two .... one .... Have a stretch, wiggle your toes about, rub your hands, feel the ground beneath you, stamp your feet and open your eyes.

LAKSHMI RITUAL FOR DIWALI

Diwali is the Hindu festival of lights. The date of the festival changes every year, but it is usually some time between October and November. Lakshmi, the Hindu Goddess of Wealth, is worshipped as the bringer of blessings for the new year. We celebrated the festival at Pagan Pathfinders and it was always a beautiful evening.

Fill the ritual space with many candles and colours. You could place an image of the beautiful Goddess Lakshmi on the Altar. Sweets are traditionally eaten at this time, so include some sweet treats in your post-ritual feast.

Requirements:

- Candles on the Altar and other colourful decorations
- Candles decorating the room
- Two candles to be lit during invocations
- Bell
- Flowers and sweets for Lakshmi to distribute
- Tealights (one for each person to take at the start of the ritual)
- Food to share

Roles:

- Circle caster
- Quarter Officers
- Five invocation readers
- Lakshmi

Cast the circle and call upon the Quarters to be present.

1. Invocation to Agni, God of Fire:

> O Agni, Fiery One, whose breath is a flame that lights the dark places. Breathe now into our Temple that your Light may dispel the Darkness. *[Light candle]*
>
> As your Flame lights our Temple,
> So does it also light our hearts and minds.
> Fiery One, Agni, we greet you!

Bell.

2. Invocation to Lakshmi, Goddess of Good Fortune, Wealth and Wisdom:

> Lakshmi! Lakshmi! Lakshmi!
> Thou who art the Mother of the Gods, the Mother of Worlds,
> The Mother in the heart of every woman and man.
> Lady of Light, we see thee in the dawn sky,
> In the glint of sun on dewdrop, in the light in the eye of a friend.
> When the heart swells with joy at the beauty of the world,
> Thou art present.
> When there is food on the table and good company,
> Thy gifts are before us.
> When we are filled with love, compassion
> And generosity of spirit, thy blessing is upon us.
> O Lakshmi, Goddess of Beauty and Abundance and Generosity,
> Be here present tonight. *[Light candle]*

Lakshmi steps forward and stands by the Altar.

Bell.

3. Lakshmi teach us gratitude:

> O Lakshmi, teach us to value with full gratitude all that we have received of thine abundance, whether it be material wealth, or the food of the soul that comes through friendship and love, or the inner gifts of intelligence, joy and creativity. Through knowledge of thee do we celebrate our own lives, for all that we are, and all that we have is of thee, and our hearts are filled with gratitude.

Lakshmi hands out flowers to those present.

Bell.

4. Lakshmi - request for abundance:

> O Lakshmi, grant us the courage and humility to ask with honesty and true vision for that which we need, so that our lives may be abundantly fulfilled. We open our hands, our hearts and our minds to receive thy gifts - and we will ever strive to use them for thy glory.

Lakshmi hands out sweets to those present.

Bell.

5. Lakshmi – generosity:

> O Lakshmi, may we through this rite come to partake of your nature. Be always in our hearts so that we may show

forth true generosity of spirit. In every aspect of our lives, let thy beauty and abundance flow through us, so that we may forgive those who wrong us and become the source of love and harmony.

All take their tealight to Lakshmi who lights it with a taper or another candle that she holds.

Bell.

Allow time for meditation on these gifts. Then thank the Gods and the elemental powers and bid them farewell, then close the circle.

PATHWORKING TO MEET YOUR LUNAR SELF

Spoken by the Guide:

Put your attention on your breathing and let yourself relax even more deeply, feeling completely centred within yourself....

And now imagine it is night and you are in a little rowing boat on a lake. The full moon shines overhead. The waters of the lake are smooth and dark, almost black like a dark mirror. There is a hidden current in the lake and the boat drifts very slowly towards the centre of the lake. Little wreaths of mist weave here and there like diaphanous moon veils in the almost still air. The petals of water lilies gleam palely among the dark pads of their leaves. All is silent, and you feel caught in a timeless, magical moment as the boat drifts almost imperceptibly across the lake .... You look up at the moon and seem to feel the moonlight penetrating right down into the inner reaches of your being – to that reflective, intuitive, emotional, watery lunar aspect of yourself, the very depths of your unconscious mind. And you become aware that the boat has stopped, that it has reached a still point in the centre of the lake. The mists have cleared away and the water is absolutely still and black. You lean over the side of the boat and in the moonlight you see the reflection of your own face looking back at you. Your reflection seems to glow with a silvery light and the lips seem to move. You lean a little closer and you seem to hear faint unearthly music and, almost lost in it, the voice of your lunar reflection. Listen carefully and hear in your mind's ear what this aspect of yourself has to say. Its message may come as a thought in your head, words coming into your mind, or you may seem to hear a whispered voice. Listen carefully and, however cryptic the utterance may be, remember and treasure it ....

Allow 2-3 minutes for this, perhaps playing some quiet and dreamy music.

And now a little breeze ruffles the surface of the lake, breaking up the image of your face. You take a deep breath and sit up in the boat and find that once more it is being carried by the current .... You reach the furthest shore of the lake and step out of the boat onto a grassy bank. You raise your arms to the full moon in a salutation to the Goddess of the Moon and to your own lunar self. And you recall the communication from your lunar self and something of its particular relevance to your present life becomes apparent to you .... And in fact when this session is over you will write down the words or draw a symbol of the message you received from your lunar self and you will keep this paper by you, letting the message continue to work within your mind until you have absorbed it and understood it and completely accepted the message ....

And now it is time to return to the everyday world, so take three very deep breaths and return to the here and now.

Spoken by the Guide:

Relax. Find that deep, quiet spot within and breathe .... Now imagine yourself walking out into a forest. Feel the soft, forest floor beneath your feet, and hear the wind rustling in the great trees that surround you. The place is ancient and full of magic. The sun is setting as you make your way along a path deeper into the forest. You hear birds settling down to roost and calling to each other.

Suddenly ahead of you in a glade you see a great stag with towering antlers. He stands proud and strong, the Lord of the Forest. You approach him, feeling he is welcoming you and bidding you step forward. As you look into the stag's eyes, they seem so human, so full of deep understanding, you see great wisdom and strength within them. As you watch, he seems to be changing, shifting into human shape, until at last before you is Herne, Pan, God of the Greenwood, Lord of the Wild Things. He is the male virility of the Autumn time that impregnates for the Spring birth. He is the cut corn that is sown for next year. He is the seed that falls into the ground. He is goat and ram, bull and stag. He is strong and proud in his maturity, in the fullness of his masculinity.

He is that within you, whether male or female, that is potent and activating. He is also that seed that is your potential, seeking the fertile ground within which to grow. And he arouses within you, whether you are male or female, that ardent response, that active and open reaching to receive, that yearning to grow.

And as the music plays, you become him and also receive him, so that the mystic marriage that fertilises your potential can take place *[Play music]* ....

[Stop music] .... Now let those feelings of strength and activation sink deep into you, knowing that you are one step closer to reaching your potential, knowing you have the power of Pan, the great stag, to aid you ....

Then as I count from ten to one, begin to walk back out of the forest in your mind's eye and back to the outer world. Ten .... nine .... eight .... seven .... six .... five .... four .... three .... two .... one .... Have a stretch, wiggle your toes about, rub your hands, feel the ground beneath you, stamp your feet and open your eyes.

WINTER

EARTH MEDITATION AND PATHWORKING

Spoken by the Guide:

Just contemplate how at ease you feel with the element of earth. Do you consider that too many commitments and obsessions with things weigh you down, or do you evade commitment? .... How do you feel about such things as your home? Are you very attached to it, or do you move house easily? .... Consider other stable things in your life such as your job and income, your money. All these things, that are the stability of your life, are they security, or are they a trap, or a bit of both? .... Do you feel you need to strengthen aspects of the element of earth within you, or do you need to curb aspects of it, or perhaps strengthen some and curb others? ....

Be aware that any faults we have in the element of earth are probably just virtues taken too far, or in the wrong context. Procrastination or inertia are maybe just caution and forethought taken too far. Obsession might be just perseverance and concentrated effort taken too far.

Maybe there are some areas of the element of earth that you feel are too weak, that you could do with more earth .... Is there any particular problem in your life that you feel is to do with the element of earth, that you need guidance on, more earth strength within you, or something of that sort? ....

And relax and breathe and let yourself become more relaxed in mind and body, deeper and deeper ....

Imagine that you are walking through ancient heath land. There are hills around you, springy turf under your feet, the purple of heather and the gold of gorse, being aware of the earthiness of the place, the spacious landscape with old stones around, a track way that you follow that has been trodden by many people for thousands of years.

Ahead of you now you see your goal, which is a level space on which are some standing stones. This place is an ancient spiral maze of standing stones between which grow heather and gorse bushes. You step into the entrance and follow the spiral path around and around. As you tread the path you become even more deeply relaxed. The smell of the heather is more clear, more real. You touch one of the stones and feel its cold, rough surface. You hear a lark singing high overhead. All your senses seem to be becoming very acute as you tread slowly, spiralling round and round and round until you reach the centre.

You stand there at the centre of the maze and it is as if in this place time stands still. You feel how ancient this place is and yet the stones themselves are even more ancient. In this still place you review your problems in the element of earth dispassionately, seeing them as though from a great distance ....

Then you glance down and notice that you are standing on a flagstone, in the centre of which is an iron ring. You step backwards and grasp that iron ring and pull and the stone swivels up easily. It is beautifully made and beautifully balanced and you see within spiral steps leading down. You feel that this is a place where the powers of the element of earth are immensely strong. You step through onto the spiral staircase and start to walk down. You go down, becoming yet more relaxed, more deeply within the powers of the element of earth and you go on down and round and down and down until you come to a door. This door looks very ancient and you take the ring handle and twist it, but it is hard to open. Perhaps the door represents your own problems with the element of earth, things that you don't want to look at. So take courage and trust yourself and push that door. Inside is a chamber, dimly lit with a green glow. As you enter, the glow gets brighter and you see on the floor a pentagram within a circle, a symbol of the element of earth. You go and stand within the centre of that pentagram and feel the powers of earth build up around you, the green glow, very intense and pulsing around you. You let go of any aspects of the element of earth that you need to release, perhaps procrastination, or obsessiveness, or inertia.

Feel them falling away and draw in perseverance and stability, reliability and confidence. Draw in the practical wisdom of the element of earth ....

If there is a decision that you have to take that you find difficult, or something that you want to do that you find difficult to get on with, consult the element of earth, tap into its wisdom. Learn from it. Let it teach you .... The element of earth teaches us that we have to make hard choices. We have to choose what we give priority to, what really matters, what we really want to do, where we want to put our energies and our time and we have to recognise that common human failing of thinking you can do it all and that it won't take very long. So draw on the element of earth to help you make the decisions you need to make, not just now, but in your life ahead. Remember how important the element of earth is.

Feel the powers of the element of earth building up even more strongly, balancing its virtues within you, nourishing you, enabling you to make your choices. Within this sacred place of the element of earth, a vast silence develops and in that silence feel the blessing of earth. We discover that that silence is blissful ....

Now it is time to leave this sacred temple, so give thanks to the element of earth for the blessing and the gifts and make your way up that spiral staircase, knowing that you can always visit this deep place again if you wish. When you get to the top, close the flagstone door down and follow the spiral path back out of the maze. As you go round and round you are coming back up from that deep place, back to the land of light and air and the fire of the sun and the flowing rivers and seas .... The scene fades and you become aware of your body again, sitting here in this room. Still staying very aware of your body and your sensations, your breathing, your hands and your feet, when you are ready stand in a circle and partake of the gifts of the element of earth.

Share food and wine.

HECATE, GODDESS OF THE UNDERWORLD PATHWORKING

Requirements:

- Tealights and lighter

Before the pathworking, each participant is given a tealight. Ask the group to stand in a circle, holding their tealights. Go around the circle and light each one, telling the group to think of it as their own inner light, their soul fire, a representation of their creative force, joy, love and positivity. Ask them to focus on these qualities as you go around.

When all the lights are lit, allow a small time for contemplation and stillness while you switch off any room lights. Ask the group to sit comfortably, close their eyes and then begin the pathworking.

Spoken by the Guide:

Now be ready to go down into your own inner darkness to journey to the underworld, so blow out your tiny lights. We each travel alone. See before you a portal, a closed portal. Now that portal slowly opens and you see a path within, which has its own faint luminescence and this is the path that you must follow to your own inner depths, a path that leads into a new birth, a new path in your life, a path that leads to your fulfillment and potential ....

As you travel this path you may meet monsters, your shadow creatures, creatures that gibber and claw at you and try to hold you back, prevent you changing. Each one that you meet, give it a name so that you disempower it and make it an object. It might be your old fears, or old resentments, beliefs about yourself and the world you live in that limit you. So step boldly onto this faintly illuminated path and confront these creatures that gibber and claw at you ....

And now you are reaching a great underground room, a temple. This is the temple of the underworld goddess, Hecate, and she is seated on a throne, a tall dark presence. You draw near, taking your symbol to her and asking her for her wisdom and her strength. She is the soul's teacher. She can help you to realise how to deal with all those monsters, how to find your inner wisdom, how to reach your goal of your potential. Feel her creative strength permeate you and let her voice speak in your inner ear, telling you how you can discover your own strength and wisdom and what you need to do to change your life. So now spend a few moments listening to her, presenting to her your problems. She teaches you that all problems and barriers are opportunities for growth, for gathering wisdom and she values you in your uniqueness, your own mixture of strengths and weaknesses. She knows that each person is uniquely perfect in their own way; that is who they are and she treasures every bit of you. She knows you have your own unique path to tread and she will help you find it ....

Now it is time to leave her, taking her wisdom with you. Follow the path further onwards, now upwards, bringing you up from the underworld back to a new life and new opportunities opening before you, new strengths, new determination ....

As you emerge back into the light take some deep breaths and open your eyes.

THE RITE OF BAST

The Ancient Egyptian Goddess Bast, the Cat Goddess, was one very close to Jean's heart as the owner of many feline friends. Bast is a nurturing, playful, sensual goddess, beloved by the common people of Ancient Egypt. In 'The Gods Within' [1] *Jean writes this of Bast:*

> "The cat is surely the best loved animal among modern Pagans, and Bast is one of the most beloved of Egyptian goddesses .... [Statues] are often placed in personal shrines and revered as representations of the Goddess herself, though more properly they are her sacred animals .... She was 'The Lady of the East', associated with the dawn aspect of the sun when its heat is mild. Sekhmet is the fierce destructive heat of the noonday sun; Bast is the gentle fructifying heat and light that encourages germination, growth and healing .... Bast is usually depicted with a sistrum in her right hand, a musical rattle also sacred to Hathor with whom she shared a joy in music, dance and revelry .... Bast was a goddess of the people rather than of the priesthood, who did not regard her as one of the High Gods; her powers were seen as particularly relevant to the concerns of the home and everyday family life .... Bast was thus also a goddess of sexuality, fertility and childbirth. She became one of the goddesses of the birth house and many amulets bear prayers or spells concerned with safe delivery of a child or the healing of women or children. One statue is inscribed, 'May she grant all life and power, all health and joy of heart' .... Cats are playful, charmingly interactive with humans, always lithe and graceful, sensuous, responsive and alert. They have the ability to relax totally and yet to become fully alert in an instant. They are small enough to sit on one's lap, to be stroked, to play with children; yet they are always independent in attitude and manner. They can inexplicably vanish from sight and as suddenly reappear, nonchalantly licking their coat as though they had never left. They are intrepid defenders of themselves and their place: they can fluff themselves out and arch their backs to make themselves look twice their size, and they can yowl and hiss alarmingly .... Bast is a model

[1] Jean M Williams and Zachary Cox, 2008.

for any woman who wishes to develop her sexuality, sensuality, social charm, flexibility, capacity for motherhood, yet retain her independence of spirit. The Greeks identified her with Artemis, 'Woman whole unto herself'. But Bast is less of a rebel against the conventional roles of women as wives and mothers, and decidedly more sexual, nurturing and pleasure-loving .... Bast is not a goddess of the intellect but of the emotional and sensual nature. She puts us in touch with the wisdom of the body, celebrating its physicality. She teaches us to dance the dance of life on swift light paws. Evoking the cat within can enrich men and women of any age .... Bast can enable us to enjoy being alone, to be emotionally and physically self-sufficient and relaxed. But, above all, evoking the inner cat can help us in virtually every type of inter-personal situation. Bast enables us to become alertly perceptive and responsive, assertive yet sensitive and delicate."

Requirements:

- Candles and incense
- Altar/Shrine with statue or image of Bast (if possible) and pictures of cats.
- Sistrum/percussion instruments
- Chair to be Bast's throne
- Chalice/goblet of wine
- Cakes and wine
- Music

Roles:

- Circle Caster
- Quarter Officers
- Narrator
- Priest
- Priestess/Bast
- Wine bearer

Begin by casting the circle and invoking the Elements.

1. Pathworking to the Temple of Bast – prepared in advance by the session leader.

2. Procession and circle dance around the space, shaking the sistrum/ percussion instruments, clapping and chanting "Bastet" *[All]*

3. All kneel before the Altar/Shrine of Bast. The Priestess enters and sits on the throne.

4. The Priest takes the sistrum, stands before the Priestess and invokes Bast:

PRIEST: Beloved of Ra, Mistress of Heaven and Regent of the West;
Thou art the All-Mother, All-Lover.
Thy beauty is a flowing stream, resting the traveller.
Queen of Night and Mystery -
Thou art the Eye of Ra that guards the Earth
While thy great Lord traverses the Underworld
And wrestles with the Serpent of Evil.
Yet art thou the Mistress of revelry -
Lady of Youth and Joy, who dances amid the stars,
The sensuous dance in which all life joins.
We are thy people and we dance thy dance.
Grant us the Wine of Life that we may worship thee.

The Priest then hands the Priestess/Bast the sistrum and steps back and kneels.

All whisper "Bastet" three times with intensity.

5. Bast replies:

BAST: I am the Beloved of Ra,
Mistress of Heaven, and Regent of the West.
Naught is hidden from me, the Eye of Ra;
For I see in all the dark and secret places.
Beware my sharp claws, for I am swift to scratch!
I am the Huntress of the night;
Let all evil and venomous things beware!
Also do I hunt down the weak and timorous.
Yet will I nurture you who are my children and my people;
For in you the flame of my passion burns brightly.
And I will treasure you and heal your hurts.

Bast rises and shakes sistrum vigorously.

I am the Queen of Night and Mistress of revelry!
I open for you the secret door of youth.
Come, join my dance!

6. Bast leads all in a wild, sensuous, cat-like dance.

7. Bast returns to the throne; all kneel.

8. The Wine Bearer presents the chalice of wine to Bast.

9. Bast blesses the wine saying, "Behold the of Wine of Life!". She drinks then hands it to the Wine Bearer saying, "Drink and be Blessed".

10. Everyone comes in turn to pay homage at the shrine of Bast and drink her wine, drawing in her power to awaken their cat nature.

11. All send the power of Bast out into the world to protect all cats. Here someone could read a poem or statement of intent before sending out the protective energy.

12. The Priest closes by saying:

PRIEST: Beloved of Ra, Mistress of Heaven and Regent of the West,
We have drunk thy wine and received thy blessing.
Always will we hold your creatures sacred.

The Priest drinks some wine and places the chalice on the Altar. He takes both the Priestess's hands, raises her and kisses her to release her from the goddess.

13. Close the Quarters and open the circle.

14. Share cakes and wine.

EMBER OF TRUE WILL PATHWORKING

Spoken by the Guide:

Now discover that you can relax yet more deeply, letting yourself sink down to the psychic plane, using whatever image you like that you feel takes you to a deep level of complete relaxation of mind and body, a relaxation in which your everyday mind is shutting down and your imagination, your dreaming mind, your creative mind is coming to life ....

So as I count from one to ten, with each count let yourself sink more deeply to the psychic plane. One .... two .... three .... four .... five .... six .... seven .... eight .... nine .... ten ....

Let come into your mind some intent you have, something you want to do but find difficult, that you tend to procrastinate about, or don't know quite how to tackle, or are reluctant to make a start on, it seems a bit too difficult, or too demanding in time. It might be something that you want to do very quickly, very soon, or some longer term goal .... Imagine that you have achieved this. See an image or have a feeling of you having achieved this, or of actually achieving it as you wish now ....

And then let yourself sink down within the dark inside you, right down to the solar plexus area, and imagine that you can see there a red glow. This is the ember of your true will, so breathe into that red glow, see it becoming brighter and brighter, fanning the flame of your true will with your breath, seeing it flame and rise up, filling you with fiery light ....

Let that fiery light fill that image of yourself achieving whatever it is that is your intent. Feel the flame of your true will entering that image, entering your intent ....

Then let the image fade, but know it is there within you and that when you put your intent into action you can use that image, draw upon that image and draw upon that flame of your true will. So let that intent and that image sink deep within you, within your deeper mind, knowing that you will remember it when you need it ....

Now it is time to rise up from the psychic plane as I count from ten to one. Ten .... nine .... eight .... seven .... six .... five .... four .... three .... two .... one .... Take some deep breaths and have a stretch.

YULE RITUAL

For a Pagan Federation Open Ritual

Requirements:

- Main Altar with candles and seasonal decorations
- Smaller, portable Altar of Light with five candles/tealights
- Tapers
- Dish of water with salt nearby (on main Altar)
- Incense burner, charcoal and incense (on main Altar)
- Candles around the room
- Drums/jingle bells
- Soft music or forest sounds to be played in the background
- Lanterns or tealights
- Jingle bells, a wand and a lantern for each Elemental Officer (ie four of each)
- Tunnel (this could be a children's play tunnel, or some sheets used to form a tunnel)
- Horned staff (or something similar)
- Bell
- Cakes and wine
- Yellow 'sun' balloon tied somewhere near main Altar
- Party poppers

Roles:

- Narrator
- Circle Caster
- Elemental Officers
- Two Guardians
- Two Invokers (optional)
- God
- Goddess

Play music as people enter the room. The Elemental Officers and other ritual participants form a path of lights (using lanterns or tealights) down which the people arriving process and then fan out to form a circle. When everyone is in, the ritual team processes to the Altar. The music fades. Drums and/or jingle bells to announce the start of the ritual.

NARRATOR: Welcome. We are going to enact the death of the old and the birth of the new - all of us, not just the ritual team. To start with, we will tune in to this season of the year, using the imagery of an ancient forest. You are going to be the trees in this forest, so find a spot in the room in which to put down your roots. Use the whole room, but leave enough space round the edge for someone to walk round.

All big candles are dowsed and placed on the Altar, leaving only the lanterns and/or tealights and the Elemental Officers' lanterns.

NARRATOR: Stand with your feet about a shoulder's width apart and close your eyes. Take three really deep breaths, letting yourself relax .... Put your attention on your physical sensations, just being aware of them without trying to change anything. Notice what you can feel, what you can hear, what you can smell. Notice your breathing .... Notice the temperature of the room on your skin .... Feel the ground beneath your feet .... Be aware of the pull of gravity and how your muscles interact to hold you upright.

And now imagine that there is a piece of elastic from the crown of your head to the ceiling and, as you relax, you are drawn up taller, your neck and backbone elongating .... And let your shoulders drop back and down. Let your breathing become slow and deep. Put your attention on your breathing as it comes in and out of your nostrils and let your mind become still .... And discover that, although you are standing up, you can become very relaxed and centered within yourself, and that this relaxation allows you to expand ....

[Play forest music/sounds] Now imagine that you are a tree. Your feet are becoming great roots reaching down deep into the earth, your legs and body are the trunk of this tree and your head and arms are the branches. Feel your roots penetrating deep into the earth, drawing up moisture and nourishment and providing a firm foundation .... And feel your branches spreading up to the sky and the sun shining on your leaves .... Imagine all the elements working together to nourish and increase the well-being of this tree that is you. Feel the rain washing your leaves and soaking down into the earth releasing nourishment; the earth feeding the roots and supporting the whole tree; the sun providing warmth and light and combining with the air to nourish the leaves. Let your branches sway to the wind and reach up to the sun and your leaves rustle as all the elements combine to bring you to a state of glowing health .... *[People could move and sway, or do this in their minds.]*

Now begin to sense other trees around you in this primordial forest. Feel the ground is deep and ancient; many leaves have fallen and decayed, forming the forest floor over countless years of the cycle of death and rebirth. The tree roots go deep, connecting to the earth, reaching out to nearby trees. Think of all the teeming life just one leaf supports, or one branch, one tree, one forest; all the insects, birds and animals, as well as providing oxygen for us to breathe. All is interconnected in this ancient place, nature's cathedral .... There is winter mist in the forest and you feel the magic of the winter gods all around you ....

Now we make the forest our sacred space by drawing a circle of blue fire around it.

Stop music.

The Circle Caster walks around the room and casts the circle with appropriate words.

NARRATOR: Through the trees come the priests and priestesses who will invoke the aid and protection of the Elemental Powers.

Each Elemental Officer has jingle bells, a wand and a lantern. Each in turn jingle their way through the trees to their Quarter and invoke their element.

AIR: Might ones of the East
Powers of Air!
Cool, gentle breeze, or stormy gale
In these darker days of retreat and reflection
You blow away the deadwood
Cleansing and clearing our lives.
You gift us intellect, wit and communication,
Aid us tonight in this rite.
Element of Air, we bid you Hail and Welcome!

FIRE: Guardians of the Watchtowers of the South,
Powers of Fire!
We ask for your presence in this rite,
Your aid and protection.
In this time of cold and dark
We await the Sun's rebirth.
Lend us your Will! Fire our spirits!
Element of Fire, we bid you Hail and Welcome!

WATER: Mighty ones of the West
Powers of Water!
Cold rain, bright snow, ever-changing ocean,
We crave your cleansing presence in this, our rite,
That the waters of life may flow over us,
Gently balancing, leaving harmony of mind and body
At this time of retreat and taking stock.
Element of Water, we bid you Hail and Welcome!

EARTH: Mighty ones of the North
Powers of Earth!
Fertile forest floor, sky-reaching mountain,
Mossy bank and green meadow;
You nurture all in your womb.
You hold the secret of ancient mysteries.
Help us to be strong and grounded,
To feel nourished, even in these darker days.
Now all is harvested and it is the time for reflection.
Element of Earth, we bid you Hail and Welcome!

During the following, someone in the background should light the charcoal block for the incense to be burned later.

NARRATOR: Close your eyes again and, in your mind's eye, emerge from your tree and stand beneath it, aware of the forest all around you .... You are going on a journey down into the dark to seek the new light, the Fire of your True Will; but you are burdened and weighed down with the rubbish of the old year. As a tree sheds its leaves and deadwood, shed all your rubbish. Let it fall to the forest floor like leaves and dead branches, where it will rot down to feed new life. Name some of the things you are letting go of to yourself .... Now feel yourself light and unencumbered, ready to go deep into the womb of the Great Mother to seek rebirth, to seek the new light. But you do not need to undertake this journey alone; there is good companionship to be had on the way. So first you need to make your way to the meeting place. Visualise threading your way through the trees seeking the glade that is our meeting place .... And physically now move to the perimeter of the room, making a circle within the glade.

The Elemental Officers say in turn:

> The dark deepens; the night is long. The journey into the depths of the womb of the Great Mother challenges the Spirit. But the powers of Air/Fire/Water/Earth will go with you to guide and guard you.

The Elemental Officers place the bells, wands and lanterns on the Altar and help to set up the tunnel.

The Guardians stand in front of the Altar.

GUARDIAN 1: We are the Guardians of the Gateway to the tomb, the tomb that you must enter if you would seek rebirth and the new light. Before you enter, you must be purified by the Elements.

[Adds salt to water] The Salt of Earth conjoined with Water becomes the Great Cleansing Sea. Great Mother Ocean, grant us the blessing of your wisdom.

GUARDIAN 2: *[Adds incense to charcoal]* Sweet Air rises from the heat of Fire. Great Father, grant us the blessing of your strength.

The Guardians take up positions on either side of the tunnel and purify each person as they enter by sprinkling water and wafting incense.

CIRCLE CASTER: I will lead the way. *[Instruct them to hold hands]*

ALL CHANT: Hecate, Cerridwen, Dark Mother take us in,
Hecate, Cerridwen, let us be reborn.[2]

Continue the chant while the Circle Caster leads everyone around the room and through the tunnel.

The Goddess and God take up positions in front of the Altar, facing the exit from the tunnel and welcoming people as they emerge and form a circle.

---

2 See online sources for tune.

The tunnel is removed. The Guardians place the water and incense back on the Altar. They then place the Altar of Light ceremoniously in the centre of the room.

The Elemental Officers take up their wands and lanterns and return to the Quarter positions, inside the circle of people.

The Circle Caster and Narrator[3] *take up positions near the Altar of Light.*

CIRCLE CASTER: Queen of the Moon, Queen of the Sun,
Queen of the Heavens, Queen of the Stars,
Queen of the Waters, Queen of the Earth,
Bring to us the Child of Promise!
It is the Great Mother who gives birth to him;
It is the Lord of Life who is born again;
Darkness and tears are set aside
When the Sun shall come up early.

NARRATOR: Golden Sun of hill and mountain,
Illumine the land, illumine the world,
Illumine the seas, illumine the rivers
Sorrows be laid and joy to all!
Blessed be the great Goddess,
Without beginning, without ending
Who gives birth to him.

GODDESS: I bring you the gift of Light and Fire.
Out of my Darkness, the Sun is reborn.
To each of you, I give the gift of inner Fire,
The Fire of True Will,
That the coming year may be full of joy and purpose.

---

[3] Alternatively, this could be done by two invokers.

GOD: I am the Light that burns away Darkness;
I am the Fire in the blood, the Flame in the heart.
I am Love and Light and Laughter,
And the promise of a new beginning.

The Goddess and God are handed lighted tapers and go to the Altar of Light.

GOD: Now at this Solstice time, let us rekindle our inner Flame.

Each light is lit with ceremony by the God (or take it in turns with the Goddess) as the Elemental Officers speak:

EAST: The Light of Intelligence. *[Candle lit]*
SOUTH: The Light of True Will. *[Candle lit]*
WEST: The Light of Love. *[Candle lit]*
NORTH: The Light of Pleasure and Strength. *[Candle lit]*
GODDESS: The Light of the Creative Spirit. *[Candle lit by Goddess]*

During the above, the main Altar candles are relit by the Guardians.

ALL SING: We are one with the infinite sun,
Forever, forever, forever.[4]

Accompanied by drums, the Circle Caster leads a spiral dance during the singing. The Goddess and God return to stand in front of the main Altar. The Circle Caster goes to near the Altar of Light, bearing the horned staff.

CIRCLE CASTER: NOW is the moment of truth! NOW is when you make your New Year's resolutions! You are ready to make a fresh start in at least ONE area of your life. Close your eyes .... and formulate your resolution now!

Pause.

Bell.

---

4 See online sources for tune.

The Elemental Officers say in turn:

The Beings of the Kingdom or Air/Fire/Water/Earth have witnessed your resolution and give you their powers to fulfil it.

GODDESS: The Great Mother has witnessed your resolution, and gives you her power to fulfil it.

GOD: The Dawn Sun of the Winter Solstice, full of promise for the coming year, has witnessed your resolution and gives you his power to fulfil it.

The Goddess and God walk down to the Altar of Light and take up positions on either side of it.

GODDESS: Bring forth the cakes and wine that are the gifts of the Great Mother and her Son, that all may be nourished.

The Elemental Officers go to the main Altar, place on it the wands and lanterns and pick up a goblet of wine and basket of cakes apiece. They go to kneel before the Goddess and the God.

GODDESS: *[Raises hands over cakes and wine]* In the Name of the Great Mother, I bless these cakes and wine. May they sustain us in all our endeavours, as we throw off the burdens of the old year and go forward with courage into the new. However dark the winter, we have the promise of the Great Mother that Light and Life will return.

[Raises hands over cakes and wine] In the name of the Great Lord of the Sun, Lord of Rebirth, I bless these cakes and wine. May they sustain us in all our endeavours, as we throw off

GOD: the burdens of the old year and go forward with courage into the new. With the gradual return of the Sun, with courage we step forward and grow, just as life returns to the Earth.

The Officer of Air hands a goblet of wine to the God, who shares the drink with the Goddess before handing it back to the Officer of Air, who then hands them cakes.

The Elemental Officers distribute the cakes and wine, each starting at their own Quarter. The goblets are replenished as necessary. During this, music is played again. All join in with:

ALL: Bring in the new days, follow the old ways.

During this, the Goddess and God return to the main Altar.

NARRATOR: Before we end our rite, there is one more very important piece of magic we must perform if we are to be sure that the Sun really will rise at the Solstice. I call upon the Goddess, to come and lead us in calling forth the new born Sun.

All shout and call joyfully:

ALL: Sun return on Solstice morn,
On solstice morn be born anew.

The Goddess releases the sun balloon! Drums, party poppers and celebration.

Then, at a suitable moment:

NARRATOR: The rite is ended and we must leave the magical forest. I call upon the Elemental Officers to close the Quarters.

EAST: Mighty ones of the East
Powers of Air
We thank you for your presence here tonight,
For granting us the gift of speech and song,
Allowing us to honour our Gods
And commune with each other.
We carry within us ideas and resolutions
For the coming year ahead.
Now, as you return to your fair and airy realms,
Powers of Air, we bid you Hail and Farewell.

SOUTH: Guardians of the Watchtowers of the South
Powers of Fire
Thank you for your presence here tonight,
Your aid and protection.
With your help we go forward with our spirits warmed,
Our Will burning strong.
We carry within us the glowing hope
Of the new born, growing Sun.
Now, as you return to your fair and fiery realms,
Powers of Fire, we bid you Hail and Farewell.

WEST: Mighty Ones of the West
Powers of Water
We thank you for your presence here tonight,
For lending us the fluidity to change
and throw off old shackles,
For the blessing of compassion,
And for the secret depths from which
We may dream ourselves afresh in the new light of the sun.
As you return to your fair and watery realms,
Great ones of Water, we bid you Hail and Farewell.

NORTH: Mighty ones of the North
Powers of Earth
We thank you for your presence here tonight,
For teaching us the deep, ancient wisdom
Of Mother Earth's natural rhythm
And helping us connect to her ever-turning wheel;
For bringing us joy and comfort
And food for feasting.
As the light returns to nourish the Earth and all its creatures
We ask that we too are nourished and strengthened.
Now, as you return to your fair and earthy realms,
Powers of Earth, we bid you Hail and Farewell.

Circle Caster closes the circle.

End with all saying:

Merry meet, merry part and merry meet again!

Allow time for celebration.

MUMMERS' PLAY

As performed at the Pagan Pathfinders annual Yule Party

The Players:

- Enterer In (Lord of Misrule)
- St George
- Prince Paradise
- Colonel Slasher
- Doctor
- Beelzebub
- Groom
- Horse

Equipment:

- Staff for the Enterer In
- 'Swords' for St George, Prince Paradise and Colonel Slasher
- Two bottles of 'medicine' for the Doctor
- Bag of coins
- Club, dripping pan and hat for Beelzebub
- Bell for the Groom

THE PLAY

Loud banging at the door and the Enterer In makes his appearance. He beats his staff on the floor. When performed in farm kitchens this used to be an exciting affair with sparks flying from the stone floor and much noise.

ENTERER IN: Open the door and let us in,
We hope your favour we shall win;
We do our endeavour to please you all.

Now acting time is come and we do here appear -
The time of mirth and merriment to all spectators here.
We are not of the ragged sort but some of the royal trim.
And if you don't believe me what I say,
Step in, St George, and clear the way!

Enterer In exits as St George enters and struts about the room, saying:

ST GEORGE: I am St George, that noble champion bold,
And with my glittering sword I won five crowns of gold.
'Twas I that fought the fiery dragon
And brought him to the slaughter,
And by fair means I won fair Sheba,
The King of Egypt's daughter.
But bring to me that man that there before me stand
And I'll cut him down with sword in hand!

Enter Prince Paradise:

PARADISE: I am Prince Paradise, that black Morocco King;
With sword and buckle by my side,
Through these woods I'll ring.
Through these woods I'll brave boys,
My words I will make good.
And from thy dearest body, George,
I'll draw thy trembling blood!

ST GEORGE: What's that thou sayest?

PARADISE: What I say I mean!

ST GEORGE: Pull out thy purse and pay!

PARADISE: Pull out thy sword and fight!
Satisfaction I will have before thou goes away!

They fight and Paradise falls wounded.

PARADISE: Pardon me, St George, for I am wounded sore.

ST GEORGE: Yes, I'll pardon thee if thou go out and come no more.

Exit Prince Paradise.

ST GEORGE: I am St George, that noble Knight,
Who shed his blood for England's right,
For England's right, for England's wrong -
Which makes me carry this bloody weapon!
But bring me that man that there before me stand
And I'll cut him down with sword in hand!

Enter Colonel Slasher. Slasher and St George countermarch, clashing swords each time they pass.

SLASHER: I am a valiant soldier and Slasher is my name.
With my sword and buckle by my side,
I mean to win this game.
This game I mean to win, brave boys,
And that I will make good,
And from thy dearest body, George,
I'll draw thy trembling blood!

ST GEORGE: Oh, Hasher Slasher, don't thou talk so hot,
For in this room thou knowest not whom thou's got.
I'll hop thee and chop thee as small as flies

And send thee over the seas to make mince pies.
Mince pies hot, mince pies cold,
Mince pies in the pot nine days old.

SLASHER: How canst thou talk of hopping and chopping me
When my head is made of iron,
My body garbed in steel,
My legs and arms be beaten brass -
No man can make me feel!

ST GEORGE: If thy head be made of iron,
Thy body garbed with steel,
Thy legs and arms be beaten brass,
I still will make thee feel!

SLASHER: What's that thou sayest?

ST GEORGE: What I say I mean!

SLASHER: Pull out thy purse and pay!

ST GEORGE: Pull out thy sword and fight
For satisfaction I will have before thou goes away!

They fight and Slasher falls wounded.

SLASHER: Oh! Pardon me, St George, for I am wounded sore.

ST GEORGE: No pardon will I give but wound thee ten times more!

Slasher dies.

ST GEORGE: Now Slasher he is dead and gone,
What will become of me?
His body's dead, his ghost is fled,
No more of him we'll see!
Is there a doctor to be found
To cure a dead man of his wounds?

Enter Enterer In:

ENTERER IN: Yes I heard of a doctor the other day
Who came from France and Spain
That can bring a dead man to life again.

ST GEORGE: Ten pounds for a doctor!

ENTERER IN: Pooh! Pooh! I don't value twenty!

ST GEORGE: Bring him in!

DOCTOR: In I come who never came yet
With my big head and little wit.
Although my head it is but small,
I like my part as well as you all!

ST GEORGE: Are you a doctor?

DOCTOR: Yes, Master.

ST GEORGE: By what means?

DOCTOR: By my travels.

ST GEORGE: Where have you travelled?

DOCTOR: Through High Italy, Sicily, Germany, France and Spain,
And now I've returned to my own country again -
To cure that man that there lies slain!

ST GEORGE: What diseases canst thou cure?

DOCTOR: Oh! all diseases, come as many as pleases -
The itch, the stitch, the pain without,
Cocks with broken legs;
Bring them all to me, them I will cure!
I cured the lass with a winking eye,
A terrible sight to see.
From the lady's head to the gallows head,
A terrible thing to be!

ST GEORGE: Well, cure me that man.

DOCTOR: Yes. Master, if I can.

The Doctor goes to Slasher.

DOCTOR: Here, Jack! Take a little of this bottle,
And let it run down thy throttle.
Rise, Slasher, and fight again!

Slasher remains motionless.

ST GEORGE: Thou silly fool, that's no cure!

DOCTOR: No, you never knew a doctor to take a short job in hand

But what he made a long'n of it.
But I've got another bottle in my pocket called Alec,
And plain, that will bring a dead man to life again!
Here, Jack, take a little of this nip nap
And let it run down thy tip tap.
Rise, Slasher, and fight again!

Slasher recovers. Exit Doctor.

SLASHER: Oh! horrible, horrible, the like was never seen -
A man knocked out of his seven senses and into seventeen!
Out of seventeen and into seven score,
The like was never seen nor done before,
Neither by bull nor bear,
But by St George, I do declare!

ST GEORGE: Thou silly ass that lives by grass,
Thou thought I'd be a stranger;
I live in hopes to buy some ropes,
To tie thy nose to a manger.

SLASHER: Thou mortal man that lives by bread,
What makes thy nose so long and red?

ST GEORGE: Thou silly fool, dost thou not know?
'Tis PP ale that is so stale
That keeps my nose from looking pale!

SLASHER: What's that thou sayest?

ST GEORGE: What I say I mean!

SLASHER: Pull out thy purse and pay
For satisfaction I will have before thou goes away!

They fight but Prince Paradise comes in and steps between them.

PARADISE: Charge! Peace! For quietness is the best;
The clock's struck one, you must obey;
Put up your swords and fight another day.

Exit Prince Paradise and Slasher. Enter Beelzebub.

BEELZEBUB: In come I, old Beelzebub.
In my hand I carry a club,
In my hand a dripping pan -
Don't you think I'm a jolly young man?

ST GEORGE: Hello, Bobsjack! Are you here today?
Pray tell me some of your rigs.

BEELZEBUB: No, as I was going down the road,
I passed a private lodging house 'twixt Bristol and Birmingham.
There I saw a chamber maid peeping through the window.
She didn't beat the bed but she did beat the pillow.
As I rode my horse a little down the road,
It took boggart at a stile,
jumped nine hedges and nine ditches,
And broke all the necks it had but one!

ST GEORGE: Pray, Jack, how many necks had it?

BEELZEBUB: Nineteen and a half, two halves as good as a whole one.

Ladies and gentlemen, ere so bold
To eat plum pudding before it's half cold,
My hat is dumb and cannot spake -
Pray put something in for St George's sake!

Beelzebub removes hat and collects a little money (or other gifts) from the audience, then exits.

There is much banging and thumping; the groom rushes in ringing a bell and shouting:

GROOM: Hello! Hello! Hello!
This is to give you notice, I've brought young Ball,
And I hope he will give satisfaction to you all!
He's a fine horse, full of blood and bone, muscle and action,
And if you'd like to see him, I'll bring him in.

SOMEONE: Bring him in!

The Groom brings in the Horse and makes him face the audience.

GROOM: Make your obedience to her Ladyship.

The Horse bows three times to the lady of the house.

GROOM: And now obedience to the audience.

The Horse refuses. There is a struggle but at last the Horse bows to the audience.

All the players enter and make a ring around the Horse. They sing the song below, after which the Groom takes the Horse around collecting.

ALL PLAYERS

(to the tune of 'God Rest Ye Merry Gentlemen'):

Ye Gentlemen of England, we'll have you to draw near
And mark these lines which we have said and quickly you shall hear
And quickly you shall hear with your half-pence and strong beer
And we'll come no more a-acting until another year.

The Winter it is coming in, dark, dirty, wet and cold
And to try your good nature this night we do make bold
This night we do make bold with your 'alf-pence and strong beer
And we'll come no more a-acting until another year.

God bless the Master of this house, and the Mist-er-ess also
And the little children that round the table go
Likewise your men and maidens, your cattle and your store
And all that lies within your gates, we wish you ten times more.
We wish you ten times more with your 'alf-pence and strong beer
And we'll come no more a-acting until another year.

Go down into your cellars and see what you can find
If your barrels be not empty, we hope you will prove kind
We hope you will prove kind with your 'alf-pence and strong beer
And we'll come no more a-acting until another year.

So now we make an ending of what we had begun
For a'going a'acting, we think there is no sin
And we think there is no sin with your 'alf-pence and strong beer
And we'll come no more a-acting until another year.

THE END

The Pagan Pathfinders Yule Party was always a highlight of the year. It was a chance for everyone to socialise and celebrate the Solstice together.

As well as a Yule ritual, we would engage in all manner of silliness, such as pass the parcel, an incomprehensible mummers' play and singing these carols[5] *(with various levels of tunefulness). All of this would be followed by inordinate amounts of feasting.*

Brothers, Sisters Come and Sing

Brothers, Sisters come and sing, glory to the new born King,
Gardens peaceful, forests wild, celebrate the winter child,
Now the time of growing starts, joyful hands and joyful hearts,
Cheer the Yule log as it burns, for once again the sun returns,
Brothers, sisters come and sing, glory to the new born King.

Brothers, Sisters singing come, glory to the new born sun,
Through the wind and dark of night, celebrate the coming light,
Sun's glad rays through fierce cold burns, life through death the wheel now turns,
Gather round Yule log and tree, celebrate life's mystery,
Brothers, sisters singing come, glory to the new born sun.

The Holly and The Ivy

The holly and the ivy when they are both full grown,
Of all the trees that are in the wood, the holly bears the crown.
Oh, the rising of the sun and the running of the deer,
The singing of robin redbreast when merry Yule draws near.

[5] Many of these are attributed to the Greenwood Singers.

The holly and the ivy when they are both full grown,
Of all the trees in the green wood, ivy wears the gown.
Oh, the rising of the sun and the running of the dear,
The singing of robin redbreast when merry Yule draws near.

Silent Night, Solstice Night

Silent night, Solstice night, all is calm, all is right,
Nature slumbers in forest and glen, 'til in Springtime she wakens again,
Sleeping spirit grow strong, sleeping spirits grow strong.

Silent night, Solstice night, silver moon, shining bright,
Snow fall blankets the slumbering Earth, Yule fires welcome the sun's rebirth,
Hark! the light is reborn, Hark! the light is reborn.

Silent night, Solstice night, quiet rest, stilled the light,
Turning ever the rolling wheel, brings the winter to comfort and heal,
Rest your spirit in peace, Rest your spirit in peace.

Oh Come All Ye

Oh come all ye faithful, gather round the Yule fire,
Oh come ye, oh come ye to call the sun;
Fires within us call the fire above us,
Oh come let us invoke him, oh come let us invoke him,
Oh come let us invoke him, our Lord the sun.

Oh Lord we greet thee, born again at Yule tide,
Yule fires and candle flame are lighted for thee.
Come to thy children, calling for thy blessing;
Oh come let us invoke him, oh come let us invoke him,
Oh come let us invoke him, our Lord the sun.

Deck the Halls

Deck the halls with boughs of holly, fah la la la laa, la la la laaa.
'Tis the season to be jolly, fah la la la laa, la la la laaa.
Don we now our gay apparel, fah la la la la la la laaa.
Trill the ancient Yuletide carol, fah la la la laa, la la la laaa.

See the blazing Yule before us, fah la la la laa, la la la laaa.
Strike the harp and join the chorus, fah la la la laa, la la la laaa.
Follow me in merry measure, fah la la la la la la laaa.
While we sing of Yuletide pleasure, fah la la la laa, la la la laaa.

Ask the way the old year passes, fah la la la laa, la la la laaa.
Hail the new ye lads and lasses, fah la la la laa, la la la laaa.
Sing we merry all together, fah la la la la la la laaa.
Heedless of the wind and weather, fah la la la laa, la la la laaa.

Lord Rest Ye Merry...

Lord rest ye merry pagan folk let nothing you dismay,
Remember that the sun returns upon this Solstice day,
The growing dark is ended now and spring is on its way,
Oh tidings of comfort and joy, comfort and joy, oh tidings of comfort and joy.

The winter's worst still lies ahead, fierce tempest, snow and rain,
Beneath the hoarfrost on the ground the spark of life remains,
The sun's warm rays caress the seeds to raise life's song again,
Oh tidings of comfort and joy, comfort and joy, oh tidings of comfort and joy.

Within the blessed apple lies the promise of the queen,
For from this pentacle shall rise the orchards fresh and green,
The earth shall blossom once again, the air be sweet and clean,
Oh tidings of comfort and joy, comfort and joy, oh tidings of comfort and joy.

The Thirteen Days of Yule

On the first day of Yuletide my true love gave to me,
a gold bough in an oak tree.
On the second day of Yuletide my true love gave to me,
two lovers loving (& etc)
3rd – three pentacles
4th – four blowing winds
5th – five trees of life
6th – six ways of sensing
7th – seven cauldrons swirling
8th – eight sabbath fires
9th – nine stones for stepping
10th – ten pagans dancing
11th – eleven stags a-leaping
12th – twelve signs of changing
13th – thirteen moons of shining

WINTER GODS PATHWORKING AND RITUAL

This is a shortened version of the 'Stone Meditation' in the first part of the Workbook.

Requirements:

- Altar with candle
- A large stone, bowl of water and cloth
- Usual candles and incense
- Cakes and wine

Roles:

- Guide
- Circle Caster
- Quarter Officers

The group stands in a circle. In the centre is the Altar with a candle, a large stone, a bowl of water and a cloth. There is incense burning. Begin by drawing the protective circle and calling on the Quarters.

Spoken by the Guide:

Sit in a relaxed state and focus on the stone in the centre of the circle. Breathe deeply and rhythmically .... Now take it in turns to hold the stone and visualise any emotional pain or tension, fears, uncertainties and doubts, worry or anxiety, sadness or anger. Focus on transferring that into the stone, letting those feelings go into the stone, releasing them. Then take the stone and wash it in the bowl of water, washing away any negative emotion, cleansing your inner being and emotional self. Dry the stone and pass it to the next person. Feel the release from anxiety.

Pause to allow this to happen.

Now sit and close your eyes, finding that still centre within yourself, relaxing more deeply as you let your breathing become slow and deep ....

We find ourselves wrapped in warm cloaks, walking in a wild place. It is winter and there is a cold blustery wind and ragged clouds race across the sky. The place we are in has a group of great oaks growing amongst a tumble of huge stones. Possibly these stones are the remains of an ancient burial site. The bare branches of the oak trees look like the antlers of great stags ....

Standing by one of the stones we see two figures dressed in black. They purvey a sense of great presence, awesome. We draw closer and see that one is an ancient crone of great dignity and we recognise her as the Goddess in her winter aspect. Beside her is a tall grey man with an antler's headdress, the winter God. We cannot escape the magnetic pull of their presence and draw yet closer, feeling the aura of austere majesty about them. There is great wisdom and understanding and compassion in their faces that inspire a great sense of trust. Let us each open our heart to them. They see our weaknesses, our vulnerabilities and also our hopes, our courage, laughter and joy and the love that is within us .... We each feel the winter God touch our forehead and our minds clear and become still and calm. We each feel the winter Goddess touch our breast and our hearts are filled with warmth and courage. We know that we have within us the courage and the wisdom to deal with whatever comes to us in the year ahead. We can stroll boldly forward with warm hearts and clear minds .... The presences give a final blessing and fade away.

We return the way we came and we pause and review our intentions, our doubts and fears and uncertainties, and our plans for the future, but now with a different perspective: more relaxed, more confident, knowing that we can find within us the strength and support and wisdom that we need ....

Now we will take cakes and wine, nourishing us in heart and mind with these other gifts of the God.

Share cakes and wine and close the ritual.

NEW MOON IN CAPRICORN PATHWORKING

You could use the ideas in this pathworking to craft other pathworkings based on the zodiac symbols or archetypes.

Requirements:

- Pens and paper

Spoken by the Guide:

So that you can become even more deeply relaxed, just let yourself sink down. Just be here, now .... Let go of the past. This is where you are now. Your past experience has been harvested and its essence distilled, distilled into knowledge and wisdom and experience. We know that we learn most from the things that we have found difficult and challenging. Sometimes we hold onto regrets, those 'if onlys', those 'I should have done'. All the 'if onlys' and 'should haves', let them all go, let them all just float away .... Value all that you have experienced, the joys and the sorrows, the terrors and the adventures, the hurt and pain, and the pleasures, the anger, the delight, the boredom. Value them all because they have made you what you are now, and all your strengths.

Now you are ready to move forward, to experience, to harvest more joy and strength, and wisdom and knowledge, and love. So just feel that you are you. Just say to yourself 'I am I' ....

Imagine that you are in your room and you go to your cupboard and you find at the back of it another door, a door that isn't always there, but it is there now and opens for you, revealing a flight of old stone steps, a spiral staircase leading down. Eager to explore, you step through and start to go down and down; with each step, becoming more deeply relaxed and your impressions of the staircase becoming clearer and clearer, more real. Feel the old worn steps beneath your feet. Feel the rough stone walls with your hands. There is flickering light cast by burning torches in sconces in the walls. There is the old musty stone smell of the place and perhaps some smell from the torches burning as you go down and round, and down and round, until you get to the bottom and there is a doorway and you open it and step through and find yourself in daylight, in rocky mountainous country. There is a golden winter sun shining low in the sky. The air is cold and crisp and beneath your feet is a path of wiry grass leading through rocky countryside with a few hardy pine trees and larch trees. At this time of the year the days are beginning just noticeably to get longer, but we are getting a little more light, rather than more warmth, and yet as we walk along the path, we spot a few early primroses and snowdrops under the trees.

The path you are treading is rough and winding and quite difficult, slightly uphill and winding in different directions. It is perhaps like the year ahead of you, difficult to see very far ahead and beset with little and big hazards, rocks, canyons, easy bits when it goes downhill, more difficult bits as you climb up. There are loose rocks and stones. Now the path takes you around a corner and suddenly you are full in the sun, face to face, and it is dazzlingly bright because it is so low in the sky. You stop and take some deep breaths of the lovely fresh air and let the light bathe you, feel the stirrings within the earth in response to the light, and within yourself as you sense the gradually growing power of the sun.

But suddenly you hear the sound of falling stones and feet scrabbling on rocks. You open your eyes and see a great ram with sweeping horns scrambling onto the path ahead of you. It looks at you with its extraordinary eyes, its horizontal pupils. You hear its 'baaaaaa' deep as a bell echoing within you and then with a toss of his head he turns and goes along the path before you. His coat seems to be aflame with the sunlight. The path is getting steeper and you are panting to keep up with the ram, climbing and scrambling, exhilarated and excited by it, feeling the energy beginning to stir within you ....

Now you reach a flat plateau with a magnificent view before you of mountains and valleys and the ram is standing proudly looking over his realm and you stand by the ram, aware of his animal strength, his sure-footedness and his persistence in the face of obstacles and, as you look onto this amazing landscape, you can see your path for the year ahead, its ups and downs and its difficulties and rewards. Perhaps if you have some particular goals for this year, you can make out the goals in the landscape, some near at hand, some further away. Maybe you can even see some false trails and some blind alleys that you can get all too easily distracted by ....

The ram is still standing beside you. You put your hand on his head and you seem to hear his voice in your head giving you some advice about your year ahead, how to make your new starts ....

Now the sun is beginning to set, darkness is falling and your attention moves within as you think of your goals for the coming year. The sun slips behind the horizon. Suddenly, close by where the sun went down, you see a delicate crescent moon, beautiful, serene, a sliver of gold, a symbol of renewal and hope and inspiration. So let your focus move to the month ahead. What will you do this month to further your year's goals? Or what special new beginning can you make this month? The ram may give you a bit of a nudge here ....

Let come into your mind at least one thing that you will do maybe tomorrow, or next week. Feel that nudge from the ram again, prodding you to be decisive, to be determined, to persevere, to be brave. The power of the waxing moon flows into you, a blessing on your endeavours, your intentions ....

Now the new moon is already setting, slipping below the horizon. The ram turns towards you and paws the ground. You know he is about to depart so you thank him for his guidance and his nudges, his strength, his sure-footedness, his Capricornian gifts to you.

Now he trots away and you turn back the way you came and somehow going back is much easier and straighter, despite the darkness, and in no time you find yourself back at that doorway. You climb up the spiral staircase. As I count from twenty to one you are going up and up, coming back gradually to the here and now. Twenty .... nineteen .... eighteen .... seventeen .... sixteen .... fifteen .... fourteen .... thirteen .... twelve .... eleven .... ten .... halfway back now .... nine .... eight .... seven .... six .... five .... feel your hands and your feet .... four .... three .... two .... one .... You step back into the here and now and take your pen and paper and capture those ideas, those intentions. Write them down on your paper.

FULL MOON & GODDESS PATHWORKING

Spoken by the Guide:

Breathe and relax. Imagine that you are walking on a hilltop at evening time, the night of the full moon .... The moon is just beginning to rise above the horizon and by its silvery light you see something mysterious ahead of you. You come closer and see that there is a large slab of rock into which is carved a spiral maze and right before your feet is the entrance to this maze. You follow the twisting path that seems to double back on itself and then go forward again, sometimes deosil, sometimes widdershins, but gradually as you follow it you are getting nearer and nearer the centre and as you get nearer the centre you are becoming more deeply relaxed, your state of consciousness changing, the maze becoming more vividly real ....

Now you come to the centre of the maze and you stand there and feel a strange power. Imagine you close your eyes there and feel the power of the earth and the power of the full moon .... You feel that that maze of going round and doubling back and intricate diversions and complicated whorls is rather like life, and you yearn to tap that inner wisdom that helps you to tread the maze of your life with sure feet and sense of direction. In your heart you ask the powers of the full moon for guidance ....

Then, still feeling the rock of the maze beneath your feet, imagine you open your eyes and you find that the rock beneath your feet is no longer the maze, but is on the edge of a river and on the other side of the river you see a misty, silvery moonlit landscape and you know that is where you must reach, so you step into the water. Feel the river swirling around your legs and you ask the elemental creatures of water to support you and help you cross the river and to guide you. You seem to hear their sweet siren song in the ripples and gurgles of the river ....

Now you reach the other side and climb out easily onto the bank and follow a little slivery path until you come to a circle of small, dark cypress trees standing about 10 feet high. Before you is an opening where you can enter the inner circle of the trees. In the centre is a great rock with quite a deep dip in the centre of it. You go up to the rock and look into the water and you see there the reflection of the moon, the full moon, which has now climbed high in the sky .... You feel that yearning within your heart to understand the cycles of your life, to use them, to use all the opportunities that come to you, to learn how to get value from even difficult experiences ....

A little breeze ruffles the surface of the pool in the rock. The moon reflection shivers and breaks up and when it becomes still again, it is the face of a beautiful woman, the Goddess of the Moon. You open your heart to her, asking through her power to learn to understand, to find your way through the maze of your life. You take a few moments just to listen and see what you can hear from the Moon Goddess, what guidance you can find, what insights, what understanding and what wisdom. So just take now a few minutes to commune with the Goddess of the Moon ....

Now feel her unlocking the hidden treasures of your creativity and your imagination. Feel all barriers melting away, a sense of inner freedom, the freedom of the Moon Goddess ....

Then the full moon moves on. The face of the Goddess slides out of view and you thank her for her wisdom and inspiration, knowing that every full moon you can contact her wisdom.

Then it is time to leave the little cypress grove. Make your way back to the river and as you wade through it thank the elemental spirits of water for their support and for their music .... Then step up onto the bank and, as you do so, you become aware that you are once more in the centre of the maze. The moon is high overhead in a beautiful, clear sky. You turn and follow the spiral maze back to the everyday world. As you travel, going sometimes widdershins, sometimes deosil, looping back and forth, enjoy the adventure of your life with its twists and turns and interest and opportunity; the great opportunities for joy and love, and excitement and peace, activity and rest, a deep and restful sleep, good food, happy days ....

Now you reach the end of the maze and the scene starts to face. As I count from twenty to one, you start to come back to the here and now. Twenty .... nineteen .... eighteen .... seventeen .... sixteen .... fifteen .... fourteen .... thirteen .... twelve .... eleven .... halfway back now, begin to become aware of your body .... ten .... nine .... eight .... seven .... six .... five .... four .... three .... two .... one .... And have stretch and open your eyes.

BEST AND WORST SELF PATHWORKING

Spoken by the Guide:

Imagine that you are in your room and you go to your cupboard and open it and find at the back of it that familiar door, not always there, but it is there now and opens for you, revealing a spiral staircase of old stone steps leading down. So you step through and start to go down the steps, noticing that it is lit by flaming sconces in the walls, and as you go down and down, and round and down, with each step you are becoming more deeply relaxed and the staircase is becoming more vivid and real. You feel the worn steps under your feet, the rough stones of the walls and smell the ancient stone smell of the place as you go down, and round, and down, and down, until you come to a landing and find there an old wooden door set in a stone arch; the door to your own private magical temple.

You open the door and find your temple just as you remember it. In the centre is a little waist high altar on which burns a beautiful lamp and to the east there are two great pillars, one black and one white. Against one of the walls is an ancient chest in which you keep your magical tools and your robes. You go to the chest and take out a robe the colour of your own choice, and you find your talisman and put it around your neck, a talisman that is your great and important protection. If ever you find that everything is a bit overwhelming, or you are feeling lost, you can take your talisman in your hand and wish yourself back in your temple and you will be back safely there in an instant.

Now you stand before your altar and prepare yourself for a trip. Draw a circle of blue fire right around yourself. You can leave your everyday self safely within this circle of blue fire while the deeper level of yourself goes exploring.

Now you pass between the pillars and find another door. You open it and find a short flight of stone steps leading you down to a river bank and there is a boat to board. You get into the boat, cast off the rope and a hidden current takes the boat and takes you sailing down the river, which very rapidly broadens out into a lake. In the centre of the lake is an island and you can just make out, as it is beginning to get dark, that on the island is some sort of a turreted building and the hidden current within the lake takes your boat towards the island. As you near it, you can make out against the darkening sky the outline of a great castle. One turret is particularly high and you can see that there is a light shining through a very small window at the top.

You climb out of the boat and find before you the entrance to the castle. You walk in and feel within yourself an impulse to climb up to that light at the top. You see a staircase which seems to be the one that leads up to that tower and you start to climb up, up and round, again it is a spiral staircase, up and up. A sense of anticipation, but also of challenge. Who might be up in that tower room? ....

You feel that it is a very important entity there that you are about to meet, perhaps a guide, a wise being, a being that will ask you some difficult questions maybe. You are toiling up and up, feeling that you are reaching for your highest potential. You become convinced that that is the challenge: you are going to be challenged to reach your highest potential.

Now you are at the top. The staircase ends at a circular room and there is a being, imposing a presence of power. Perhaps this person, this being is, who knows, your holy guardian angel, a special guide. In fact it is a representation of your highest potential. It is an aspect of yourself that perhaps you hardly know. You are welcomed. You enter and you let this entity speak within your mind. You hear a special message, or advice, or a challenge maybe ....

As you listen to this entity you begin to feel that you are this entity. It is you, yourself, speaking to you. So describe this being to yourself. What are this entity's special qualities, special achievements, special goals? ....

Now, having absorbed this entity within yourself, you start to go down the staircase again, and down, and down. When you reach the ground floor you find that the staircase goes on down, down, down into the crypt. You follow the staircase down, and down, and you begin to hear strange noises, clanging, as though something is being hit with a hammer, and inarticulate bellowing and cries.

You realise that in this crypt is another aspect of yourself, your shadow aspect. You go on down with grim determination until you reach the bottom and see there another entity, a dark, shadowy entity, which seems to express all those attributes you hate or despise in other people, those people who maybe make you feel uncomfortable, or a bit scared, or angry, or embarrassed, perhaps people who are angry and dominating, or people who seem to cringe with fear all the time. You realise this is another aspect of yourself, all the things within yourself that you project out to other people and find them hateful.

So let this entity speak to you and as it speaks you realise it is a part of yourself speaking to you .... Describe yourself as this aspect of yourself .... Accept these energies, as you will find they are strengths and talents. They are only hateful when you don't own them. Feel this aspect brought in with you as you accept your shadow side ....

Now you find your way back up the stone staircase to the ground floor and follow the smell of incense into an ancient temple. You can feel within yourself the conflicting aspects of the highest you and the lowest you. Before you in the temple is an ancient wooden statue of a Goddess figure, blackened with age, but strangely compelling. In front of her has been placed a large candle and you stand before her and light the candle. By the flickering light of the candle the wooden statue seems to move and to come alive. A powerful presence fills the room. She is the primordial Goddess of ancient wisdom. She presides over the evolution of life, including the evolution of mind and spirit. She presides over humankind and animal and plant kind, but also each individual ....

Present to her the whole of yourself, your highest potential self and your shadow self. Feel under her magic you become whole. The energy of your shadow self that you have repressed and given away to others is taken back to become a part of your strength and your wisdom and your love. Feel yourself grow in stature, feel your higher self overshadowing you. Feel it towering above you like a wonderful flame ....

The more you keep awareness of your higher self and treasure your shadow self, the stronger you will be and the more in touch with your potential. Feel the powerful magic of this primordial Goddess and thank her for her gifts, knowing that with this new sense of integration you can see the potential within everybody else. You can see overshadowing them their higher self. Some people may be very unaware and out of touch with their higher self, but it is there waiting to be acknowledged, to play its role ....

Now it is time to thank that wonderful presence which fades away. Salute the ancient wooden statue and leave the castle, your step light, buoyant, confident, and then you climb into your boat and in no time at all you are back at the entrance to your temple. Quickly enter it and then take off your talisman and put it back in the chest, and your robe. Let the circle of blue flame die down and as I count from twenty to one, make your way back up the spiral staircase to this place. Twenty .... nineteen .... eighteen .... seventeen .... sixteen .... fifteen .... fourteen .... thirteen .... twelve .... eleven .... ten .... half way back, take some deep breaths .... nine .... eight .... seven .... six .... five .... more deep breaths, feel your hands and your feet .... four .... three .... two .... one.

THE COLOUR WITHIN PATHWORKING

Spoken by the Guide:

Imagine you are sitting in your own secret place, feeling very calm and relaxed. And you imagine that you close your eyes and immediately have the sensation that you are sinking slowly down through the rainbow colours – first through red .... then through orange .... and through yellow .... green .... through blue .... through indigo .... through violet .... and finally into complete darkness. And you stay within that darkness, feeling totally relaxed ...

And now within that darkness, you see a glow of colour and this colour is whatever colour you need at this moment. Colour has healing properties - there are methods of therapy that use coloured lights - but you can tap into the healing power of colour simply by using your imagination. When you contact your own psychic and intuitive faculties through deep relaxation, you are able to sense what colour you need at this point in time to bring yourself into balance.

So as you let yourself relax even more completely, let that colour emerge as a faint glow in the darkness .... Now it is beginning to get brighter and more vibrant, seeming to fill your entire body .... And imagine it glowing with particular intensity in that part of your body that most needs the healing power of that colour and imagine that colour penetrating that part of your body, bringing ease and balance and wholeness ....

And now imagine that colour going beyond your body into your aura, so that you are not only permeated completely internally with that colour but surrounded by a brilliant cloak of coloured light .... Perhaps you sense that some part of your aura seems to need that colour, a part that is dark and smoky, or pale and lifeless. Feel that colour gently but persistently invading and permeating that part of your aura, driving out any dark or smoky areas, bringing vitality to any pale and lifeless areas. Feel your aura being cleansed and repaired, strengthened and revitalised .... And be aware of the effect that this has on your sense of physical, mental and emotional wellbeing, how it strengthens you and mobilises your inner resources ....

And now observe how you feel about this colour. Sometimes one needs a particular, pure intensity of colour for only a short time and if you feel that you have had enough of that colour or that it needs a mixture of another colour to balance it, feel free to change it or add to it .... Let your aura and your body be shot through with other colours, or with white light. Let them pulsate with changing vibrant colours ....

And now let the colours become less intense and subside to a soft, pearly mist. And become aware once more that you are in your own secret place and in this place you open your eyes and look around and it seems to glow with the same softly iridescent pearly light that has the potential for all shades of healing colour ....

And now the time has come to return to the everyday world and you take three slow, deep breaths .... and open your eyes.

TAROT RITUAL AND PATHWORKING

This is a session written and conducted by Lisa Stockley, long-term attendee of Pagan Pathfinders.

Set up the ritual circle. Alongside the elemental tools, place the Aces from your favourite Tarot deck, ideally one with nature-based imagery. Make sure you have paper and pens handy, and at least one full deck of tarot cards (depending on how many people are present, more than one deck may be useful).

Spoken by the session leader:

Start with a shake, groan, stretch, to bring yourself into focus and shake off the energies of the day .... Take some deep breaths and stretch upwards, raising your arms and standing on tiptoes to stretch as tall as you can ....

Now lie down and relax. As your mind slowly clears, bring to mind a specific intent for your magical work later and take a few minutes to clarify your intention .... Relax each part of your body individually, releasing any tension from the feet, legs and so on, all the way up your body to your face. Imagine that you are lying on a beach with the waves washing over you, carrying away your stresses and leaving you feeling cleansed and open ....

The cards of the Tarot awaken our intuition and by looking at them in a ritual circle we allow ourselves to go deeper into the images and really experience them. The Tarot deck has seventy-eight cards in total. Twenty-two of these are called the major arcana and describe archetypal ideas and concepts, the energies that bring big changes in our lives. Then there are sixteen court cards, which depict people and show us aspects of our personality or sometimes the people around us who guide us on our path. The forty minor arcana cards have four suits, each with ten numbered cards, which bring the 'big ideas' of the major arcana into the reality of life. So if you get lots of major arcana cards, it suggests there is a lot shifting in your self and your life (although it may be internal and not necessarily obvious to others), whereas if you draw minor arcana cards, you are more likely to be in a phase of integrating previous changes into your life and bringing dreams into reality.

Cast the ritual circle and call the elements in your usual way, making sure that everybody who wants to has a chance to participate. One suggestion for an informal circle casting is to stand and hold hands, and visualise the circle together. Each participant imagines a sphere encompassing the whole room, protecting you all, a sacred space between the worlds. As you call the elements of air, fire, water and earth, hold up the Tarot Aces and ask that their energies be present in your circle.

When your ritual space is established, go around the circle and each call upon a guide, or a deity you work with to help with this inner work using Tarot. You can be very general, simply using the word "guide" or "higher self", or be more specific if you like. As you invoke this energy, focus on guiding your vision, awakening intuition and showing what is hidden.

Place at least one full deck of Tarot cards in the centre of the circle.

Now sit, focus on your breath and allow it to settle into a quiet, regular rhythm. Now we will take a few minutes for everyone to consider internally any particular issue they would like guidance on from the Tarot, or simply clear the mind to see what comes up .... *[allow time for this to happen.]*

Now focus your mind on the element of air, on the powers of the mind, communication and clarity. As you feel ready, everyone in the circle should pull a card, taking a few minutes to focus on the image .... *[allow time for this to happen.]*

Working with a partner, talk about your card and what you see or sense in it. This is the air of your issue, so this card shows how you communicate about it, understand it, and what you know consciously. It might also be what you need to cut away. Spend around five minutes each and try to keep in a meditative quiet state as you share your ideas .... *[allow time for this to happen.]*

Now come back to stillness and focus again on your breath. Focus your mind on the element of fire, on passion, creativity and action. As you feel ready, once again all pull a card, to represent the fire of your issue, where there is energy and passion. Take a few minutes to focus on the image and then taking paper and pen, draw or free write something about what you see in the card and how it might relate to your self and your life at this time. Use your intuition and creativity, don't think about it too hard, be as spontaneous as you can .... *[allow time for this to happen.]*

Once again come back to stillness and focus on your breath. Focus your mind on the element of water, on feelings and the unconscious mind. As you feel ready, once again all pull a card to symbolise the water of your issue and how you feel about it. Take a few minutes to focus on the image and what it might mean for you at this time. Allow yourself to really feel the energies of the card, to receive its wisdom. What emotions arise? Does it bring up any memories or spark your imagination in some way? Note down your feelings and insights on the same sheet as your drawing .... *[allow time for this to happen.]*

Again come back to stillness and focus again on your breath. Focus your mind on the element of earth, on abundance and manifestation. As you feel ready, once again all pull a card. Take a few minutes to focus on the image, the earth of your issue, and consider what you can do to bring the energies of your cards so far into reality. Choose one concrete action and commit to doing it, to manifest your desired change. Write it down on same sheet as your drawing .... *[allow time for this to happen.]*

Now come back to stillness for the final time and focus again on your breath. Focus your mind on the element of spirit, on the oneness and unity of all things. As you feel ready, once again all pull a card. Take a few minutes to focus on the image. We are going to travel into this card, to integrate the energies of all the cards and synthesise the Tarot reading we have done for ourselves. Spend a few minutes memorising the image, or at least noting the key aspects of it. Now close your eyes and visualise a door in front of you. Step through it and climb down the stairs you see before you .... At the bottom is another door, with an image of your card painted on it. Step through the door into a three-dimensional image of your card. Spend some time exploring, conversing and communing with any beings that you meet, getting to know the realm of your card .... *[allow time for this to happen.]*

Now it is time to come back and you see, close by, a doorway again. Once again step through it, climb the stairs, and step through the first doorway again back into this room .... Take a few deep breaths to come back to your body and when you are ready, open your eyes.

On your piece of paper, or a new one, make a note of what your cards were and any insights you gained from your pathworking .... *[allow time for this to happen.]*

Now it is time to close the ritual circle. Give thanks to the spirits of the Tarot and to the elemental beings for their guidance and close your circle. If you opened the circle by holding hands and visualising a sphere together, now join hands again and visualise the sphere fading.

WATER PATHWORKING AND RITUAL

After the usual grounding and centring, ask the group to start to tune into the concept of fluidity – fluidity in the body and in emotions. Perhaps get the group to move to music, feeling themselves flowing like water, becoming water.

Requirements:

- Candles
- Incense
- Tarot cards
- Pens and paper

Spoken by the Guide:

Now make yourself comfortable and take some deep breaths. Feel yourself sinking down, deeper and deeper, feeling more and more relaxed .... Now imagine you are in your own special place. You see before you a source of water that is pure, perhaps a small spring, or a well, or a small waterfall. You take a goblet and fill it with this pure water. There is blue light rising from it which seems to fill your mind and body and emotional nature, cleansing and refreshing you. Drink deep from the goblet and relax. Find yourself sinking deeper down into the psychic plane ....

Let come into your mind some problem, either a problem with your health or emotional wellbeing. Review this problem. Let the blue light be shed onto it. Feel water dissolving the problem so that it can be dealt with. Be aware of how it would feel without that problem. Feel deeply within yourself that the problem has been dissolved ....

Now the group are invited to open their eyes and stand in a circle. The ritual space is prepared, the circle cast and elements welcomed. The Guide explains the purpose of the ritual, which is to connect to water and to explore some aspect of the element of water, via a Tarot image, and to bring back some wisdom.

Evoke the element of water – this can either be done by the Guide, or by members of the group.

Lay out the Tarot cards and each member of the group should pick one. The Guide then leads a pathworking to meet the being or image represented on the card. Participants are encouraged to receive guidance, help, wisdom or emotional healing from this being.

After this pathworking, allow time for people to write down what they have learnt.

Close the circle.

POEMS AND INVOCATIONS BY ATTENDEES

It was one of the stated aims of Pagan Pathfinders to encourage attendees to tap into their own creativity and to find new ways of expressing themselves. For many this was a challenge, but these are some beautiful examples of the results. Poems and invocations were often encouraged to be written before a ritual, or after a pathworking.

Invocation of Water by Kay Bridger

I call the brimming Cup, I call the Grail.
I sing a silvery song that echoes low
And settles in a vessel-form:
A shell-encrusted cup, a shimmering sight,
The holder of a virtue - Generous Love.
For love fills the dark void
And swells the heart.
It is a thing sought out by every soul.
But generous love is of a rarer hue,
It gives not to receive, but to renew.
Powers of Water - teach us how to give.

Yemaya Invocation - Anonymous

Yemaya! I call you! I call you!
Goddess of the mighty Ocean,
Praise to Yemaya!
Praise to the Realm of Dreams,
Praise to Yemaya!
Praise to the fathomless Ocean,
Praise to Yemaya!
Praise to the face of the Moon,

To the starry sky, the axis of the constellations!
Praise to Yemaya!
Praise to the Mystery of Time,
First moments,
The calling forth of hidden things,
The quickening heart,
Enchantment!
Praise to Yemaya!
Yemaya!
Behold the Children of the Orisha bring you gifts:
Perfume to delight you,
Jewels to deck your beauty,
And flowers to enchant and entice you.
Yemaya! We call you! We call you!
We call you! We call you!
Praise to Yemaya!

Imbolc Poem by Liz Wigglesworth

The wheel of the year is spinning onwards.
Dark days of stillness in the earth
And stillness in the mind roll behind us.
Outside the greening is beginning,
The Imbolc sun is warmer,
The Imbolc moon tides are high.
The sea breathes in and out,
Ebbing and flowing, old to new.
No longer we yearn to sit by the hearth-fire,
Telling stories and dream weaving;
We yearn to be out in the air.
The Lady of the Wildwood is walking the land,
Her bare footsteps imprinted in the fresh green grass.

Hear her sparkling laugh as she rushes past you on the path,
Feel her magic in new thought-seeds and plans,
See her light emerging through the soil as beautiful snowdrops.
She casts the wild out into the world,
Calling up seeds buried in the warming earth,
Green shoots appearing, covering the fields and woodlands
And poking up through cracks on city pathways.
The wild cannot be contained.
She inspires new beginnings,
Old ideas to be hurled off our shoulders
New starts, new creations and energy bursts.
Bless us Brigid in your walking and wilding,
Bless our thought-seeds that they may grow and fruit,
Bless us all this Imbolc-tide.

Artemis - Anonymous

Artemis, great goddess of the crescent moon,
The maiden moon, the new moon,
You are strength, you are new life.
You are beauty, you are the spark of life.
You are the will to make new beginnings.
Give us the determination to create those beginnings
And to follow them through.
Beautiful and powerful huntress, we call to you,
We honour you.

Gaia - Jean Williams

Gaia the beautiful,
Glory of sunrise and sunset,
Stately grace of trees,
Chuckling streams and roaring seas,
Great rocks and jagged mountains,
Birds and lions and beetles,
Lizards and leprechauns,
Amazing plenty of life feeding on life,
Life feeding on death.
Gaia the beautiful,
The amazing,
The joyous,
We are of you.

To Gaia - Anonymous

So long before we were, you were.
Long after we have gone, you will be.
We have always known your beauty,
As we get older now we know your complexity.
Before it gets too late for us
May we comprehend your generosity;
For all we have ever done is take from you
And all we have ever returned
Is our poison and our rubbish.
One day perhaps we will grow up
And live with you in peace.

Dark Goddess - Kay Bridger

Drawing in, drawing down
Strength and beauty buried underground.
Rot and blackness follow after fruit,
Death the inevitable twin of ripeness.
Lady now you start to show your teeth –
Blackened, honed sharp on the death of days.
Shadows deepen, chills stir in the air,
Yet your heart is whole and full of love.
Cleansing is the winter cold that breaks the soil down.
Loving is the Goddess in her winter guise.

As the maiden you were promise, purity and hope,
But now your real beauty teaches balance,
Dark to your maiden sister's light.
You are the peace of winter days,
The chill that makes the hearth light warm.
And your consort, Lord of dark and shade,
Stands beside you at the mouth of the earth.
Here is wisdom, experience's fruit.
Dark in the womb of earth his dark eye gleams.
He is your lover and your trusted page.
He is the hand that reaches after death.

Lady and Lord of Winter,
Chill and skeleton tree.
Teach us to love the balance of the darker days.
We are not here to play our days in childhood,
But to find balance and the peace of heart
That owning the darkness brings.

Moon Goddess Invocation - Anonymous

Lady of Magic,
Queen of the realm of night,
Silver radiance and ruler of the seas,
You are mistress of our inner tides,
Give us your gifts,
Your strength,
Your power.
Reveal our inner depths
Of creativity love and joy.
Lady of magic we call to you.

Moon Priestess - Anonymous

Hail, Lady of Night, arising in beauty.
The magic of thy light touches, transmutes us.
Thy sweet radiance turns all to silver;
Shadows and mystery surround us in your realm.
Open to us thy secret places,
Arianrhod, Selene, Diana,
Silver Enchantress who commands the mighty oceans;
We dance thy dance, that thou mayest come to us.

Fire - Anonymous

Bright flame
Burn away doubts and fear.
Consume the dross of outworn habits,
Light the fire of will
That I may move forward on my path
With courage, energy and focus.

Fire, in your still heart
The heat is greatest
And there shall we find your wisdom.

Lady of Flowers - Anonymous

Come comely lady, white as May blossom,
Bluebell, violets, forget-me-nots,
Lovely, delicate and precious as wood anemones.
Come, Queen of Flowers
You who dance through the woods,
Beautiful in the breeze,
Lay down against the green, intermingled.
Turn your face to the sun,
But hold secret in the moonlight
Your promise of fruit, of seed.
You who dance and smile with your lover
As the animals hold court.
Lady of life and promise,
Be with us and lead our dance.

Sea Invocation by Chris

Oh mighty, deep and moving sea,
That ebbs and flows continuously,
Thy emerald shades of mystery,
Come to me, come to me.
Clear blue transparency,
Cleansing, enlivening, still,
Lapping on the sandy shore,
Return to thyself once more,
Thy ancient mystery we adore.

Water Invocation - Anonymous

Oh, mighty power of water
I invite you to come to us,
As a deep pool, still and calm in the moonlight,
As a mighty ocean that stirs us to passion,
As a brook, bubbling and merry that fills us with life,
As raindrops joining together and flowing to the sea,
As a warm bath that soothes and comforts us,
As a drink when we are parched and dry.
Let us flow with you and feel your qualities within us.
Blessed element of water, be with us.

Untitled by Lisa Stockley, written following a Blind Walk

O Sun King! Great Lord of Light!
At the zenith of your powers,
Bathe us in your golden fire
As we feel your warmth and your heat,
Awake within us the flame of our true will
That we too may know the zenith of our powers.

Earth Mother, you are ripe and green,
Made fertile by the warming power of the Sun,
Enjoying the fullness of your sensuality and creative power.
Awake within us our own creativity
That we too may bloom, full of vitality and growth

Moon Invocation - Anonymous

Silver Lady of many faces,
Which face will you show us tonight?
What gift will you give from your cup?
Filled with wonder,
We wait for thee,
Here in the moonlight.
Sparkling dew-light on every blade,
Flashing like diamonds.
Stars are your jewels.
Lady of Night
Mistress of Tides
Our hearts are open
Our hands reach out.
Come to us, come, come,
Here by the sea
Where the tides are deep;
Here by the old stones,
We await thee.
Come to us, Lady of the Moon.
We are ready –
She is here.

Afterword

WHY DID PAGAN PATHFINDERS WORK SO WELL, AND LAST SO LONG?

When people reminisce about Pagan Pathfinders (PP), it is with great fondness and a huge appreciation for the wonderful group they were a part of. I think, like me, many didn't realise quite how special it was until it was no more. PP ran every week from the 1970s, with very few exceptions, and Jean quietly taught us discipline, dedication and so much more. We learned a huge range of mind-expansion techniques, as well as opening our minds to the many different branches of Paganism and their associated mythologies. We learned what we could do, developing our own potential, working on aspects of ourselves we struggled with and growing in confidence and happiness. We learned how to connect with the earth and all its mysteries. Celebrating the turning of the Wheel of the Year with the small group was magical and many felt a great sense of fellowship. Most agree that Jean's way of teaching was so subtle, so gentle, that you didn't even realise how much you were learning until reflecting on it later or talking with others about similar groups or methods. Jean had no ego at all and until I read one of her books late in my time at PP, I had no idea she was such a respected Wiccan elder, or about all the other Mystery work she was involved in. It wasn't in her character to put herself above others. Unlike other groups I had been to, there were never any boasts or power struggles. Jean had a wonderful way of filtering people, which I think must be hard to achieve, but she always made sure she checked people out first. It was her home after all! Once you had joined, she made you feel welcome and at ease and even though sometimes you were challenged to step out of your comfort zone (dancing around like a crazed goblin for example), the experiences were truly profound and I learned a huge amount, as well as making some lasting friendships.

Thoughts from other 'Peepers'

Rosie

For me, PP is a scheduled opportunity to learn and practise the skills that benefit one's inner spiritual journey. Attending PP means that I am putting time aside specifically towards this goal. There are many bonuses – such as a warm welcome, making new friends and a little performance art on the side!

Fiona

I started out at PP way back in 1994 ... I have very fond memories of those wonderful Monday evenings. Jean taught me so much and I'll always be grateful to her for them.

Alexandra

I became interested in fairies and wood nymphs some time ago, and [after] some lurking around the 'fairies and wood nymphs section' in the local bookshop I was eventually led to the Pagan Federation, which in turn led me to find Pagan Pathfinders. Only later did I discover that I'd stumbled across one of London's longest standing and most respected Pagan groups, and, brilliant, it was only on my doorstep (Monday nights find people travelling from all corners of London to meet at the feet of the most respected member of the Pagan Federation, who apart from her wisdom, conducts each week with humility and love – I only had to walk down the road) ....

Jean Williams' living room becomes all things. A sacred forest, a ritual circle, a meditation room, a dance floor, a place in which to trance, pathwork, heal and find oneself. From the first meeting, standing (like a tree) in the darkened candle lit space, to the weekly chats on astrology, tarot, the different gods and goddesses, the pathworkings, the magic, to the rituals celebrating the moon phases, the sabbats, and even Diwali, it lightened and enriched my soul ....

Over the years we have covered talisman magic, had talks on NLP, had sessions on the relevant astrology sign to the week, sessions with yoga, chanting, toning, chakra opening and polarity healing. We have worked with tarot, danced Five Rhythms and done a huge variety of rituals .... We celebrate the turn of the wheel each season, finding the earth's energy and using it to help, guide and inspire our life's path within a ritual context and it has been my privilege to run these rituals over the last couple of years, which has been an empowering but hugely humbling experience. The people in PP are focused, interested and very willing participants which adds considerably to the workings. And I can without fail say that everything that I have intended within the format of a ritual since I have been at PP has come to pass. I never have to wonder how or why but once placed in the context of a ritual setting, with those people whose energy and focus help to inspire my own, whatever I wish for eventually happens, almost unconsciously .... After putting my energy and desire into a ritual, over time my life is guided until I look back and realise I'm exactly where I wanted to be. Its no coincidence that the desire has been placed in a sacred and ritual format that gives it its energy and strength, and I have to thank PP for providing the space and time and place in which to do that.

Liz Wigglesworth

It's very hard to put into words the effect PP has had on my life. Before PP I would still have considered myself an insecure, confused novice in the Pagan world. I'd dabbled around, spent a bit of time in groups and read lots of books, but it was only in PP that I felt I was in a truly comfortable environment. The group energy was so welcoming and so warm. It was through Jean's teaching that I finally realised that books cannot teach you everything and that going with the flow of what feels right is far more important than worrying about prescribed rules and rituals. I have learnt a huge amount about different religious systems, Gods and Goddesses and festivals that I may never have looked into on my own. I also made some wonderful friends at PP who became the first people I had ever had to share my Pagan beliefs with. I have learnt so much from them as well.

I really appreciated the fact that PP was so varied. One week we'd be doing a pathworking that transported us to the hot, dusty Egyptian desert and the next we'd be in a dark, cold cave, drinking knowledge from Cerridwen's cauldron. It enabled me to realise what resonates with me as well as what doesn't (although that was rare!).

I very much enjoyed marking and celebrating the seasons with everyone at Jean's and I will never forget the parties. Who, once they have experienced it, can forget the chaotic country dancing and the mayhem of the Maypole .... That Jean opened her house and heart to us for so long is something I will always be grateful for.

Izzy

I found PP gave me more confidence about following my own path, instead of trying to fit in with other people. PP seemed to me to blend together so many different strands, and they all fitted, all had value, were all worth thinking about. I found it a real inspiration.

Jon

The group was very committed, it obviously changed over the years but Jean was an incredible facilitator. She was someone who could bring out the best in people; she was able to give people confidence in what they did. She had a very gentle and non-intrusive way of doing it so for me when I joined PP, the last thing I would have thought of was becoming a witch. If someone had said that to me I would have laughed, thought they were joking.

Jean never preached Witchcraft, by the way. She didn't even preach Paganism. She gave you experiences. 'You come along, work with me'. It felt very natural, almost like kid's games. We did polarity healing, read cards. Some of it was quite funny, some was quite deep. It was very dependent on who was there at the time. Jean facilitated and I didn't realise at the time just how profound it was.

The one thing that did strike me about Jean though was her voice. Her voice was incredibly magical. She could do a pathworking and send people on a journey that they would become totally immersed in. She did it in such a way that I can't think of anyone else who managed it. Jean's ability to take people on a journey was absolutely magical. And even now I am not quite sure how she did it, apart from her hallmark of visualising the Golden Light, or the Golden Bubble. This technique effectively re-vitalised you. Learning how to do this was quite profound.

I went there for over 15 years and each session was unique. There were new exercises, or variations on a theme. But one of the things Jean did for me, which helped me immensely was understanding the Elements. In PP the way you would invoke elements wasn't the way you would do it in most magical systems. You would build up a very clear visualisation and then share it with everyone in the group. At first PP could be quite intimidating but after a while it became very natural. The elemental visualisations were different every time – even if they were from the same person because they were telling what they saw. In effect they had a much stronger elemental contact than in most conventional magical systems. It was in effect elemental discovery from an intellectual, emotional, physical sense and how you could use it within you for elemental balancing. Jean was an absolute master in this and yet at the time it almost seemed like a game. It wasn't 'Now we are going to do some profound magical work ...' – Jean would say, 'Now we are going to do a little exercise...'

She also did exercises – for example, imagine you are a tree. In fact, there were many exercises ... I think she used her background in Humanistic Psychology, the structure, but she was also incredibly intuitive. In this sense she was a true witch, really in touch with herself and the astral and she was able to draw down energies and derive inspiration from it. She seemed to use the filter of Humanistic Psychology so that she could devise exercises and training programmes.

What I really liked about PP was that Jean never once talked about the theory or magic or whatever. Everything was about experience. In a way you built up your own theory during the experience. Only when we talked/evaluated things would we write things down. Only then would we collectively come to some kind of theory. We might have an idea of 'the best techniques' about understanding the polarity of healing.

About polarity healing. You could do that physically by, for example, rubbing your hands together, or by visualising energy being drawn into you and taking it through into your hands, or a combination of both. Then you'd place your hands on the person and literally massage their aura. You'd then focus on the spot that needed attention. It was a very simple, natural form of healing.

Very few people at PP thought of themselves as healers. A few may have thought that they had had a bit of experience of healing, but they didn't consider themselves healers. What it made you realise was that everyone has the gift of healing. What we don't have is the confidence to use it, or any idea of how to bring it out. I found that PP gave me the confidence to do quite a bit of healing, through polarity healing, using hands and direct touch and massage – and a combination of both.

We also learnt how to give massages at PP, often in a meditative state, often releasing tension. There were many exercises done at PP. They were not just designed to help people but also to help people develop their own skills, and confidence. Some exercises helped people to develop their psychic abilities – for example by reading psychically cards other people were holding. None of the exercises were long and there was a fair bit of dancing, stomping and physical exercise.

At PP we would always start with an attunement where people would start with a particular note, and then bring it up. It was a very powerful way of getting the group mind working.

Even though the people changed over a period of time there was always a very strong group mind. It felt like a safe and sacred place to work in, even though it wasn't a group of initiates. The power of Jean's personality created such a strong bond between the people that it felt like a very good place to work in; a place where you could take risks, expose yourself and your personality, and really go outside your comfort zone within a context that people wouldn't laugh at you, or ridicule you. That was another thing about Jean; she made this possible. It was her personality – I don't think these people would have been so comfortable without her. I don't think we can model her personality, but many of the techniques she taught can be learnt and replicated.

Bin

Pagan Pathfinders was a doorway for so many people and such an important point on so many people's journeys. For those who worried about what they might find there, there was tea, an abundance of cats, and a beautiful warm energy weaving around the place which was all down to Jean and her magic. Things looked normal but weren't! It was a safe haven and an important piece of many people's spiritual development.

I can't recall exactly when I first started going to PP, it could have been as far back as 1994. How I heard about it I can't remember either, but my two possible contact points would have been either a Talking Stick pub session in Soho, or Pagan Federation open rituals. I think that I was a regular up until around October 2003, at which point I pretty much uprooted from the UK for a bit, and subsequently moved to Cornwall.

I am not the most fearless extrovert joiner of groups, or in general someone who joyfully mingles with total strangers, but in my mind there didn't seem to be that angsty 'first day at new school feeling' when I first turned up at Jean's house on a Monday evening. The whole 'vibe' was always so low-key and relaxed. It was probably calculated to be that way to an extent, as Jean was so well-versed in human psychology. Unless you were a bit late (but arriving after the official session had properly kicked off wasn't really OK) you would arrive ahead of time and sit round the large kitchen table, sharing tea, biscuits and other nibbles. During the 'ante-chamber period', you could therefore acclimatise to the group (which had regular weekly attendees or members who turned up more randomly) and begin to form friendly bonds by easing into the conversation. Jean used to subtly assist with the ice-breaking by being around the table to kick-start conversation from new members, but in a very innocent way. I think Elizabeth Windsor could have learned a few things from Jean!

Another part of the setup that made for this relaxed dynamic was that regular attendance wasn't obligatory. Even if your appearances were fairly sporadic, it didn't matter as it wasn't a group with a formal structure. Apart from Jean, no-one had a fixed role (unless you were down to be the animator or organiser of the evening's themed activity) so therefore, nothing would be compromised or interfered with if you couldn't make it to a session. (However, regular attendance was encouraged if possible to aid group cohesion.)

With hindsight, the whole PP package was quite remarkable and unique, and the house played an important part. The ground floor (comprising living room, kitchen, back extension and garden) was effectively the temple, annexe and reception area. It was the 'safe space' and ceremonial/ritual venue not only for PP but for other more tightly-constituted groups; but the rooms and spaces involved morphed effortlessly back and forward between esoteric chambers and a normal living area for Jean and the other residents of the house. The temple or meditation room identity was a simple transformation requiring two or three volunteers to roll up a carpet, move a TV set and drape a cloth over it, and then light candles in holders or sconces that were already subtly present in the décor of the room. Following a session, the space was then quickly and easily transformed back into a cosy parlour where Zack could resume watching a repeat episode of Star Trek. The house was a kind of suburban Tardis concealing a discreet and non-metallic Star Gate to various different parallel universes.

PP worked on a number of levels. It was a 'gateway drug' to following a committed Pagan spiritual path, both for people new to the 'Pagan scene' and for people new to the UK itself! It was 'generic Pagan' in its orientation and I believe anyone could feel engaged whether they were perhaps inclined to The Fellowship of Isis, or interested in Ceremonial Magic, or The Norse deity pantheon and the use of Runes. In a word: Eclectic! It resolved what would have been an issue for many Pagans: the PP offer was a safe space in which someone who was essentially a solo observer could nevertheless dip in and out of a loose group that actually celebrated all the seasonal festivals and, when synchronised, many of the full moons during the course of the year, but at the same time there were also members who treated it as their regular, permanent celebrant group (within those ranks, people who didn't want the more rigid or hermetic commitments of, let's say, a Wiccan Coven or a Druid Lodge, people who had belonged to more formal groups but had become 'homeless' and people like myself who moved into an initiatory group but still enjoyed additional celebrations and workings on top of the regular 'path' commitments). For all categories of participant (apologies to people who wouldn't consider themselves fitting one of my categories) it was an opportunity to learn and encounter things that they wouldn't have otherwise encountered. This was of course facilitated by Jean's huge breadth and depth of knowledge and experience, but also because she was very empowering - she was aware of the diversity and depth of the experiences or expertise of the members, and constantly encouraged people to share their relevant talents and experience.

There were certain points or fixtures in the PP year that the followers clearly regarded as 'must-do', such as the celebrated Yule party and its attendant parlour games, things that were for some a great nostalgic throwback to childhood, such as pass the parcel and bobbing for apples. Likewise, the annual outing/picnics to sites of interest as far afield as Wiltshire or the Sussex Coast, some memorable days out, and an opportunity to cement friendships old and new.

I would say in tribute that the group provided an outstanding and genuine social networking space where I for one met a lot of people who became good friends. Many of us who were regulars and lived in North London would meet up and do things socially or ritually, quite independently of the group. With hindsight we realise, I hope, that this was a very liberal and easy-going club that enabled real social bonding in the often alienating and impersonal environment of a mega-city. Can people say that any online 'social networking' compares?

I haven't really talked much about the core content of PP. Once again, I think that others may have ample material to contribute, but before I quit with the Memory Lane, I will say a bit about my personal highlights. Uppermost in my mind: Jean's Pathworkings. These were an always reliable excursion or time out from the workaday world. My involvement in PP and Paganism happened during the last decade of my life in London. There's an irony: if I hadn't been a Londoner, I probably wouldn't have come across the richness and breadth of the traditions I tapped into. But ultimately, I believe that I was experiencing an alienation from the natural world and a way of life that was more tuned into the elements and changing seasons. The experience of pathworking and other rituals helped me to tune out of what was to me the oppressive surroundings of concrete, machine noise and bad air around me. I miss PP, but I don't miss London!

I loved my first 'blind walk' session, in which the group paired up, one person would be blindfolded and then led around the garden on a spring or early summer evening by their 'buddy'. The sighted guide would lead the blindfolded one to objects or plants around the place, inviting an experience of smell or touch and after 15 minutes or so, the tour would finish and the blindfold would come off. This led to a sensory explosion, in which the world flooded in with a psychedelic intensity! Then there was an indoor session involving a dynamic meditation. Again, we paired up. One person would visualise themselves as a tree with roots stretching down into the earth - thus so far so 'routine' in PP land. Then, we were directed to visualise a 'green energy' below, draw that up into the trunk and then up to the branches, i.e. an extended arm and hand. Once infused out to the fingertips with the green energy, then the other player was to grip the outstretched hand/arm firmly and try to gently pull it down. It was almost impossible to shift the arm in this mode! I remember that very clearly. My partner couldn't really budge my arm, nor could I shift my partner's. These are things that began in the mind but manifested in the physical world. That's the whole crux of it all, no? Thanks for those many gifts, Jean, wherever you roam, and thanks also to the other people that I travelled with and taught me things. I think you all know who you are. Cheers!

Hannah

Growing up with a 'pagan' spirituality, I had always felt isolated and apart from others. At school I kept my beliefs secret and chose to keep myself separate. I often felt lonely but not as lonely as I felt with others with whom I could not share myself honestly. In my teens I had my fingers burned with some 'occultists' I fell in with and afterward vowed to keep what was most sacred to me hidden. A stubborn solitary one might say!

When I moved to London in 2006 a chance happening found me hearing about Pagan Pathfinders. I was reticent but [Jean] being so close geographically and so welcoming, I felt a real draw to come along and give groups another chance. Whilst I was still pretty defensive, scared and mistrustful, I found the gentle rhythm and warmth at Pagan Pathfinders imbuing me with hope and optimism.

As it happened I unexpectedly became pregnant and left the group probably much sooner than I would have liked but my hope in finding a spiritual family remained. Thanks to PP!

Charles

In 1986, two years after arriving in the UK from South Africa, [my partner] and I had both found jobs in London, and we'd settled in Horley, in Surrey. She was a Craft-seeking missile with inborn witchy gifts, which hadn't yet found a focused outlet, and I was her lucky life partner. On her relentless quest, she found a booklet called 'The Q Directory', in which Pagan Pathfinders was listed and so found your magical house and you, dear Jean.

Like so many before and after us, we made the journey each week to PP, had tea and chats in your kitchen, often with Zach surprising us by appearing in karate kit, or in full Swinburne-quoting, Billy Graham-loathing flow. Then we went through to the drawing room, where we relaxed, we explored our own and each other's auras, you gave us mysteries to ponder, and we followed your pathworkings wherever those fantastic journeys of discovery led.

One evening, when we'd reached the stars and come face to face with the Goddess, you invited us to dance with Her. I did. It was my first experience of transcendence, and not only have I never forgotten it, I still remember it exactly, with the original mixture of awe and joy.

My personal temple, my talisman (which I have since drawn many times and sculpted in clay and fired), and my way down the steps and through the temple, and out into the realms of magick are with me whenever I need them and are among my most precious possessions. And I discovered all of them at PP, under your gentle and powerful guidance. Thank you.

Farina

So many nights of magic, solemn meditation and wondrous pathfinding. Thank you so much for your guidance. I think, especially, the Imbolc journey will stay with me for a long time.

Lucy

[Jean] set me on the path by walking it so humbly and with such humour. I remember the Christmas Mummers plays and Zach as the Devil (of course), biscuits and tea and beautifully magical conversation. I remember the intimate ritual and deep pathworkings and being encouraged to hold the space for all. The elementals were always playing up in your house and the cats were more mischievous than you and Zach put together! ....

You welcomed me as a young witch and my partner at the time came too for a while. In the mid-nineties when I was in my mid-twenties your home became my weekly place of exploration and training for a while and I was so lucky to be granted such wise counsel and knowledgeable training ....

Your depth and quiet acceptance and warm tolerance were the signs of a soul that is awake and alive with the mystery. You allowed me a place to dwell in that mystery and a firm belief in the magical nature of reality allowed my intuition to blossom and my love of magic and consciousness to show itself more and more fully. I owe you a great gratitude and I honour you from the depth of my heart.

Skip

I heard about Pagan Pathfinders from a friend of mine and first went along to a meeting in early 1991. I'd been involved in Paganism for a few years and knew that PP provided a wide range of teachings and practical work for those searching for their own Pagan path. I'd also heard really positive things about Jean who ran the group from her home in north London.I worked with PP for over a year then left for a while and came back again, working with it until 1997, but still kept in touch with friends I met at PP and with Jean.

I found PP a lovely safe space to work in. It offered the opportunity to learn about different aspects of Paganism and to work with different techniques and practices, using simple exercises, pathworking, and ritual. Everyone was encouraged to provide some input into the running of the group at some time - to prepare a pathworking, a simple ritual, or run a complete session. This was great fun. Sometimes the work was very serious and very focused. Sometimes it was very light-hearted. Part of the magic was when energy was raised by everyone falling about laughing. Oh, those memories...

I remember the embarrassment of the first ritual I prepared for the group. It included a part where one of the group would, in the course of the work, be lifted up overhead by four people. This didn't happen though. We did the work, we started the levitation, and nothing happened - no movement, nothing, we couldn't even move the person off the floor an inch. So we improvised and carried on. I learnt a lesson that day. Always check your work before you put it into practice. And avoid any special features unless you are not 100% but 200% sure they will work.

Because people coming along to the group had different interests we could be doing work in Wicca, Northern tradition, Kabbala, Hermetics or anything that came under the general heading of Paganism. Some of the sessions were very simple, some more complex, some very practical such as learning to dowse or having a study session on Tarot – but each one provided the opportunity to learn something new. It was very gentle and very lovely. We always started with a warm up exercise, followed by a visualisation, followed by the work of the evening. Grounding work was done after by having cups of tea and some food – when I started going to PP this was simple biscuits and snacks, but by the time I left it could be a huge feasting session.

One of the highlights of my time at PP were the yule parties where we did some country dancing, played wild party games including tunnelling (eventually stopped for safety reasons!), pass the parcel, sang Pagan carols and performed the mummers play. Great fun. Another highlight was the summer outing which was a day visit to somewhere with Pagan connections and having a picnic there.

I genuinely miss those sessions at Jean's house. Even though I've moved on with the work I do and the knowledge I've gained, I still remember with great fondness the times I spent at PP. There was something really special there and I learned a lot – about Paganism, about magic and spirituality, and last but not least - about myself.

Ruth

PP gave me so much – not just a fantastic grounding in nature spirituality, but also a deep sense of belonging to a family. Having a

PP baby made it harder for me to come, but every time I look at her, I remember the group!

Claire

I look back on the ten years I spent with PP as a golden opportunity for my spiritual growth and one I am so grateful to have had. The rituals, the fun, the laughter and the companionship, I feel I was truly blessed!

Irina

I'll always remember the Monday evening in 1998 when Ruth, Martin and I came together to PP for the first time. You made us feel so welcome! Little did I know then that I would be coming to your house for the next 11 years, once a week. PP (and mostly you) taught me so many things, from trusting my own gut feelings, to trusting in the spiritual work at hand, including the frequently invoked effervescent sparkles. Gradually I learned to fully embrace my own spiritual journey with confidence. It was not always easy considering that I was brought up in a communist family. At times it took all my courage to overcome certain taboos that were imprinted in my childhood. I am so grateful for your guidance and the safe environment you provided for me. I particularly enjoyed the once a year blind walk through your garden in summer. I always have felt this to be the very garden of the Goddess. What inspiration I gained from the smell and feel of the plants.

Katie

Back in 2015, between the publishing of the Rainbow Bridge book and Jean's last period of illness, she asked me to help out with a talk she was giving about PP. My instructions were to create something I'd learnt at PP. I racked my brains, thinking of my time there. How could I single out one particular thing I'd learnt, and more importantly, how could I put that into words and actions? I needed to create something which envisioned the kind of lessons Jean was so good at teaching. The walk down that north London hill in the dark or twilight always held the promise of another spiritual experience, another lesson as I climbed the steps and knocked on that big front door awaiting the scent of the hallway. There was always a lingering aroma of incense mixed with quality tea and the gentle hum of chatter of those who'd already arrived.

Thinking through everything I'd learnt I asked myself what was the greatest lesson Jean taught me through her calming voice and encouraging smile? After much soul searching I realised the most important thing Jean ever taught was the lesson of how to be a High Priestess. The rituals we undertook at PP were never oath bound; there were very rarely long lines to learn and instructions to follow. We learnt by osmosis, by the action of watching and this is how she taught us to lead; through observing. Jean facilitated rather than taught. She created activities where we could discover and understand our own needs and selves. Every part of PP was a learning experience from the tea and biscuits and discussions before we started right through to the sharing at the end.

Holding space: Jean was a master of holding space. We felt safe in her presence and safe in the group. It was about more than just simply taking hands and calling names, rapport building was so slow and delicate no one realised they were doing it. Tea and biscuits started the process, with Jean ensuring everyone had a chance to speak and feel comfortable before we started. The steps into a ritual space were slow and repeated each week – the golden bubble for example created an element of togetherness and safety. Nothing was forced or labelled, it was simply there.

Slow removal of the comfort zone: We worked on some very deep themes in PP but they were always just the right amount of challenging. We also did some frankly ridiculous stuff which would have left me cringing and whinging in other circumstances. The comfort zone was slowly broken down. Jean added the awkward first – we swayed like trees, we meowed like cats, we hopped like bunnies. We felt silly, but we trusted. When the heavy subjects came, either on the same night or several weeks into the term, we'd broken the ridicule scale. The trust was established, the hard work possible.

All at the right time: Jean taught by immersion, you watched Jean and more experienced members of the group time and time again before one day she'd announce it was your turn. Of course you could always volunteer but if you didn't and she felt you were ready you'd be volun-told. It was never the wrong time, Jean watched and knew exactly the point someone had witnessed enough and was confident enough to give it a go. This could be as simple as calling a quarter or a request for you to run the next week's session.

Mentoring: Jean had plenty of advice and guidance, but you never really knew whether it came from her or from your own heart. She listened and encouraged and mentored in a way which never came across as patronising or preachy. When she directed rituals she did it with a raised eyebrow here, a smile there, and a nod of the head. We all knew where we were supposed to be standing just by glancing over to Jean. There was never any need for raised voices or spoken instructions, everything was orchestrated with perfection.

Tailored: I'm sure it's been said before, but for twenty-five years Jean sat and wrote a new session nearly every week. Very occasionally she tasked someone else with leading, even more rarely she recycled from years gone by. The themes were often similar – the wheel of the year, Divali, springtime, shadow-self; but each week was carefully planned using her intuition of what was needed on that occasion. It showed. Her thorough organising meant she could tailor to the current cohort and the challenges of the day. Facilitating a group like PP is about more than following a script, it's about rewriting that script once a week if necessary.

Removal of ego: Jean stood back. She let the voices of the group be heard, strengthening the quieter ones and encouraging the louder ones to listen. PP was her baby, some would say her life's work, but very rarely was it labelled 'Jean's PP'. She let the strengths of her creation show rather than the strength of her personality. Everyone who worked with Jean knew how amazing she was, but she focused on the group and the work rather than her own self-identity. By this instant the group followed and everyone had space and room.

Positive reinforcement: I don't remember Jean giving critiques. It was rare anything was truly appalling but whenever things needed work Jean focused on the positives and on suggestions. That didn't mean she was never displeased – the slight frown at the corner of her mouth told you when she was. But she focused on change and improvement rather than criticism. It also didn't mean she was a pushover – far from it. Everyone fell into line through the respect they had for Jean. She had an enormous presence and strength, commanding reverence through the sheer nature of her being. If you were late you'd only be late once because the activities would have started without you. If you missed a week you'd be told how much you were missed and would endeavour to make it next time. Jean was always keen for PP to become bigger than just one meeting in her north London borough, but I don't know if she realised the magic she brought to it personally. In the different splinters of my life when pondering on a teaching or coaching problem I still think back and consider how Jean might have dealt with a similar situation. And Jean's words when I explained what I'd learnt at PP? 'Who is this pariah?'

I spent about six years attending Jean's PP every Monday night, in term time (1999-2004). When I first met Jean at a Pagan Federation Imbolc I had no idea how much she would influence me. When I left London I still didn't completely understand what I had been given (so freely) over six years of Pagan Pathfinders. This would come later, when I discovered that very few Pagan leaders are her equal in humility, compassion and gravitas.

Jean's gentleness and generosity with time and knowledge seeped in quietly. I had no idea for years how pivotal she was in the Pagan community. Her humility was exceeded only by her unerring ability to persuade you out of your comfort zone. My first PP found me growing from an acorn into a mighty oak to some unutterable seventies soundtrack with labrador-like acquiescence. Was that really me?

Jean was a truly magical being, with laser like willpower beneath that disarmingly soft mop of hair and Alice band. Under Jean's power of intent, two manky blankets became the 'tunnel of transformation' at many a public ritual. Her capacity for holding magical space was just immense and looking back I realise how osmotically she taught us, just through proximity.

I feel so lucky to have seen Jean every week for six years. The commitment she made to Pagan Pathfinders was a true path of service: opening her home and fostering a wonderful group. It was one of the few places I have ever felt to be 'home'.

Jean was a mentor: a spiritual parent, of the best kind. I felt her confidence in me and her quiet insistence that I explore and challenge myself. And Jean seemed to do this for everyone around her.

Jean inspired people. She inspired them to find their true path; to do crazy-assed silliness (thoughts of a tiny room full of grown-ups manically expressing their 'inner goblin'); to take their part in nurturing the Pagan community; and most of all to be better people.

Who could bear to disappoint Jean? Bitchcraft could not survive in the air she breathed and she inspired devotion without a trace of her own ego. Teacher, mentor, inspiration, light-bringer, cat-whisperer, wisewoman and friend.

I have never met her equal, but the sparks of light she inspired in others are so many that I feel her leaving us can never be a darkness. She truly lived her spiritual path.

May Jean be memorialised in the replication of her humanity, kindness and wisdom. I know I will try to carry that with me all my days.

Mani

Dear Jean,

Thank you for opening the door, so generously, warmly and wisely.

'She dances with the sun on her forehead
The moon on her breast
And her skirt sewn with stars'
(From a Bulgarian ritual song)

Ian

I first met Jean in 1994, when I was new to Paganism. PP was a very good place to meet people. It started in 1975 and was very much Jean's thing. She did say that the aim of PP was to combine Humanistic Psychology with Paganism, so she was certainly using her background as a psychologist. She used it in such a subtle way that most people would never have even noticed. She could lead very quietly. She had a quiet, gentle authority. She made suggestions where others would command. Psychic mugging as Jon [another Peeper] would fondly call it.

She would try and put people off. You had to be there at a certain time with a packet of biscuits. The first thing she did was the exercise with the Tree. If they couldn't be a tree, they didn't come back. It was Jean's way of filtering people.

We would meet once a week, continuous from 1975 until about 2007. There was a summer break though. She would start in late September and run to the Christmas party, with traditional games etc. Then there would be a summer party in July, followed by a break.

PP was always held at their home, which was a very magical place. It was filled with cats. The rituals were always indoors. The circle was oval and was affectionately called the 'PP sausage'. The Altar was in the centre and the PP weapons on it were often quite quirky, touristy souvenirs. However, the garden was used once a year when we had the Blind Walk. People would pair up with someone else and then be led around the garden to smell, or touch the flowers, the bark of the tree, etc.

PP was for beginners but also people who were very experienced would go as well, which would include Wiccan initiates. They would go along because it was just a very good group.

The way Jean led the rituals was superb. Sometimes PP did the open seasonal ritual for the PF. There would be 70-80 people attending. She was amazingly good at running larger rituals like that as well; directing the energy, the way she did.

I remember sometimes being the one who fell asleep during pathworkings. Although contrary to popular belief, I wasn't always asleep. Sometimes I went very, very deep into the pathworking, but I always came out when Jean brought us back, so I can't have been properly asleep. Sometimes I couldn't remember a word, which is actually called 'trance amnesia'.

A funny thing happened back when I first started going to PP. I had just started dating a girl. We had only been seeing each other for a couple of weeks I think. At that point we discovered that we had both, independently, been in touch with Jean and been given the same date to come along to a PP meeting. It felt like a good sign.

I was very, very quiet when I started going to PP and it brought me out more. Jean did comment on this a few years ago, that I had changed quite a lot over the time of going to PP. I became able to do things I would never have contemplated doing when I started – ritually speaking.

When I was there the PP group got very tight. People became friends outside PP and would socialise and do other things. There are people that are still friends, even quite a lot of years later. Various people had little groups going on the side as groups of like-minded people formed.

I have fond memories of the regular PP parties. The Yule party was great fun. We used to perform a Mummers Play with Zach [Jean's husband] as Beelzebub, carrying an old battered frying pan as a prop. There was country dancing, which there was no opting out of, but it was actually fun when you got going. Jean would come into the kitchen where people might be hiding and say 'Has anybody not danced?' At Beltane we would get out the handmade PP Maypole, which was utter chaos. People just couldn't get the hang of going under, over, under, over. We made our own one for the new PP. It uses a garden umbrella base filled with water to hold it down, which is more secure than the old one which was in a base of sand!

For me going to PP every Monday for lots of years was a regular social thing I did. Even some Mondays if I didn't feel like it, I was always happy I went. It is the same now. It is a good place to meet people and connect with people, both on a personal friendship level and a spiritual level.

"Song for Jean's Birthday" by Kay Bridger (To the tune of 'Amazing Grace')

It's PP night, the stars are bright,
We're on o-u-r way to Jean's;
To gorge on chips and swing our hips
And sleep thro-ugh the pathworking.
It's Jean th-at tells us what to do,
And trustingly we obey.
In perfect love and perfect trust,
We pretend to-o-o be goblins.

We might be blindfold round the back,
Or dusting the tunnel off.
We could be sacred sausaging
Or learning our elements.

It's PP night, the stars are bright,
We're on o-u-r way to Jean's;
We want to thank Jean very much,
For think-ing up PP.

"Ode to PP" by Skip

Darksome night and shining moon
Gathered us all in Jean's front room,
Lots of toil and never trouble
Protected by our Golden Bubble.
We worked, we sang, we laughed, we ate,
Started at 7(ish) and finished late.
Jean, thanks so much for running PP
With love and blessings from Jake and me.

"Jean's Birthday Song"

Once a lovely Pagan opened up her circle,
Invited all the neophytes to come for free.
And she sang and she danced as she waited while her incense burned
Who'll come and open the quarters for me.
Open the quarters, open the quarters
Who'll come and open the quarters for me
And she sang as she danced and waited while her incense burned
Who'll come and open the quarters for me.

Along came a Kabbalist clutching his pistachio nuts
Hoping to learn to climb life's tree
Next came to muggles with their packets of biscuits
Seeking the answer to life's mystery.
Open the quarters, open the quarters
Who'll come and open the quarters for me
Next came to muggles with their packets of biscuits
Who'll come and open the quarters for me.

Then came three Pagans dressed in multicoloured black
To join the magickal university
Last came four Wiccans wearing designer pentagrams
Searching for Gardnerian depravity
Open the quarters, open the quarters
Who'll come and open the quarters for me
Last came four Wiccans wearing designer pentagrams
Who'll come and open the quarters for me.

Each in their own way summoned up an element
With blowing, stamping and necromancy
Standing like a tree they dozed through the pathworking
Shut down the quarters and joined Zach for tea.
Open the quarters, open the quarters
We'll come and open the quarters for thee
Standing like a tree we'll doze through the pathworking
Shut down the quarters and join Zach for tea.

BIBLIOGRAPHY

Bardon, Franz, 'Initiation into Hermetics', Verlag Hermann Bauer, 1956.

Bloom, William, 'The Endorphin Effect', Hachette, 2012.

Bosschart, Johfra, 'Astrology', V.O.C-Angel Books, 1981.

Cade, Maxwell, Cecil & Coxhead, Nona, 'The Awakened Mind: Biofeedback and the Development of Higher States of Awareness', Delacorte Press, 1979.

Crowley, Vivianne, 'Wicca: A Comprehensive Guide to the Old Religion in the Modern World', HarperCollins, 2003.

Dawkins, Richard, 'Unweaving the Rainbow: Science, Delusion and the Appetite for Wonder', Penguin UK, 2006.

Farrar, Janet and Stewart, 'Eight Sabbats for Witches, and Rites for Birth, Marriage and Death', Phoenix, 1988.

Fortune, Dion, 'The Sea Priestess', Inner Light Publishing Company, 1938.

Goodman, Linda, 'Sun Signs', Pan Books, 1972; RosettaBooks, 2011.

Gunther, Bernard, 'Energy Ecstasy and Your Seven Vital Chakras', revised reprint by Newcastle Publishing, 1983

Harvey, Andrew, 'The Direct Path', Rider, 2009

Huxley, Aldous, 'The Doors of Perception: And Heaven and Hell', Harper & Brothers, 1954.

James, William, 'The Varieties of Religious Experience: A Study in Human Nature', Longmans, Green & Co., 1902.

Jung, C.G, 'Memories, Dreams, Reflections', Exlibris, 1962 (German); Pantheon Books, 1963 (English).

Jung, C.G & Kerényi, C, 'Essays on a Science of Mythology', Princeton University Press, 1969.

Jung, C.G, edited by Aniela Jaffe, 'Memories, Dreams, Reflections', Pantheon, 1963.

Jung, C.G, 'The Structure and Dynamics of the Psyche', Routledge & Kegan Paul, 1970.

Leopold, Aldo, 'A Sand Country Almanac and Sketches Here and There', Oxford University Press, 1968.

Lovelock, James, 'Gaia: A New Look at Life on Earth', Oxford University Press, 1979.

Maslow, Abraham, 'Religions, Values and Peak Experiences', Ohio State University Press, 1964.

Maslow, Abraham, 'Motivation and Personality', Harper & Brothers, 1954.

Maslow, Abraham, 'A Theory of Human Motivation', published in Psychologial Review, 1943.

Masters, Robert & Houston, Jean, 'Mind Games', Dell Publishing, 1972.

Miller, FG & Kaptchuk, TJ, 'Placebo Effects in Medicine', New England Journal of Medicine, 2015.

Moseley, JB, 'A Controlled Trial of Arthroscopic Surgery for Osteoarthritis of the Knee, New England Journal of Medicine, 2002.

Nichols, Sallie, 'Jung and the Tarot: An Archetypal Journey, Red Wheel/Weiser, 1985.

Pratchett, Terry, 'Discworld' series, Transworld and others, various dates.

Rinpoche, Sogyal, 'The Tibetan Book of Living and Dying', HarperCollins, 1992.

Sharman-Burke, Juliet & Green, Liz, 'The Mythic Tarot', (new edition) Rider, 2001.

Starhawk, 'The Spiral Dance', Harper & Row, 1979.

Tart, Charles, 'Altered States of Consciousness', Wiley & Sons,1969

Steinbrecher, Edwin, 'The Inner Guide Meditation', Aquarian Press, 1982.

Valiente, Doreen, 'The Charge of the Goddess', (expanded edition), The Doreen Valiente Foundation, 2014.

Williams, Jean & Cox, Zachary, 'The Gods Within: The Pagan Pathfinders Book of God and Goddess Evocations', Moondust Books, 2008.

Wise, Anna, 'Awakening the Mind: A Guide to Mastering the Power of Your Brain Waves', Jeremy P Tarcher, 2002.

L - #0151 - 041122 - C0 - 210/148/25 - PB - DID3415263